OVER THE TOP SECRET

OVER THE TOP SECRET
A FUNNY SPY ADVENTURE

ALEXA TUTTLE

This is a work of fiction. Names, characters, places, and incidents either are the product of the author's imagination or are used fictitiously. Any resemblance to actual persons, living or dead, events, or locales is entirely coincidental.

Copyright © 2023 by Alexa Tuttle

All rights reserved. No part of this book may be reproduced or used in any manner without written permission of the copyright owner except for the use of quotations in a book review.

Published by
WonderCorp, LLC

www.alexatuttle.com

For my fellow goofballs...

CONTENTS

	Prologue	1
1.	Keep Calm and Take a Quiz	7
2.	Wakey Wakey, Scared and Shakey	16
3.	Recycled Air Farts	19
4.	Critical Failure	38
5.	Sh*t Happens	50
6.	Loosey Goosey	60
7.	Test is My Middle Name	74
8.	Code Red	96
9.	T.O.P.S.E.C.R.E.T	105
10.	The Prince of Weapons	111
11.	The Not-so-Safe House	120
12.	Crème Brûlée	126
13.	What's HapPENning?!	133
14.	Total ReCALL	142
15.	Not Your Grandma's Panties	149
16.	Tout le Monde	155
17.	A Buttery Betrayal	163
18.	Getting to the Bottom of it	170
19.	Into the Dungeon	175
20.	Out Snooping, Call Back Later	185
21.	Oh Rats!	197
22.	Another Damn Experiment	206
23.	Krav Maga	215
24.	Follow That Rat!	223
25.	Up, Up and Away	230
26.	Look Before You Fall	234
27.	Puke Breath	243
28.	Triggered by the Trash Man	247
	Epilogue	255
	Dear Reader	267
	Your Words Matter	269
	About the Author	271
	Also by Alexa Tuttle	273

PROLOGUE
MISSION REPORT

"Hi. My name is Julie Richardson, and this is my first ever mission entry. Mission log? Mission... review."

I roll my eyes at the image of my recorded self and press the "delete" key again. How long have I been doing this? My stomach growls. Another deep breath. This time I press the space bar a bit more pointedly. The little red dot blinks at me. I smile at the camera.

"Hi there. My name is Julie Richardson, and I have absolutely no idea where to start. The last week has been..." I search for the right word, replaying everything that's happened in the last few days. The logical part of my brain insists it must have been a fever dream induced by the stress of graduating, and yet the constant aching in my bones and the disheveled, baggy-eyed girl staring back at me suggest otherwise.

Has it really only been a week? I shake my head at my reflection. Time flies when you can't remember what day it is.

"Insane," I say, decidedly. It's the only word that fits. Especially when you consider there's absolutely no way anyone in their right mind would believe me if I told them. Not that I'm allowed to.

"Anyway," I continue, "the last week has been totally bizarre and incredibly dangerous. I'm still not entirely sure if things will ever go back to normal. The Director says my situation is only temporary, but I think she's just trying to convince herself that's the case. I doubt Simon has any plans to remove his experiment from my brain, no matter how many times The Director tells him to." I purse my lips, wondering if he's planning another life-threatening test as I speak. "Honestly, I'm not holding my breath. But I guess that's something we'll find out in time. Assuming I live past this next assignment."

Behind me, a head of short, jet-black hair pops into my video frame, followed by the annoyingly handsome face and ridiculously svelte body of Eric Shaw. He's wearing his usual—a black leather jacket, white cotton shirt, jeans, and black boots. A single black ringlet juts out from the rest of his luscious waves, curling against his forehead as if to say, "Look at me!" I wonder if he spends time every morning perfecting the look, or if it's au naturel. Probably the former. He gives me his signature crooked smile and swaggers over to my desk.

"Don't say that," he says with false empathy. "You know you'll survive because it's my job to save your ass." He grabs my laptop and looks into the camera with a smolder. "Hi, my name is top secret, and you're watching the lamest thing I've ever seen." He winks, then shoves the laptop back in my hands.

I stab the pause button and give him my annoyed look, which he's become oh-so-familiar with. "Ever since you appeared in my life, everything has gone to shit, and I'd really appreciate it if you could give me at least a minute to myself." He smirks. "Maybe even two," I add. He's still standing in my personal bubble. "That'd be great."

"Julie," he says, leaning close to my face. His beautiful hazel-eyes stare into my turd-brown ones. "You're the one who screwed with my life, so you might consider thanking me for saving yours on multiple occasions." Why does his breath always smell minty fresh?

"Thanks for continuously putting my life in danger and making everything worse along the way," I say, batting my eyelashes sarcastically. We stare each other down for a moment. Is he going to kiss me? I'm not sure if I'd like that, or if I'd slap him.

He backs off. I realize I'm staring at his lips. So does he. He gives me a smug look. Damn it, why does he always win? What are we competing at, again?

"I'm not here to eavesdrop on your pathetic vent session about the spy life," he says as he saunters back toward the door. "I only came in here to tell you to hurry up. Pizza's here, and we have surveillance to review."

A furious surge of heat shoots through me. I growl through gritted teeth. "What did you say?"

"I said pizza's here." He steps toward the doorframe of my temporary bedroom. It's somewhat shorter than most door frames. I'd deemed the compact safe house "cozy" when we first arrived, but after a week and a half of living in the same three cramped rooms with the same antagonizing mission partner has given me severe cabin fever. Looking at Eric's judgmental expression reminds me how much I want to punch him. "Are you on your period?" he asks.

Ohmygod. "Eric, this is a safe house. Meaning we're supposed to stay low, so we stay safe." He gives me a blank stare. "Meaning, don't order food to be delivered to a T.O.P.S.E.C.R.E.T. location!" I wonder how he's managed to survive this long. "Also, did you forget for the umpteenth time that I'm lactose intolerant?"

"Relax, I got you a salad."

I squint suspiciously. "What kind of salad?"

"Come and find out," he says with a sexy smirk. Yeah... there's definitely cheese on it. Or dairy-laden dressing. Or both.

Sigh.

Eric grins at my scrunched-up face, then heads back down

the hall towards the living room, his voice echoing back to me. "Tick-tock, tick-tock..."

Technically his surveillance isn't worth anything to us unless my messed up "McGuffin" brain is triggered by it. He can enjoy his pizza alone, thankyouverymuch. I've got my own work to do.

I turn back to the computer, shaking the image of his perfectly toned butt out of my head. Damn him.

I un-pause the recording.

"Sorry about that. Alright, back to business. I haven't been briefed on how to correctly do a mission log, or whatever it's called, so I'm just going to treat this as an opportunity to vent through my traumatic experience with T.O.P.S.E.C.R.E.T. I can't tell my parents or my best friend because, well, you know. It's T.O.P.S.E.C.R.E.T." (Though, truthfully, if there's anything I've learned from my time at T.O.P.S.E.C.R.E.T., it's that everything they do is anything but).

"And you've just witnessed the incredibly self-centered Eric Shaw who would rather have nothing to do with me, so I can't very well confide in him either. I'm sure you picked up on his lack of listening skills." Major eye roll. (By now it's become an unconscious bodily reaction to the mere thought of him.)

"Which leaves you. The computer. Probably not the best idea, after everything that's happened with me and computers this past week. We're currently on a mission in—" I stop short, realizing it's probably not a good idea to reveal our whereabouts, even if it is in a T.O.P.S.E.C.R.E.T. mission log on a T.O.P.S.E.C.R.E.T. computer.

I conspicuously check over my shoulder anyway, double-checking the blinds are all closed. Will I ever be able to relax again?

"One sec," I tell the camera. I dart to the door and softly guide it shut, careful not to alert Eric. Actually, I better lock it, too. Don't want Eric to know what's going on in my head, though it seems pretty pointless since everyone at T.O.P.S.E.C.R.E.T. is most likely dialed into my brain waves right now. I wonder if Simon has figured out a way to read my thoughts yet. I blanch at the possibility that he could be reading them right now. STOP RIGHT THERE, SIMON! I think loudly. Then I realize he never listens to me even when I'm right in front of him. Well, it was worth a shot.

I take a second to gather my thoughts. "It's probably best if I start at the point where everything went terribly wrong. The first time. Here goes…"

1 / KEEP CALM AND TAKE A QUIZ

"This entire life-altering sequence of events started when I was Face-Timing my best friend, Nicole. She's a Physician's Assistant at GERIATRIC GENERAL in FL, graduated two years early from college due to her insane accumulation of honors credits. And here I thought being top of my class was something to brag about. She was telling me all about her day in the ER, but I couldn't handle the gory details…"

"Eew, Nicole, please!" I drop the phone, my vision crowding with dark spots. Her melodic laugh rings through the tiny speakers.

"Okay, sorry." She takes a giant bite of her Publix Sub. "I can't believe you still get queasy with this stuff," she says through a full mouth.

I blink until the spots go away, taking short, quick breaths. "It's not something I can particularly control, remember? Aren't you supposed to be the medical expert?"

"Vasovagal Syncope is just a fancy way to say 'prone to fainting.'" She takes another bite of PubSub and waits for me to pick the phone up again, her beautiful caramel eyes waiting expectantly.

Nicole is wearing her signature look—hospital scrubs with a creative updo and no makeup. She doesn't need it, the way her flawless dark skin glows. "Well, the whole point is I'm finally getting to work in the ER with the handsome Dr. Reeves. It will be glorious, but unfortunately, I'll be working the entire time you're here."

I almost drop the phone again. "For real?" I stifle a childish whine.

"They always give crappy shifts to newcomers." She shrugs, then shoves another large bite into her mouth.

This means I'll be spending the whole week of Spring Break with my retired parents, mainly my worry-wart mother. Not exactly what I'd planned on, but at least I'll be back home in Beechmont, Florida, with no school assignments to worry about.

I physically wave the thought out of my mind and continue packing with Nicole in one hand and a box of Lactaid tablets in the other. I've opened every cabinet and drawer in my spotless apartment bedroom to make sure I can see all my options for packing. Everything is organized first by season, then by color, then by style. I've already emptied my undergarment drawers and the cabinet full of hand-me-down fanny packs, having stashed them neatly in my carryon. You can never overpack on the essentials, especially when pockets are involved. Plus, who doesn't love a good fanny pack?

The Mickey Mouse clock on my recently dusted mirrored dresser tells me I've been at this for the last two hours, but seeing as I've only had to re-pack a total of four times, I'd call this a successful packing session. Well, four and a half. (I'd thought about including my hand-pump antibacterial soap, but it wouldn't fit with all my travel-sized hand sanitizers and backup toothbrushes, so I settled on just three hand sanitizers and no hand soap. I've got two at home anyhow. Best not to overdo it!)

"It's all good, really. I'm happy for you and Dr. Handsome." I continue counting Lactaid tablets as I place them neatly in my carry-on suitcase, solving the Tetris packing puzzle as I go. "I mean, you're living the dream, really. Think about it." I grab my toiletries bag, full of every mini-sized item found in the travel aisle at Target. "You're doing what you love and getting paid for it, working alongside your future husband, and saving people's lives." She smiles at the future husband part, cheeks full.

"And what will the great Julie Richardson be doing after graduation?"

I stop folding my shorts, close my eyes, and imagine my future. My great future, the one that I've been working toward for the past twenty-two years. Sacrificing free time and any kind of social life for the endless study sessions, extra credit assignments, and mandatory volunteer hours that would deliver me a future of success.

Success in what, though? I still haven't decided what to do with my generic business degree. It's always been the same plan: work hard in school to ace your classes so you can get into the next set of classes and so on and so forth. Until now.

Oh my God.

"Julie?" Nicole's voice turns serious. I can't respond.

Suddenly, I see myself sitting on my parent's couch with a graduation cap and gown. I'm waiting for my only friend to get off work from her incredibly important and useful job in the real world with absolutely nothing on my own agenda (now that homework's not a thing anymore) while my mother updates me on all the morbid news stories going around on Facebook.

I shiver. And start hyperventilating.

"Julie! What's wrong?" Nicole's distant, high-pitched voice weakly makes its way to my brain, and I realize I'm now sitting on my bed, having dropped the phone on the floor. I quickly pick it up, slightly lightheaded.

"Sorry. I just…" I just realized my entire life of GPA-driven ambition has totally ill-prepared me for whatever comes after shaking the dean's hand at graduation—other than a good dose of hand sanitizer.

"Julie, please tell me you're not still thinking about our suturing discussion earlier." Nicole stares at me with a face that says she's disappointed in my theatrics.

I shake my head, still unable to form words. How could I have come this far in life without a plan? I always have a plan! Maybe I've just forgotten the plan. What was the plan again?

"Julie, speak!" Nicole shakes the phone, probably pretending it's my shoulders.

"I'm sorry. I think I'm just having an existential crisis." My voice is monotone and barely there. "I'm fine."

"What are you talking about? Julie, you kick ass at everything you put your mind to."

"Oh my God, you sound like my mother." Who I'll be roomies with all too soon.

"Seriously, where did this come from?"

"I don't have any idea what I'll do after graduation!" Nicole furrows her brow, narrowing her eyes at me. "How could I not have seen this coming?" I continue, mostly to myself.

"Obviously, I'm going to graduate, and at the top of my class, most likely. But then what? Have I really been so blind?" Nicole purses her lips, and I can tell she doesn't have a rebuttal. Because I'm right! "I've forced myself to forgo any kind of life outside of school in exchange for being top of my class, but now that just means I'm an inexperienced, naive goody-two-shoes entering a world where grades don't matter and GPA doesn't count!"

I'm shaking, my hands trembling so badly that Nicole's

image on the phone is jittering like my grandma's TV stuck between channels.

"Julie, take a deep breath and try to calm down. It's okay, it's all going to be okay."

I drop to the floor and hug my knees to my chest, fighting back tears. "Easy for you to say," I mutter.

"Excuse me, but we're talking about you here," Nicole chides. "You're a badass." I scoff. No one has ever described me that way before. "I'm not the one who decided to go to college across the country," she says with a half-smirk before I even get the chance to argue.

"I'm not a badass. And you would have, too, if you wanted to get away from your overbearing mother."

"You keep telling yourself that, but we both know you could have stayed and gone to UF or FSU or UCF or USF like everybody else we know."

I purse my lips. "I suppose you're right," I say, not entirely convinced it was a "gutsy" move. Regardless, my blood pressure begins receding to its usual pace.

Nicole scoops up the remaining innards of her PubSub and licks them from her fingers. "Especially if you're right about not having a plan for life after college. That's pretty brave, girl. Going across the country just to take a bunch of hard-core classes for the hell of it."

Just when it seemed she was being helpful.

"Hang on," Nicole says. Her screen pauses for a second. I suck in a shaky breath. She's back in a moment, and she has bright eyes.

"Dr. Reeves is calling me! I can't not answer," she says, bubbling over with excitement. She stops bouncing at the sight of my ashen face and turns to me, serious. "Are you going to be okay?"

"Yes," I say, though my head is shaking, "no."

She doesn't seem convinced. "I'll call you right after." I nod, but it's unrecognizable amongst all the involuntary shaking. Nicole hangs up.

Holy snap.

Okay. Nicole's right, it's fine. I mean, I'm Julie freakin' Richardson! The Master of Plans. The Acer of Tests. The twenty-two-year-old who's never been on a real date or done anything just for the hell of it.

This is ridiculous. I need a plan.

In my small apartment kitchen, I grab a glass of ice-cold water and plant myself at my desk. My ancient laptop hums to life. It's as old as the scratched silverware in my drawers and the chipped china in my cabinets. And the stained placemats on my table. All gifts from Mom, who wanted to make sure I felt her motherly touch in my one-bedroom apartment across the country. At least, that's what she told me. But I know it's because my parents are cheap as hell. Who would want a new mattress that isn't stained from childhood bed-wetting, anyway? At least it was an opportunity to put my triple backups of baking soda and dish soap to use. Maybe when I'm forty and can pay for it myself with my grown-up real-world job.

But that's assuming I make it past graduation.

The hunk of technology screeches at me, letting me know it's finally awake. Hello to you, too. As soon as the Internet connection is established, I immediately begin searching online for career quizzes.

Don't judge me.

Oh! Here's one that doesn't look like a thirteen-year-old made it.

As I fill out the questions page by page, the faint, familiar sense of purpose comes back to me. I read the questions aloud.

"You spend most of your free time socializing, at parties, shopping, etc." HA. Unless burying myself in textbooks at the school library counts as socializing, that's a NO. Click.

"You take pleasure in executing tasks when a clear and

detailed plan is in place." You're speaking my language, quiz. Click.

"You quickly get involved in the social life of a new workplace." Hmm. I've never really had a job, what with all the studying and such, but judging by my general lack of social skills, I'm going to go with NO. Click.

"You think and reflect first before taking action." I take a look around the room in thought. Oh, ha! Guess that answers the question. Yes, as should everyone. Click.

"You are capable of making decisions based solely on logic rather than feelings." You're preaching to the quire, buddy. Click.

I sit back in my seat, relax my shoulders a bit, and take a newfound comfort in the fact that this quiz appears to have been made for me. Perhaps I'm not as much of a lost cause as I'd thought. Maybe there is a job out there for me. I continue reading through the questions with fresh optimism.

"You enjoy working alone or with a small team of others." Either way, I'm always the one who ends up doing everyone's workload. But, honestly, if you want something done right... YES. Click.

"You can think quickly and adapt to situations creatively." Hells yes. Nancy Drew PC games will teach a person a thing or two about creative problem-solving. Click.

"You'd be willing to travel the world as part of your job requirements." I stop to think about this one for a minute. The traveling-to-new-places-and-learning-about-other-cultures part sounds glorious, but the germ-riddled-means-of-transportation-and-recycled-air-farts part does not seem like a great time. I decide the quiz is referring to a perfect world, void of air farts. And who knows, with no air farts I might even be able to picture myself working at a job involving a private jet. In which case the answer is YES. Click.

"You are multilingual." I did rack up five years of AP Spanish and French studies, but I haven't ever used that knowledge in a single legitimate conversation. Meh, I suppose all those conjugations collecting dust in my brain have to count for something. YES. Click.

The next question actually makes me snort with laughter. "Prolonged time away from family or loved ones is not a deterrent in your career decisions." In all seriousness, I barely ever see my parents or Nicole, save for time off school anyway. YES. Click.

"You are capable of packing light and moving fast." I glance over at my suitcase, overflowing with so much underwear you'd think I was planning to poop my pants every day. Definitely a NO. Click.

"You are experienced in the arts of Krav Maga and general self-defense." An oddly specific question. I don't think the yellow Tai-Kwan-Doe belt in my childhood memory box counts. Plus, I've never thrown a punch. NO. Click.

"You are not bothered by a slight invasion of privacy." Umm... Yes? Or no? Which one's the double negative? They should just use true or false. Click.

"You are comfortable working with ambiguous or incomplete information/data and guessing its meaning." Nancy Drew PC games for the win, again! YES. Click.

The next question sends a prickly feeling to the nape of my neck. I sit upright and make sure my oversized Stitch plushie isn't looking before reading it to myself. You can keep a secret. To this day, no one knows I had a little help from my textbook on that take-home Biochemistry quiz... I mentally berate myself for that, once again, and quickly click YES, suddenly eager to get this quiz over with.

The screen loads for a moment, calculating my future. I take a deep breath, my fate resting in the hands of whichever twenty-something created this time-waster. It's still loading.

Oh crap, it looks like the screen is frozen. Darn spam sites. I should have guessed this quiz would give my computer a virus. I press the escape key, but nothing happens. A sudden thought pops into my head—the entirety of my senior year projects lives on this hard drive.

My heart rate soars through the roof. "NO!" I shout at the computer, furiously pressing 'escape.' "Please don't die," I whisper.

As if on cue, the screen turns black. A small white square blinks in the middle of the screen. I stare at it through my fingers, unwilling to watch the terrible fate unfold, yet not able to look away. After a few moments of frozen terror, the blinking stops. I sit, glued in place.

At least now I know what I'll be working on over Spring Break.

Like a sudden jolt of electricity to the brain, a wave of images zaps into my head. Fiery explosions, silhouetted figures, and lethal, handheld weapons of all kinds flicker behind my eyelids. Hundreds of lines of green computer code and random words written in mismatched fonts and sizes flash across my vision like a movie on fast forward. Clips of gruesome violence play in my head as if they're my own memories, knocking me to the floor in a heave of uncontrollable spasms and twitches.

My Vasovagal Syncope kicks in.

I pass out.

2 / WAKEY WAKEY, SCARED AND SHAKEY

GHASP!

I bolt upright, heart racing, covered in pools of my own cold sweat. The shriek of my iPhone alarm slowly seeps into my consciousness. I whip my head around in search of the blaring alarm, sending a sharp pain throughout my whole body.

"Agh!" I cover my eyes with my shaky, clammy palms. What happened to me? Slowly, I reach for my phone. The screen brightness temporarily blinds me. This must be how vampires feel when they've just turned.

It's 1:30 pm, my battery is at 10%, and I have an hour until my flight boards. Holy smokes, I must have really knocked out last night! Uncharacteristically, I decide to ignore the little red bubbles telling me I have twelve missed calls from my mom and sixteen unread texts. I cautiously stand up, fighting a wave of nausea. The room wobbles beneath my feet.

What exactly happened last night? Looking around, I see the curtains are still open, suitcase overflowing, lights on, laptop dead.

A cold tingle trickles down my spine at the sight of the laptop. The virus.

What kind of computer virus makes a person spasm uncontrollably? How could it have affected my brain like that? Maybe I had a seizure. Or perhaps it was just another case of Vasovagal Syncope. More likely, though, it was my existential crisis going into overdrive.

I shiver at the memory of my ridiculous outburst. I'm fine. I'm fine. Everything's fine.

My phone vibrates. A FaceTime call from Mom. If I answer, she'll see I haven't left my apartment yet and start hyperventilating at the thought that I might miss my flight home.

Oh, right—I have a flight to catch! Decline.

I rapidly type a text message to her saying I'm heading to the gate now (not entirely untrue). Love you. Yadda yadda. That should hold her off for at least another 10 minutes.

I shove the overflowing contents into my father's hand-me-down suitcase and button it shut (apparently, they hadn't invented wheels or zippers back then). Slip a few extra chewable Lactaids into my travel fanny pack (the kind that you put on underneath your clothes so pick-pockets can't get to your goodies—especially your Lactaids. It's the most practical replacement for a cumbersome purse), and jam my feet into some sneakers.

Suddenly I'm freezing. Large sweat stains begin forming under my armpits, adding a dense layer of sopping chilled grossness to my situation.

I change into a long-sleeved shirt and grab a handful of wintery layers to take with me on the plane. Looking around my apartment one last time, I cringe at the mess I'm leaving behind.

Shake it off, Julie. I rush out the door with a dairy-free granola bar in-hand.

As I race to my car in the apartment parking complex, the sight of my neighbor's motorcycle makes me stop dead, against my will. My shoulder jerks upwards and my neck and eyes twitch as images related to the ones from last night flash through my brain. The throttle of a motorcycle engine. Gunshots ripping through flesh, blood pounding in my ears, a silhouetted figure emerging from an explosion. The images are gone as quickly as they arrived and the intensity of the moment causes me to trip, sending my suitcase sliding across the floor.

A terrible realization grows inside me as I lie on the unswept parking lot, panting with my arms and legs outstretched. That was no ordinary computer virus. Whatever happened to me was not normal, and it definitely wasn't a pathetic episode of Vasovagal Syncope.

Fighting another wave of the shakes, I start my Honda Civic's engine and speed toward the highway, silently vowing to never take another online quiz again.

3 / RECYCLED AIR FARTS

"Fasten your seat belts, please. We'll be taking off in just a few moments."

I do as she says, cinching the germ-riddled airplane seatbelt another half-centimeter closer to my abdomen. That's as far as it'll go against all my layers of inappropriate winter clothing. It's eighty degrees on the airport tarmac, but I look like a snow bunny with my fluffy outer coat and touchscreen-friendly gloves. Even with all the superfluous apparel, I'm still freezing my ass off and shaking uncontrollably.

Thank goodness there's no one else in my row. I don't know if I could handle a five-hour airbus ride squeezed between two strangers and their germy airplane breath. At least I managed to nab the emergency exit row, with glorious extra space for my long legs.

My iPhone buzzes in my pocket (I can't believe I forgot to put it in airplane mode). It's a text from Nicole.

Nicole: Hey girlie. Feeling better? Did you make your flight?

Me: Yges, on yhe farmak niw.

Turns out the gloves don't work as well as advertised.

Nicole: I'm glad. Tell you all @ my call w/Dr. Reeves later. Have a safe flight!

I tap over to the other conversation with my mom, the one with now twenty-five unread messages. I scroll to the most recent ones.

Mom: Are you through security?

Mom: At the gate yet?

Mom: Why aren't you responding??

Mom: Julie, call me, your father and I had a change of plans.

Mom: Please tell me you got a friend to drive you.

Mom: You know I don't like you riding on Uber.

Mom: Horror story in the news today about a girl in the Uber.

Mom: Julie! Answer me!

I type a generic response.

Julie: Yes, in tge flught now. Sew yoo sppn.

Half a second after the text goes through, my phone buzzes with a call from mom. I better answer it this time.

"Hi, mom."

"Julie!" My name sounds like a breath of relief when she says it, followed by her shrill worry voice. "Why hadn't you responded this whole time? That is not like you at all."

"Sorry mom, I was—"

"Oh, never mind. Julie, listen." Her voice is as taut as always. "I hope you won't be too angry, but you'll have to ask Nicole to pick you up from the airport when you get here. Your father and I can't make it because—"

"Nicole won't be able to pick me up, either. But that's fine, I'll just take a taxi."

"A taxi?" I pull the phone away from my ear with a cringe, my eardrum still vibrating from her screech. "You can't trust a taxi driver, Julie. You know this!" I roll my eyes.

Why hasn't the plane taken off yet? There aren't any other passengers loading in and I already have to pee. "What was it you wanted to tell me, Mom?"

"Oh, right." She takes a loud slurp of something through a

straw, then lowers her voice to a conspiratorial whisper. "Your father and I can't pick you up because we're going on a cruise to the Bahamas."

My mouth drops. "Since when do you travel?"

"I wasn't too excited about the idea at first, but now that we're on the ship, I have to say," she hiccups loudly, "these Pina Coladas are delicious."

"You're already on the ship? You're drinking? And you didn't invite me!" I look to my side with an expression that says, "Can you believe this woman?" but no one is there to share in my moment of disbelief. For a split second, I'm disappointed. Then the germ-riddled airplane AC kicks on, reminding me how grateful I am to not have to breathe my seat-mate's recycled airplane breath.

"It was a last-minute decision," she says. My mother never makes last-minute decisions. Or drinks soda, let alone alcohol. I don't think I've ever seen her have fun at all, actually.

I shake my head in disbelief as she continues. "Julie, I haven't seen your father like this in years. He was so excited when he came home from his last day of work yesterday, he went straight to the computer and booked the cruise!" Behind her, a loud horn rips through the air, followed by a chorus of enthusiastic cheers. Mom shouts over the noise, "He even started dancing with me in the living room, can you believe it?" She giggles. Giggles! "Oh, I hope you're not mad, dear."

"I'm not mad, really." Just shocked out of my mind.

"With you graduating soon and moving on into the world, well, your father and I got to thinking. We don't want to live the rest of our lives on the couch while you're out there," she hiccups again, "taking the world by storm. You've inshpired us!" she lisps.

Who is this crazy woman, and what has she done with my mother?

The flight attendant gives me a warning look and motions

for me to hang up the phone. But I still have so many questions! I tell her with my eyes. She shakes her head, "no."

Fine. My interrogation will have to wait.

"Uh, mom, I have to go—"

"Julie? Honey, your father wants to go wave goodbye to the land-folk as we leave the port. Oh, and here he comes with another Pina Colaaadaaaa!" She sings that last part. My face is frozen in a permanent look of bewilderment. "Enjoy having the house to yourself this week! I love you." She gives me a sloppy kissing sound and hangs up.

I stare at the phone in my hand.

This is so not like my parents. Could they really be so relieved to be kicking me out into the real world that they've changed personalities entirely? No, I know. They've been suffering this whole time as parents, worried and up-tight about raising a child, and now that I'm an "adult," they can go back to loving life. And here I was, thinking my parents were the fun-suckers!

I let my head fall onto the germy headrest behind me without hesitation as I close my eyes. How many times can plans change in one day? All these stressful unknowns are driving me crazy. Ugh. Once I'm back home, with the quiet house all to myself, I can make a master list and figure out what the hell is going on in my life. With a well thought out list, everything works out. I nod, more to comfort myself than anything else. Lists have never failed me in the past. In the meantime, I take a deep breath and focus on the few things I do know.

Let's see here: My parents have been replaced by Pina Colada-loving hippies, and my best friend is moving on up as an essential addition to the real world. At the same time, I still have no idea what I'm good for, and I'm sitting here with a cryptic ailment screwing me up from the inside out.

Oh, and my thesis projects have been destroyed because I broke down and turned to the internet for advice.

Hmm. That wasn't as reassuring as I'd hoped it would be. At least no one is here to watch me suffer.

"Ehem."

My eyelids fly open. An extremely handsome young man with a Tom Cruise vibe is standing in the aisle looking right at me. He chuckles at my shocked expression, his jet-black hair bobbing up and down.

"Excuse me. My seat is right here." He flashes a brilliant, crooked smile and slides into the aisle seat next to me. I doubt he's much older than me, maybe twenty-seven or twenty-eight. His smooth, black leather jacket fits his lean, muscular torso perfectly. Black boots extend from the bottom of his tight-fitted jeans. He expertly fastens his seatbelt in one swift motion with the most superbly trimmed fingernails I've ever seen. Besides my own, anyway.

He gives me a sideways glance that says, "I know you're checking me out." I should probably take advantage of this unusual opportunity to enhance my flirting skills. Right when I open my mouth to say something saucy, a wave of nausea sends my stomach halfway up my throat. I pinch my lips together and turn away, thankful I haven't puked on anyone. Yet. Looks like the mystery virus taking hold of my body is not letting me function today. I glance around at the rest of the plane.

Why couldn't he have picked literally anywhere else to sit? The plane is practically empty! Well, except the very front and back rows where a handful of burly men sit.

They're all wearing matching black trench coats. For some reason, none of them have taken their sunglasses off. One of the men is much taller than the rest, and he appears to have a hunched back. His blond hair is gelled back into a ponytail that reaches a centimeter away from the ceiling above him. He and his bald buddy are flirting with the flight attendant, who's flirting back. The other trench coat guys in the back of the plane are flipping through the in-flight magazine, stealing glances here and there every now and then.

What's with the weird outfits and suspicious behavior? And why isn't anyone else boarding this plane? Surely a bunch of Californian college students would trade Laguna Beach and Disneyland for a week of humidity and bug bites? Ha. Not even if the Disney World Mickey Mouse were to personally lube 'em up with sunblock.

Probably there's a trench coat convention in Orlando. Duh.

Hot Guy watches me, no doubt curious about my eclectic ensemble and finicky movements. He asks, "Planning to do anything fun in Florida?"

You mean besides having an existential crisis? I blink the running sweat out of my eyes. As I stare at him, I wonder if he can tell that I'm struggling to respond without throwing up. I lick my cracked lips before answering, "Spring Break. Home."

Am I smooth or what?

He lets out a short laugh-y breath through his nose. "Nice. You going to wear that getup to the beach?" We both look at my outermost layer of fluff, dark pools of sticky cold sweat already forming under my armpits.

I force a laugh, the sound of a heaving dog. "Don't feel too well." I bite my tongue. The less talking, the better. He smirks, clearly entertained.

The plane lurches forward, heading toward the runway. I take deliberate, short breaths. In through my nose, out through my mouth. With each breath, the plane gains speed. I glance out the window and immediately regret it. The sight of the black tarmac rolling by mixed with the fluorescent lights and the roaring, shaky plane sends my vision spinning. We're about to lift off. I clamp my eyes closed.

My head throbs and my eyelids ache from shutting them so tight, but I don't dare move until the plane reaches the electronics-approved altitude. I can feel Hot Guy staring at me, probably hoping I don't puke on his chiseled chest. The plane roars as we speed down the runway. Recycled air intoxicates my head. I focus on willing my body not to combust. Deep breath...

The plane surges into the sky. My knuckles are white from giving the armrest a death grip.

"Ladies and gentlemen, you may now use the approved electronics listed in the back of our in-flight magazine," says the flight attendant. The middle-aged white woman is angling her body toward the trench coat men in a totally desperate position that leaves as much of her ashy skin revealed as possible. She ends the message with a giggle, her artificially-wound red curls bobbing up and down as she does so. She notices me staring and purses her purple-pigment covered lips at me with a look that says, "You better not be a problem, ya hear me?" Then she gets back to flirting.

I let out my deep breath through clenched teeth. Slowly, my shoulders release their hold on my ears. Now all that's left is the ride there and the landing, I tell myself.

My eyes are still closed when I hear, "You can let go now," from my right.

I peek a glance at him. Hot Guy is still watching me, a smile tugging at the corner of his lips. "Right," I say.

My claw-like fingers gradually return to their human shape as I let go of the armrest and shove my hands into my lap.

I look like an idiot.

I feel like hell.

Ugh.

Out the window, tiny cars and houses fade away as we rise above the clouds.

A few minutes pass. The cabin pressure stabilizes. It begins to feel like my head might not explode, just yet.

Hot Guy points out the window. "Check out the mountains."

I turn to see brown peaks poking through a blanket of fluffy white clouds. It's quite pretty.

I sense movement behind me. I turn back to see Hot Guy reaching for something beneath his seat. He sees me noticing him.

Slyly, Hot Guy places a mystery object in his pocket. He gives me a tight-lipped smile, then tilts his head at something at the front of the plane. I follow his eye line. The hulking blond man, whose head is almost pressing into the roof above him, is staring intensely back at Hot Guy. The blond man turns to his bald friend and whispers something in his ear. Together they glance over their shoulders once more at Hot Guy, then return to flirting with the flight attendant.

Is it me, or did Hot Guy just grip the mystery object in his pocket tighter?

My entire body floods with heat. The zipper on my outer layer won't budge, trapping me in an oven. Crap. I yank at the tiny metal handle again and it breaks off. Shit! I'm going to die in this fluffy coffin! I wince at the thought of what needs to happen next: Me, splashing some cold, reprocessed plane water on my face. Gulp.

You gotta do what you gotta do.

"'Scuse me," I mutter, struggling to sidestep my thick torso past Hot Guy. He reaches his hand out, stopping me.

"I wouldn't do that if I were you," he says.

"What, go to the bathroom?" I ask. He glances at the front of the plane, his features hardened. "There's no one in there," I whine, motioning to the green restroom sign near the bathroom, a mere fifteen or so rows away, indicating it's open for use.

Hot Guy doesn't move his hand.

"I have to go." I push past him, waddling my way into the aisle. His eyes bore into the back of my head as I walk to the front of the plane. Weird.

Just a row or two from the bathroom entrance, the trench coat guys sit totally enthralled by the flight attendant, who is twirling her ringlets around her pointer finger and batting her false lashes as if there's acid in her eye. She's leaning against the bathroom door in the hallway, giggling furiously, showing off her low-cut purple uniform to Blondie and his bald friend. They quiet down as I approach.

Now that I'm closer to them, it's much clearer how enormous Blondie really is. He's like a rugged, beat-up version of Fabio, but on steroids. His muscles threaten to burst through his black trench coat, his face covered in scars.

Through his totally unnecessary shades, I can make out his beady, dark eyes staring me down. He grimaces, revealing rotting teeth in pressing need of some flossing. The intensity of his gaze sends all the liquid to the forefront of my bladder.

I gotta go. Now.

In a flurry of waddled motion, I yank at the bathroom door that the flight attendant is leaning on. She dramatically "trips" into Blondie's lap. He grunts, then gives her a tight-mouthed grin, causing her to burst into another fit of giggles, the shrill of which makes me wince.

I shoot her a look that says, "You're welcome," and tug the bathroom door closed in a jerky motion. In a matter of two seconds, I lock the door behind me, rip off my outer jacket, and throw some cold sink water on my face.

Surprisingly, it helps a lot. I can almost hear the water sizzling against my burning forehead, and now I don't even have to pee anymore. Wait a minute. I whirl around, searching my pants all over for a pee stain, and thanking my former self for packing so many extra pairs of underwear.

Huh. None. Guess I was imagining that I had to go.

I dry off with some tissues. The cheap, thin material sticks to my face. As I pick off the fluffy white remnants, I notice my hands are shaking. Like Jell-O in an earthquake. I shove them between my legs and clamp them together with my thighs.

What the heck is wrong with me? I've ridden in planes before and I've dealt with a lot of Vasovagal episodes in my life, so what's with all the sudden nausea and twitching and seeing things that aren't there? And the imaginary needing to pee? I gulp down the frightful suspicion that it all stems from that damn career quiz and come up with a more realistic suggestion instead. Perhaps the giant stress ball in my stomach has finally exploded after all these years. That's much more likely.

While using the restroom once for good measure (after all, I'm already in here and I don't trust the phantom pee urges), sounds of shouting and grunting seep into the tiny room from under the door. It sounds like someone is struggling in the cabin.

Ain't no way I'm gonna be stuck on the toilet if something crazy goes down on this plane.

I yank my jeans up and hold my breath while the airplane toilet sucks all the air out of the room. Then I use the rest of the soap and dry my semi-shaky hands on my jeans. After a moment of fumbling with the door lock, it swings open, and I step into the aisle.

It's as if time has frozen. Baldie is crouched in his chair, aiming something toward the back of the plane. Blondie stands with his back to me, his large body blocking the aisle and most of my view.

From what I can see, it looks like the other trench coat men have left their seats. Everyone is looking in the general direction of the emergency exit row. My row. They're all tense.

I feel like my presence paused some kind of action-packed movie.

The flight attendant rounds the corner of the small pantry. I jump at the sight of her, and she jumps at my jump, dropping mini pretzel packages all over the floor. I help her pick them up, paying no attention to her pissed off glances, and when I turn back to the cabin everyone is sitting in their seats, entirely back to normal.

Have I imagined this now, too? Jesus, I need to get home.

I can't shake the feeling that everyone is eying me suspiciously as I make my way back to my seat. I squeeze past Hot Guy and plop down next to him. A moment passes. He, too, watches me from the corner of his eye.

Ignoring the stares, I check my watch. Only seven minutes have gone by. Great. Another four and a half hours left. My skin prickles in the quiet moments that follow as my thoughts become obsessed with the weirdness of this plane. Have I found myself in the middle of some kind of airborne drug war? I wondered why not many people boarded this plane. Oh my god, what if I've accidentally boarded some drug cartel jet and—

Oh, get a grip, I scold myself.

I jiggle my leg nervously. Look out the window again. A sea of clouds and heavenly sunlight look back at me, almost mockingly. I reach over and shut the shade, suddenly very upset by all this discomfort.

It occurs to me that maybe I'm dying. My heart stops at the thought. Then I remember all the research I have to do over break. I will my body to keep it together, at least for now.

Hot Guy's stare bores into my side as he watches my every move. I turn to him, fueled by an unexpected burst of anger. "What is your problem?"

He raises his eyebrows. Even I'm shocked by this outburst.

"Stop staring at me," I hiss. "I'm not that interesting," I add.

He chuckles. "Quite the contrary," he says, then points to his cheek. "You have tissue on your face, by the way."

Damn it. I wipe my face angrily. Now I'm hot again. I struggle to pull my next layer off.

"Would you like some help?" he says.

I finally get the jacket off and shove it under the seat in front of me, rolling my eyes at him. "No, thanks." Out of nowhere, my nausea is replaced with an intense need for water. My mouth is incredibly dry, my tongue stuck to the roof of my mouth. I search my purse for a water bottle.

Oh yeah, security made me throw it away.

Silently, I curse T.S.A.

Hot Guy pulls an ice-cold water bottle from the same mysterious place under his seat. He knows I'm eying it.

"Thirsty?" He untwists the cap. He inches the bottle to his lips. Before he can get his mouth on it, I snatch it from his hands and gulp the entire thing down. He stares, half amused and half appalled. The hell is wrong with me?

With a full stomach of chilled water, my body simmers down again. I sit back in my chair and let out a deep, satisfied sigh.

He looks at me, incredulous.

"Sorry. I don't know where that came from. I just…" I search my brain for a logical reason, but none can be found. Shrugging, I finish my sentence. "…couldn't control myself."

"I'd say." The corner of his mouth raises in a handsome, although crooked, grin. Then he runs his hand through his black hair and winks at me.

"Look, I'm not in the mood for this, okay?" Maybe if I get real with him, he'll leave me alone. "Something weird is going on here, and I'm not exactly sure what it's doing to me."

"It's called attraction." He leans back in his chair, nonchalantly.

Who does this guy think he is? "Actually, I think it's called repulsion." Take that.

"Body language doesn't lie." He looks me up and down with a grin. Everything about me is turned toward him. I'm leaning dangerously close to his personal bubble.

Oh, snap. It looks like Hot Guy's right. I let out a "Hmph" and unbuckle my seat belt in a huff.

"Where are you going?" he asks.

I stand, defiantly. "To one of the hundred other empty rows." I gesture with my hand to the rest of the plane. The trench coat guys turn toward us, alerted by my raised voice. Hot Guy grabs my jacket.

"Don't do that," he says. "Just sit down, Julie."

"Excuse me, but I—"

Did he just say my name? I don't remember telling him my name. Before I can speak, Hot Guy pulls me back into my seat.

He speaks in a low voice. "Julie, you need to stay put."

I gasp. He said it again! "What's going on here?"

"It's safer if you just remain here," Hot Guy says. "I'll let you know when the situation is diffused. Until then, stay out of the way."

He glances back to the front of the plane. Blondie isn't in his seat anymore. The flight attendant is heading our way. With Hot Guy leaning toward me, I can see the handle of a gun poking out from his inside jacket pocket. I suck in a shaky breath, eyes bulging from their sockets. My whole body shivers.

"You should buckle up. This might get ugly," he says.

Before I can even start to flip out, the plane forcefully tilts to the side. We both fly across the aisle. I smack into the flight attendant, taking her and her bags of mini pretzels to the ground again.

Sorry pretzels.

Hot Guy lands a few aisles back. We lock eyes for a moment, and the genuine look of warning in his eyes tells me I need to hide.

Hot Guy jumps to his feet while the flight attendant rushes right past me to her foldable turbulence seat near the cockpit. Welp, looks like it's every woman for herself. I scramble past the forgotten pile of pretzels and right into the closest safe place I can think of—the bathroom. I lock the door behind me.

Am I hallucinating? I splash water on my face again. "Wake

up, you turd!" I tell my reflection. The plane struggles through the turbulence. Then—

BAM!

Something small ZOOMS right over my head, bursting through the bathroom walls and leaving two small, jagged holes in its wake. The plane jerks to the side, then lurches downward, filling me with the same stomach-dropping sensation of a roller coaster (except, not fun).

I shove my feet into the corners of the cramped room, grabbing hold of the edge of the plastic sink. Outside the bathroom, there's muffled shouting. A breathing aid drops from a compartment above. The crackle of the on-board sound system fills the air as the flight attendant comes back on.

Her voice is high pitched, and she's talking rapidly. I can only make out the words "pilots," "down," and what ominously sounds like "die" before her voice is replaced with a gurgling sound, and she's gone.

Stay calm, Julie! I shove my face right up to the shattered hole in the wall facing the cabin, trying to get a clear view.

Hot Guy stands in the middle of the plane's center aisle. Trench coat men surround him on all sides. Hot Guy raises his fists, ready to fight, and the trench coat man behind him lunges first, hand outstretched with a sharp knife poised to stab. How the heck did he get that thing past airport security? Oh, right, and Hot Guy got a gun onboard, too. The whole drug cartel idea is starting to sound more plausible by the minute.

I gulp as Hot Guy bends forward and kicks behind him, sending the trench coat man crashing into the back wall of the plane and the knife clattering to the ground, disappearing behind another row of seats.

Hot Guy smirks and raises an eyebrow in a look that says, "Is that all you've got?" Trench coat man number two races forward and throws a mean-looking punch. Hot Guy expertly dodges the attack, grabs the man's meaty fist and twists him around, forcefully shoving his exposed neck upwards against the overhead compartment with a loud CRUNCH. The man crumples into the empty row of seats beside them.

Holy shit! Did that just happen? I can't tear my eyes away from the insanity unfolding before me.

With a flurry of motion, the trench coat men take turns attacking Hot Guy. Lunge, block, attack, attack, hit, swing, jump, SMACK. Then they ambush him like a pack of hyenas pouncing on their prey.

With surprising efficiency, Hot Guy keeps them at bay. He rips off a seatbelt from the row nearest him and forcefully swings the metal end at his closest attacker. It makes contact with a sickening CRACK. The bald man falls to the ground with a thud.

Another trench coat man pounces, gun raised. Hot Guy spins aside, kicks the gun out of his hands, and jabs the attacker with a dagger sticking out of the heel in his boot.

I blanch. Turns out I've been silently rooting for Hot Guy this whole time, but now I don't know what to think!

One after another, the trench coat men attack Hot Guy, each one coming from a different angle. Hot Guy punches, jabs, dodges and kicks them all. They drop to the ground like Cicadas dropping from the sky on a hot summer's night.

Then, somehow, they all get right back up and attack him again with gusto, covered in a fresh batch of cuts and bruises. It's like they're not even human.

Who are these people?

Just then, one of the trench coat men flies across the cabin and smacks right into the peephole. I shriek.

I peer into the other hole. It's facing the cockpit. The pilot on the left lies limply in his chair, head dangling over the back in an unnatural angle that tells me he's gone.

As in... dead. The cold, paralyzing grip of fear roots me to the ground. I smack my hand over my mouth to prevent anyone hearing me hyperventilate.

Keep it together, Julie. You're not going to die in a restroom. Not today. Well, hopefully not ever. Though, crapping myself out of fear might be an option. And not even my life-saving Lactaid could prevent that.

I maneuver my head to get a better view of the second pilot. He's alive! Hallelujah! Tears sting my eyes and I'm shocked at my own relief. Just the sight of the uniformed pilot taking action to stabilize the plane makes me feel like there may just be an ounce of sanity on this flight after all.

The pilot presses a ton of buttons on the complicated dashboard, calling "Mayday" into his radio. He pulls at the yoke and manages to stabilize the plane again. Reaching as far as he can, the pilot struggles to flip a switch on the other pilot's dashboard.

Finally, he manages to flip it open with the tip of his finger, revealing a big red button labeled 'autopilot.' Just before he can press it, the pilot lets out a dramatic sigh and hunches forward, limbs completely slack. His head knocks into the yoke, sending the plane into another nosedive.

My heart stops.

Holy snap—the pilots are dead, and we're all gonna die!

THUMP— something massive hits the bathroom door, restarting my pulse and sending an electric stab through my heart.

Through the other hole, the trench coat body from before slowly falls down the wall, revealing Hot Guy standing a few rows back. There's not a scratch on him, and his shiny black hair is still perfectly in place.

He watches as his last attacker falls to the ground. Then, a booming voice erupts from right outside the bathroom door.

Blondie takes a step forward. His enormous bicep blocks my

view as he lets out a deep, disturbing chuckle that reverberates the bathroom walls.

"Give me The McGuffin," his low voice rumbles.

"You mean this?" Hot Guy pauses. "This is Top Secret property, Greyson. I would never let it fall into the hands of an idiot henchman like yourself."

I lean against the door to hear better. Henchman? Or did he say Frenchman? This is an international drug ring; I just know it.

"How many times have you let The McGuffin get away this week?" Blondie laughs. Or should I say, Greyson? "Such an amateur."

"I wouldn't do that if I were you," Hot Guy says. I lean closer to the door. He wouldn't do what?

Just then, the bathroom door swings open, right as the plane does another shaky jerk to the left. I fly into the wall across from me, my crash made more intense by the increasing amount of G-force pulling us to our deaths. The walls are shaking, and the roar of the wind drives my heartbeat into my ears. How long will this flimsy airplane be able to hold itself together?

"Julie!" Hot Guy yells. "Stay down—"

Blondie takes that one moment of distraction to charge. He slams right into Hot Guy, tackling him to the ground. A small metallic rectangle flies through the air, landing right at my feet.

I cautiously pick it up. It's a sleek, silver piece of metal, about half the size of my hand, with the acronym T.O.P.S.E.C.R.E.T. engraved on it.

Blondie sees it in my hands. We exchange looks, his of determination, mine of terror. He charges right at me. I shriek.

Before I can even scramble to my feet, Blondie lifts me off the ground by my neck with his giant hands.

"Let me go! Let go of me!" I scream. He presses his thumb into my windpipe, silencing me. As his grip tightens, black dots crowd my vision. What's the point in choking me when we're all gonna die any minute now? My heart pumps faster and faster against his calloused palm. I lash out at him, I wriggle, I kick his rock-solid body, but I'm no match for Blondie's iron grip. Just before I die in the most unexpected way imaginable, an idea pops into my head.

I'm still holding the piece of metal he's after.

With every bit of energy in my veins, I chuck it as hard as I can toward the cockpit. Almost as soon as it leaves my palm, the speed of the plane whips it right back at us. The small metal square lodges itself in Blondie's eyeball.

He releases his grip with a cry of pain.

I drop to the ground as he staggers backward. He claws at his face, then slams into the plane's exit door.

Recycled air never tasted so good. I relish the stale taste of oxygen while wheezing and coughing like an old lady smoker.

Somehow, the lack of an eyeball doesn't affect Blondie. He rips the square from his face, then holds the blood-covered piece of metal triumphantly.

"HA!" He lets out a victorious laugh.

With dramatic flare, Blondie rips off his trench coat, revealing a bunched-up parachute strapped to his back, atop yet another trench coat. (So he's not a hunchback after all! The realization strikes me as a slight betrayal. I mean, just when you think you know a person.) The tiny chute looks like a toddler's backpack on his ginormous body. I can't imagine it would actually hold him in the air. Regardless, he kicks the door. The furious wind finishes the job and completely rips it off the side of the plane.

Hot Guy gets up just in time to see Blondie salute us with the middle finger. "No!" Hot Guy cries. Blondie jumps.

One second Blondie's there and the next he's gone.

Hot Guy races over to the window. "Shit," he mutters. He rushes past me into the cockpit, shoves the dead pilot out of his seat, takes his earpiece, and confidently grabs the yoke, pressing a few buttons arbitrarily here and there. A second later, he gets back up, shakes his head. "Yeah, there's no saving this poor baby," he says. "We've got to get out of here."

As if I don't already know this! He grabs me by the arm, pulling me to my feet.

"What's going on?" I yell.

"No time to explain." He pulls a small round gadget from his jeans pocket and slaps it onto my upper back. In a second, it transforms into a metallic backpack with an attached helmet, fastening itself around my torso and head. What the heck?

"What is this?" I yell. My voice sounds tinny from inside the helmet. In front of me, Hot Guy's own backpack and helmet duo form around him. He speaks in my ear through a tiny speaker.

"Hurry up and follow my lead," he demands.

He heads to the open exit, but I grab his sleeve and yank hard. He turns to me. "What?" he says, his tone clipped.

"Who are you?"

Hot Guy lifts his head dramatically, the wind blowing behind him, the sunlight silhouetting his figure. He says, "Eric. Eric Shaw." Then he waits, expectantly.

I stare at him quizzically. "Is that supposed to mean something to me?"

He grunts. "Just jump!" He motions to the clouds below us. I gulp.

"Wait! I can't just jump!" My breathing shallows. Stars dance in my eyes. "I don't even know how to use a parachute!"

Eric sighs and checks his watch. "We don't have time for this."

And then he shoves me right out the door.

4 / CRITICAL FAILURE

I plunge into a freezing cold free fall. The wind rips through my clothes as I plummet through layers of fluffy white clouds. I'm flailing, frantically trying to make sense of the endlessly spinning sky. I don't even realize I'm screaming until Eric's voice escapes the speaker in my helmet.

"Julie, shut up! I'm trying to concentrate." I squirm around, searching so I can adequately glare at this jerk.

Aha! I make out Eric's poised figure falling below me, slightly to the left. He's fast approaching another falling object—Greyson (AKA Blondie). How the hell did he get down there so fast, while I'm still wind-milling up here like one of those floppy car dealership balloon guys?

Eric slams into Greyson's back, wrapping his arms as far around the giant's torso as they'll go. Greyson turns around to face Eric, and the motion sends the two men spinning through the air.

"Not so fast," Eric says, struggling with his grip on Greyson's giant forearms. He grabs hold of the greasy blond ponytail whipping him in the face instead. Greyson roars in response to Eric's enthusiastic tug, and the distraction gives Eric a moment to shove something into one of Greyson's rapidly flailing trench coat pockets.

"Hey!" Greyson says. At least I assume that's what he says when he slaps Eric's hand away and grabs him by the neck. Eric knees him in the groin. With that, a skydiving match of fisticuffs breaks out and the two men start throwing punches mid-air. I can hear Eric grunt in my ear as Greyson swings his hefty fist and misses.

"Nice aim, clueless," says Eric. "Oh shit." He probably just noticed Greyson's bloody eye. Eric takes advantage of Greyson's blindness and effortlessly snatches the silver square from the giant man's clenched fist.

"What did the idiot say when he lost The McGuffin?" Hot Guy pulls Greyson up close to his helmet, delivering the punch line right to his face. "Eye have no idea." I can hear Eric's self-satisfied grin as he laughs and pushes off from Greyson's body. Eric spreads his arms and legs wide, creating distance between himself and the behemoth.

Some fifty feet above, I'm still spinning and watching it all unfold, my stomach clueless as to which way is the right way to throw up. To my left, the plane heads straight for the mountains. It seems to move in slow motion, it's elegant white body gliding through the air, tilted almost entirely to the side now. I almost forget I'm free-falling, mesmerized by the sight of it heading for the mountains. I have to squint as the plane passes the sun. In a matter of seconds, the giant vehicle crashes into the edge of the mountain, nose first in a massive explosion of fire, black smoke, and metallic debris.

I scream again.

"Stop yelling!" Eric flips his body around, so he's facing me from below. He's too far away for me to see his expression, but I'm sure he's smirking. "And what the hell are you doing?" he asks, probably referring to my squirming like an insect.

"I don't know!" I yell.

He grunts at my piercing voice. "Just put your arms and legs out like this."

I do as he does, creating as much surface area for my body as possible. The spinning immediately slows. I let out a high-pitched squeal.

"Great. Now watch out for Greyson." He points below us, to my right. Greyson's trench coat whips around behind him, but his body is unaffected by the wind. He's like a giant boulder plummeting through the sky.

Just then, Greyson turns around and BAM! A bullet ricochets off Eric's metallic backpack strap, flying off somewhere behind us.

"Ugh, this guy." Eric flips back around and pulls something out of his inner pocket. "The baboon really thinks I'd let him get away with The McGuffin." He laughs wickedly. Click.

As soon as Eric presses the button on his handheld device, an aggressive explosion of orange flames ignites from Greyson's trench coat pocket, engulfing his entire body. He turns into a ball of fire and gracefully passes behind a mountaintop, out of view.

I jerk my head away. The slight movement sends me spinning.

Crap.

I shoot my extremities back out in the "flying squirrel" position. That's better. Okay, no panicking.

Just when I start to get the hang of this "free-falling" thing, Eric says, "Prepare to deploy your chute."

A hot surge courses through my veins. I frantically search the metallic backpack for a button or zipper or something. "How?" Pretty sure my voice comes out higher than if I'd just sucked the helium out of an entire birthday balloon.

"It's a Smart Chute," he says as if that explains things.

"What the heck does that mean?" I ask, letting out a whimper of fear.

He sighs. "Just say, 'engage automatic deployment' and sit tight," he says. "The suit will deploy for you automatically, once we reach the right altitude."

Sit tight? Does he think we're just hangin' out in a waiting room somewhere? I clear my throat and say the simple command as if I'm speaking to Tony Stark's techno assistant J.A.R.V.I.S. A moment later, a smooth female voice speaks into the helmet. "Automatic deployment engaged."

"Here it comes. Brace yourself," Eric says.

Below, a silver cloud explodes from the back of Eric's figure. The parachute POOFs into shape, catching him gracefully in the air. Now he's falling at half my speed. I continue zooming forward.

"Reaching deployment altitude," the helmet lady says.

My screen suddenly lights up with green letters and numbers. It's some kind of algorithm factoring my altitude, speed, GPS location, and some other calculations I don't recognize.

"Ten, nine, eight..." the voice counts down. My heart races. Teeth clenched, hands clenched, butt clenched, I'm ready for the impact of the chute. "Two, one... deploy."

A moment of silence. I hear nothing but the rush of wind past my helmet, the digital ticking of the altimeter, and the racing beat of my heart.

PING! Something small and incredibly forceful lodges itself into the back of my chute pack.

"Critical failure. Critical failure..." the calm voice chants.

Damn it! Greyson's bullet.

An emergency alarm rings through the helmet. The green calculations turn red, and a giant "CRITICAL FAILURE" warning flashes across my screen, totally blocking my vision.

I scream, naturally.

"Would you stop scream—"

Just then, my body rips through Eric's parachute. I smack

right into him, and together we tumble through the air, drawing closer and closer to the mountains and the desert floor.

"Damn it!" he yells. We squirm against each other, trying to pull apart from the ropes entangling us. "Stop moving, you're making it worse!"

"I can't see anything!" I yell.

"Critical failure," the voice continues.

We both struggle against each other. Eric pushes me away. I spin through the air, farther from him, unable to control myself. I curl into the fetal position.

If I landed in a pool right now, it'd be one hell of a cannonball.

"Keep your arms out!" he yells, but I can't quite hear him over the warnings in my helmet. I'm falling way faster than him now. "You're gaining too much speed," he says. I put my arms out, but it does nothing. So much for the flying squirrel. We're fast approaching the sharp mountaintops.

"Shit," says Eric.

He presses a button on his chest, releasing his ropes. Then he puts his arms and legs by his side, turning himself into a human torpedo. He zooms through the air, right past me. Once he's a few feet below, he flips around and puts his arms out, catching the wind. He slams into me, face to face.

Oof.

"What should I do?" My voice is all over the place.

He ignores me, searches my body for something, his hands patting me down like a T.S.A. agent. He pats my butt.

"Hey!" I say.

He rolls his eyes. "There you are." He grabs something on the back of my chute. I can't see what he's doing back there. He pulls the dagger from his boot and starts sawing away at something.

"Critical failure, critical failure," the voice continues.

Yes, I know! It's quite clear we're going to crash in a matter of seconds. "Hurry!" I urge, though I've no idea what Eric is doing.

"Got it." He puts the dagger back and wraps his arms and legs around me. Then he stares into my eyes. "Hold on."

I wrap myself around him as best I can, interlacing my hands behind his cold metal pack. The mountains fly toward us, like a giant, teeth-cracking Toblerone. There's no way we'll make it. I hold my breath. Eric punches a button on my pack—

The parachute immediately escapes into the air, trailing wildly behind us. Half a second later, it catches in the wind.

Eric's body pulls against mine, but we manage to keep our grips. The chute slows our descent for a moment, just long enough for us to share a look of hope. Could this possibly work? Are we going to get out of this insane situation alive?

The heartbreaking sound of a metal CREAK sucks the breath from my lungs. Our combined weight is too much. The parachute completely rips away from us, and with it our fleeting pipe dream of survival, sending us to our deaths.

Eric and I free fall for another few seconds, then BAM! We smash into the mountain. Our grips break, and we tumble down the rocky slope at high speed toward an empty ravine. Dirt and pebbles fly in my face. All my layers of clothing bunch up behind me, leaving my bare back totally exposed. I skid over sharp rocks, desert cacti, and dry, pointy shrubs. One sharp object after another sends shooting pain through my body. The world is sky and earth, pain and…goddamn what is with these cacti?

If I somehow survive this, I'll be bruised for life.

I can't see Eric anywhere, but maybe that's because the damn "Critical Failure" badge is still flashing across my helmet. Give it a rest, helmet lady! Just then, my head smacks into a rock, cracking the entire screen into a million spider-webbed pieces, silencing the helmet lady for good.

I dig my heels into the ground in an attempt to slow my fall.

My feet catch on something jutting out the side of the mountain, jolting me into the air.

A second later, the mountain smacks into me hard. I tumble some more until my flailing body crashes into another out-of-control human body—Eric.

"Agh!"

We spill over one another until, finally, we hit rock bottom. Literally.

I fall hard on top of Eric. The inertia smacks my giant helmet into his unprotected chin (his helmet must have come off in the fall) with an audible THWACK. We lie there, motionless, our bodies bent in unnatural angles sprawled across the sharp, rocky ground. Dust clouds form above us as small rocks trickle down the mountainside.

We lie like that for a while, staring at the sun and listening to the pebbles trickle down the mountainside like crumbs. After all that commotion, the quiet of the desert feels eerily calm. It's actually kind of peaceful for a moment. Until Eric wheezes back to life.

The sound of him gulping down air makes me jolt with surprise, sending electrifying pain to every square millimeter of my body, and reminding me that, yes, I am unfortunately still alive.

Eric groans angrily and pushes me aside. I roll onto my back, gasping for breath just as he did. I wonder if I'll ever walk again. Can I move my toes? I mentally send a signal to my extremities. None of them budge. I hope I'm not completely paralyzed.

"Jesus Christ," says Eric. He sits up, moves his shoulders around. Stretches his neck. I watch in bewilderment as he jumps to his feet, full of energy and seemingly unharmed, save for the part of his lip where I smacked him with my helmet.

Yep, that's gonna leave a nice little bruise.

Meanwhile, every move I make sends increasingly painful lightning bolts through my body. It's like my nerves are awakening with each breath, telling me whatever just happened should have left me dead. Yes, I know, I tell my limbs. I wince with every inhale, gingerly pulling my heavy helmet off. My thick brown hair is matted to my head with sweat. I suck in the fresh air, fueling my bruised limbs through the motions of standing up.

As soon as I straighten out my spine, nausea and heat flashes and the shakes all come back at once for one final blow. I double over and vomit.

There goes my breakfast bar.

Eric checks his pockets and pulls out a small silver square, the one Greyson had stolen on the plane. It glitters in the sunlight. He admires it for a moment with a sigh of relief, then puts it back.

"Follow me, Julie," he says, then turns on his heel and heads further down the ravine, as if he knows exactly where he's going. As if everything that just happened was no big deal.

"Excuse me." I wipe my mouth with my sleeve. "What the hell just happened?" He doesn't answer. "Uh, hello?" I watch slack-jawed as he completely ignores me, walking confidently into the middle of nowhere.

"Did you hear me?" It occurs to me that maybe he actually didn't hear me. Perhaps he's in shock. I hustle to his side, sidestepping around the fallen rocks, and tug at his sleeve.

He whirls around with electric eyes and a snarl more gnarly than a stray dog. "How could I not? You haven't shut up this entire time."

"What is wrong with you?" He gives me a disgusted look. It floods me with so much hatred that I slap him. I know it's a good slap because the sound echoes through the desert.

He grabs my wrist, pulling me into his personal bubble.

"The question is, Julie, what's wrong with you?" His breath smells minty fresh. "Every single unfortunate turn of events that led us here could have been avoided if it weren't for you."

I gawk at him. He's seriously blaming me. "You mean how you shot the pilots, killed those passengers, and crashed the plane?"

"I didn't shoot the pilots," he corrects me.

"Oh, excuse me," I say. "Who the hell are you?"

He shakes his head. "You have no idea what you've gotten yourself into."

"You know what? You're absolutely right. Why don't you explain it to me?"

"I can't do that. Just be quiet and follow me." He drags me after him, marching forward through the dusty, rocky ravine. The sun blares down on us. I whip my head around, squinting into the distance in search of any familiar landmarks to get my bearings. Where the hell are we headed? All I see are mountains, mountains, and more mountains. A small orange lizard scurries behind the shade of a nearby pile of rocks, then pokes its head back out to watch the unusual action unfolding in his front yard. I glance at him, telepathically asking if he knows where we're heading. His bulging eyes stare back at me as if to say, "Hell if I know."

That does it.

"I'm not going anywhere until you tell me what's going on!" I rip my hand from his grasp and plant my foot in the ground. The motion sends a breath-catching sharp pain through my hip.

Ouch.

"Listen," he says. "It's my job to take you to headquarters. Once we're there, all our questions will be answered, and you might even get to return to your normal, boring life. Either you willingly come with me, or I make you."

Hmm… follow this crazy kidnapper to some creepy underground lair where who knows what will happen to my body? No, thank you. I shake my head.

"No," I say. Eric's eyes narrow.

"You think I care if you die out here?" he says. "I'm just following orders."

"Orders? From your creepy ring leader?" I say. The mention of any nearby ring leaders has panic building in my stomach. "Then I guess you'll just have to fail your mission."

His eye twitches. Clearly, he doesn't like the sound of that.

"Highly unlikely," he says. Then he straightens up. "You want me to leave you out here to die of dehydration? That's fine with me. I'll be doing the entire agency a favor."

And with that, he stomps away, leaving me in the dust cloud that follows.

Well, that took an unexpected turn. I look around once more. The mountains tower above us. They seemed so scary when I was falling toward them to my death, but now, in the pinkish glow of the setting sun, they look like a Bob Ross painting. It's peaceful, but I know once the sun sets, it'll be a different story.

I'm suddenly hyper-aware of the dryness in my mouth, and my lack of survival skills.

Damn it.

"Wait," I call after him. He turns around with a smug look on his face.

Whoever this "Eric Shaw" guy is, he's really pissing me off.

"Well?" he calls, fifteen feet away from me.

"I'll go with you, but only if you answer my questions first."

He considers this for a moment. "You get one question."

Ugh. Fine. I nod in agreement.

"What do you want to know, Julie?" he asks.

"That! Right there," I say, pointing my finger at him. "How do you know who I am?"

"That's classified," he states, matter-of-fact.

"Seriously? That's your answer," I say. He shrugs. "What are you, a spy?" I'm only half-joking.

He says nothing. Then I consider all the signs.

The Tom Cruise looks, the cocky attitude, the hand-to-hand combat, and cheesy one-liners…

"Oh my God, you're an asshole!"

"Close, but no cigar," he says, proving my point. "Let's go." He steps toward me.

"No way!" I turn around. "I take it back. You're insane." I dart the other direction down the ravine. Pebbles rush forward, threatening to take my feet out from under me.

Not a good idea.

Eric bolts after me. He reaches my side in two seconds. A firm pair of hands grab me by the waist and hoists me over his shoulder.

I kick and scream, right in his ear. He covers it with his free hand.

"Give it a rest," he grumbles. "There's no one else out here."

That's probably true. I scream louder, just to defy him.

"Agh!" He drops me on the ground and reaches into his inner jacket. He's going to shoot me, I know it.

He pulls out a small black box.

"What are you doing?" I ask.

He opens the box to reveal a mini syringe. Just the sight of it makes me woozy. He notices this, of course, and lifts the needle into the fading light of the sunset, showing off its green-tinted clear liquid.

"What is that?" My voice cracks as I scuttle backward.

"This is a drug that will knock you out immediately after injection," he says.

I struggle to stay upright. Blurriness creeps in from the corners of my eyes. Of all the unfortunate moments for my Vasovagal Syncope to kick in. I gulp. "Now, wait just a second —" I say.

"I'm not the bad guy, Julie. Remember that." He squeezes the handle, squirting the liquid out the end of the needle. He steps closer, his hand on my shoulder.

The thought of the needle penetrating my skin makes my entire body turn to Jell-O. My muscles begin spasming randomly like someone connected an electrical current to only my right bicep and my left butt cheek.

He brings the syringe right up to my inner elbow, pushing his thumb into my arm to wrangle my erratically pumping vein into place. He pierces my skin with the needle and I struggle to remain conscious against the mental image of that greenish liquid rushing into my venous pathways, reaching closer to my heart with each pump of blood...

Oh, screw it.

5 / SH*T HAPPENS

Beep... beep... beep...

The steady drum of digital beeping gently awakens me. My entire body is heavy, surrounded by comfy fluffiness. I slowly regain consciousness, the constant flow of breath in and out of my lungs a comforting rhythm.

Man... what a crazy dream I had. I must have been entirely out of it on the plane ride. But how did I get home?

My stomach grumbles. I'm starving. The low hum of heavy electrical equipment seeps into my ears. I take a slow, steady breath.

It smells... sterile, like cleaning supplies. Mom must have gone on a cleaning spree before my arrival. Oh snap, I must have imagined that whole pina colada thing, too. I take another deep breath. The motion brings awareness to my incredibly sore ribs and stomach muscles. In fact, all my muscles are sore. It's as if I fell down the side of a mountain.

Wait a minute...

I try to open my eyes, but I can't. They won't budge. I stifle a scream.

Where the heck am I?

Think, Julie, think. I fight to calm my pulse, which is threatening to break the light barrier. Okay, if I can't see, then I'll just try to hear. I focus on the sounds, even the smallest high-pitched whine of... is that fluorescent lighting? A faint scribbling noise flows through the air from behind me, a pen on paper. Is someone else in here with me?

Ohmygod. Someone is in here with me!

I try to open my eyes again. Nothing. Open, damn it! My left eyelid flutters open. I blink the blur out of my vision until the space around me becomes clear.

I frantically take in the space in search of the mystery person. I'm lying on a single bed in a large, white room. Frosted glass walls reach from the shiny white tiled floor to the metallic ceiling about fifteen feet above. Fluorescent rectangles shed bright white light down into the room, adding to the cold atmosphere.

But I don't see anyone.

The AC kicks on with a whir, drawing my attention to the silver, cylindrical ventilation system lining the perimeter of the ceiling. A few monitors stand to my left, displaying my heartbeat and other vital functions alongside a whole slew of readings I'm not familiar with. It looks like a combination of numbers, colorful patterns, and squiggly lines.

Is this some kind of hospital?

A door opens behind me.

"... but I got it back, of course. I'm telling you, she's a pain in the ass." Eric's boisterous voice fills the room.

My God, it was real! The realization strangely calms me for a moment, as it proves I wasn't imagining it all. Then my pulse beats in my throat again because that means I've been abducted by a man who explodes planes and people midair.

"She doesn't listen, she's unpredictable, and her voice is annoying," he continues.

"You clearly put her in a horrific situation, Eric." A woman's voice. She sounds older, maybe in her late forties. "I'm just relieved you managed to get her back here alive." The door shuts. "Hello, Simon," she says.

"Good afternoon, Director. Eric." This voice sounds like a teenage boy. He must be Simon.

"Look, it's clear she's not the right person for this," Eric says. "We're going to have to find someone else."

I want to shout out, "I'm not the right person for what? Where am I? Could you move a little closer so I can see who I'm dealing with, here?" But my voice is strangled within me and I can barely keep my one eye open.

The woman sighs. "Let's see what we have here first, alright?" says the woman. "Simon, were you able to learn anything while we were gone?"

"Actually, yes," the teenage boy says. He speaks with an air of knowledge like that of a Star Trek doctor. "Though, it's inconclusive due to her being unconscious. However, I'm quite excited at what my initial readings suggest." The energy in his voice increases as he talks. "It looks as though she is experiencing an allergic reaction to the transfer of information. She's capable of retaining much more data than my simple test message contained. Look at this." He steps around to the front of my bed.

I quickly close my eye, suddenly not too eager to reveal that I'm awake. These people are clearly using me for something, and I want to know more. But if Eric sees me awake, he'll surely stick me with his needle again. Gulp. More footsteps follow.

"Do you see this pattern at the bottom, here?" Simon asks.

"What is it?" Eric says.

While I suppose they're all focused on the monitors, I sneak a quick peek.

A short, pudgy red-headed teenager points to the screen. This must be Simon. His wavy red hair stands out against the stark white of his lab coat, and his bright, wide eyes take in the data on the screens excitedly. It's oddly off-putting for such confident science talk to be coming from so young a person. He continues to talk, his pudgy hands becoming as animated as his freckled face. I don't have a clue what the mumbo-jumbo he's saying means.

He's about a foot shorter than Eric, who's standing beside him with his arms crossed, frowning. Eric is wearing exactly what he was wearing when I met him, but it's a clean set of clothes. His closet must be a collection of the same white cotton shirt and black leather jackets. Which, honestly, I can understand. I mean, why not keep wearing what works? I'd probably do the same if I knew what worked for me.

Behind Eric, a tall, tan woman with slightly frizzy shoulder-length brown hair squints at the screens, holding a clipboard. She's wearing a pantsuit with a silky violet shirt underneath. Her name tag reads "PENELOPE BARNES, T.O.P.S.E.C.R.E.T. DIRECTOR OF OPERATIONS." The bags under her eyes, combined with her slumped over posture, give her an air of exasperation.

"These consistently flowing shapes show me that her brain is working out the data right now," Simon explains impatiently. "The oscillating colors suggest there's something unusual about the way her mind is interpreting the information. I'm guessing it's her brain's way of organizing the data, but I'll have no way of knowing until she wakes up." He says the last part with palpable anticipation.

"Or her brain is about to explode." Eric snorts. Simon's eyes light up, as if he hadn't considered that outcome. The Director gives Eric a pointed look, but he ignores her. If I could, I'd slap the excitement right out of him. "I'm telling you guys, she's clearly not the right fit for this."

The Director turns to him. "Yes, obviously, you were the agency's first choice, Eric, but you didn't make the cut."

"Test me again," he says, like a threat.

"My data was entirely conclusive, Eric," says Simon. "Your brain is not capable of handling the information—"

"Yeah, yeah. Fine. Let's just mess with her brain, wipe her memory, and send her home."

"Eric, why are you so against this?" The Director asks. "Julie is the first person to respond at all to Simon's test. Don't you at least want to know why?"

He presses his lips into a thin line.

"She's quite a unique specimen," Simon says. "Once I learn what makes her so special, I plan to initiate the next stage of the project." He smiles with a hundred thoughts dancing behind his eyes.

The Director adds, "With my approval, of course."

Her voice snaps Simon from his daydreams. "Of course," he nods.

"I'm excited, too, Simon," The Director says. "If it isn't a fluke, I think this could be the biggest breakthrough in modern history."

Jesus, they're talking about me like I'm some kind of lab rat. As if I'm not right here next to them.

My breathing turns shallow. The beeping on my heart rate monitor increases rapidly. They all shift toward me. I squeeze my eye shut, trying to make it look like I'm in the middle of a fascinating dream.

"She's waking up!" says Simon. He rushes over to his desk and rifles through some papers. "We need to prep the truth serum."

Truth serum? What the...

A buzzing sound alerts The Director. She checks her phone and gives another deep sigh. "I'm being summoned elsewhere." She shoves her phone back in her pocket and adjusts her clipboard. "Let me know when your testing is complete," she says, blocking Simon's path out of the room and forcing him to look right at her as she continues. "I'd like to meet her."

Simon nods and pushes past her, collecting more papers.

The Director turns to Eric. "Eric, could you please file an official damage report for all the unnecessary destruction you left in your wake—again."

"It was one plane, Penelope. Just take inventory of what I dropped off in the debrief room. You'll see what I used and what I didn't."

"You need to call me 'Director,' and that's the kind of information that should be in your logs. Please leave them on my desk in the next half hour."

"Can't. I told Simon I'd help him with the truth serum." Eric puts an arm around Simon.

"You did?" Simon asks. Eric steers him toward the door.

"Let's make it extra strong, and add some muscle relaxants, too," Eric whispers, leading Simon out into the hall. "She's surprisingly feisty."

"Ooh, tell me more," Simon says as the door closes behind them.

The Director closes her eyes. Her watch beeps and she taps the touch screen. A digital male voice says, "Time to relax! Let's get that blood pressure down. Begin simple breathing exercise—"

She silences the message with a forceful jab of her finger. After a moment of standing with her eyes closed and her lips pursed, The Director straightens her posture and scribbles on her clipboard papers, her heels click-clacking as she walks down the hallway. The door shuts behind her.

Silence, except for the heart rate monitor betraying my inner worry. I give myself a minute to figure out what I should do.

If this is real (why am I kidding myself, I know it is), one thing's for sure—I need to get out of here before Simon starts messing with my brain. Though, I have to admit, I'm actually pretty curious. What kind of test did I pass? What information is in my head? What's that tingly feeling?

A prickly sensation spreads through my toes. Then my fingertips. I cautiously test their functionality and am happily surprised to find them twitch back to life! Ha! Like an onslaught of pins and needles, the feeling washes over me from head to toe. I carefully stretch my whole body out. Everything feels bruised, but I can finally move again. I lightly touch my face, feeling for any kind of weird wires or (eek) needles.

There are a few round pads stuck to my temples. They're connected to cables that run into the monitors. If I take them off, will Simon and Eric be alerted?

The threat pales in comparison to being subjected to truth serum with Eric in the room. Screw it. I need to get out of here pronto.

I rip the wired pads off my forehead and remove the heart rate monitor from my finger when I notice there's a band-aid on my inner elbow.

Oh, God—they took my blood! I squeeze my eyes shut when the room starts wobbling. Now is not the time, Julie! Deep breath. I swing my lower half over the edge of the bed. The cold floor immediately wakes me up from my feet to my brain. I take in my surroundings with both eyes this time.

The only thing I couldn't see before was a large metallic desk sitting against the wall behind me. The entire wall is covered in monitors and computer screens showing all kinds of scientific information. Half of it looks like computer code and mathematical equations. The other half seems like a combination of chicken-scratch notes and hastily scrawled doodles. I'm caught between being overcome with curiosity (what in the world is this information regarding?) and terror (have I gotten myself involved in a conspiracy theorist's operation?)

There's loose-leaf paper strewn all over the desk. Each page contains more notes and images of what looks like brains, DNA strands, and question marks. Right in the middle of the desk lies a large red button. The button reads,

"LAUNCH," and it's sitting right beneath a monitor with a single image on it that says, "Project McGuffin." Above the desk is an air vent.

Ha! I'll crawl out, just like in the movies.

As I sneak over to Simon's desk, I notice my butt feels cold. Why does my butt feel cold? I look down—I'm wearing a hospital gown. Damn these crazy strangers! They took my clothes and my blood. And my fanny pack! Wait. Ohmygod—did they see my bare ass? I push away the unnerving thought and instead focus on the task at hand. Maybe they hid my things in Simon's desk.

I yank open the metal desk drawer closest to me, half expecting to spot my granny panties and my fanny pack right away. When all I find are pens and more loose-leaf paper, my stomach drops. Damn! There's no time to investigate, though. Simon and Eric will probably be back any second.

I climb on top of the desk and unscrew the surprisingly flimsy vent with the only weapon on me—my thick fingernails. Then I use all the sore muscles in my body to hoist myself up and into the vent. I try to distribute my weight as evenly as possible atop the thin sheet of metal.

So far, so good. The space is actually much bigger than I thought. It's almost as if these vents were made for escaping.

Guess that's why everyone always does it in the movies.

Carefully, I screw the vent back in place while coming up with a plan of escape. I'll crawl until I find a room with windows to the outside world. Then I'll drop down when no one's looking, break through the window, and run home. My stomach drops at the possibility that I'm on a secret prison floating in the middle of the ocean, in which case there would absolutely be no running home. Either that or I'm still in the middle of the desert and I'll die of exposure. Best not to think of that until I find the window room.

Alright. Which way should I go? Left. That seems like the

way out. With my first crawling movement, my knee makes a crater in the metal.

What is this made of, aluminum foil?

I better move fast before the floor gives way. Just as I take another crawling step forward, the door opens to the room below. I freeze.

"What a fascinating new subject," Simon's voice enters the room below me. "I cannot wait to start diagnostics testing—and just when things were getting boring around here!" I realize he has a slight lisp when he says, "fascinating" and "subject." Through the slits in the vent, I can see he's holding a tiny vial of purple liquid.

"Let's try to keep the science talk to a minimum," says Eric. They stop in their tracks at the sight of my empty bed.

"Where'd the test subject go?" Simon gasps.

Eric groans. "I'll tell security to seal the exits."

My other knee creates a second dent with a loud "THUNG." Eric and Simon look to the ceiling. The metal groans, echoing through the entire vent system.

Turns out, the movies were lying.

SCHOO! I fall right through the vent. My bare ass lands smack-dab on Simon's launch button.

I topple onto the cold floor. Immediately my brain is flooded with images, just like in my apartment after the career quiz. Except for this time, it all feels much heavier, much more real.

Flashes of all kinds of colorful information flicker before me in an uncontrollable surge of information.

High-tech futuristic weapons designs, blueprints for buildings, and gadgets I've never seen before command my attention.

Vehicle breakdowns, mugshots, zoomed-in photos of a thousand different people, and text files with so much redacted information there's barely anything readable in them—they all fly by under my eyelids at a hundred miles an hour.

Clips of silhouetted figures robbing banks and building weapons, and videos of violent acts as if I'm the one committing them bring tears to my eyes.

My eyelids flutter, my muscles twitch, and I'm pretty sure I'm drooling.

"She just launched Project McGuffin!" Simon cries. "My God, the possibilities," he murmurs.

Eric says, "Unbelievable." I tell my spasming legs to kick him in the groin, but they smack him in the ankles instead.

Close enough.

I can only hope my convulsing expressions convey that I'm glaring at him.

"Do you have any idea what you just did?" Eric asks me.

6 / LOOSEY GOOSEY

By the time the sedative part of the truth serum mixture starts to kick in, Eric and Simon have already managed to wrangle my flailing body back into the hospital bed.

They hastily re-attach the electrodes to my temples and clip the heart rate monitor to my twitching pointer finger.

Surges of foreign information continue to flash across my vision, sending waves of nausea and throbbing pain through my entire body. With each spasm, the fast-paced beeping of the monitor flatlines for a few seconds, then returns to normal.

My eyes flicker back and forth while more and more images sprint across my brain. Gap-toothed grins and evil laughs, pools of blood and handheld rocket launchers, silhouetted individuals piecing together disassembled weaponry. I'm standing in hotel rooms overlooking crowded city streets amid public gatherings, I'm walking down seedy alleyways at night, protecting manila envelopes of confidential information from being destroyed by raindrops as I discreetly exchange proprietary information... It's like half of the images are random moments captured in time, as if they really happened, while the other half are completely outlandish dreams as if I'm the one performing these foreign acts. None of it means anything on its own, but somehow all of it together forms an intense feeling of dread when combined.

The sedative slowly winds its way through my veins, relaxing my tensed muscles. Simon and Eric stare with wide eyes as my uncontrollable limbs begin to calm, my breathing still heavy. The continuous surge of information gradually trickles to random flickers. Then, total blackness. My eyes shut tight, eyeballs dancing all around, still chasing the ghosts of the images that just invaded my mind.

"This is incredible," Simon whispers. "Project McGuffin is finally a go!" I can feel Simon's presence as he leans close to my face and claps his hands together. My eyelids fly open. "Stay awake. I'll be right back." Simon hurries over to his desk. "Lock the door, Eric," he adds.

I let out a whimper. Eric flashes me an amused grin and says, "Just so no one interrupts," before heading to the door.

I want to run, but there's no way in hell that's happening now. Not with all the damn muscle relaxant.

Now I'm so loosey-goosey I can't move my muscles, and my lips and tongue are numb. My head aches, and another round of sticky, cold sweat is seeping into the thin hospital gown fabric, forming dark stains under my armpits. I've never felt so attractive in my life. The touch of the cold liquid sends a layer of goosebumps across my entire epidermis.

My own sweat betrays me.

I take deep breaths. At least I can control my lungs. Stay calm, Julie. It's going to be okay.

Eric steps into the hall, looks both ways, and locks the door behind him with a loud click. He steps to the edge of my bed and leans into my personal bubble.

"Can you hear me, Julie?" Eric asks.

"Yes, jerk," I spit. Literally, a bit of drool comes out. My mouth is so numb it makes everything I say sound like baby talk.

Eric chuckles. "I can't take you seriously like this, I'm sorry."

"No, you're not." I sound like a pouting four-year-old. "What do you want from me?"

"I want to test out the truth serum," he says. "Tell me this—What's your name?"

"Julie Richardson," I answer immediately, unintentionally. I know this because I had planned on being uncooperative.

"Alright, and what's my name?" he asks.

"Eric. Eric Shaw." I try to mimic his dramatic delivery from the plane as close as possible. He just laughs.

"Okay. Where are you from?"

I want to say, "none of your business," but it comes out as "Beechmont, Florida." I guess this truth serum does work.

"And where are you now?"

"I don't know. Jeez!" I say, in an exceptionally whiny tone. Maybe the truth serum is turning me into a child. Or perhaps it just stripped me of all my remaining dignity. Though, if I'm being honest with myself, there wasn't much of that left to begin with. "Can you stop asking questions? I'm the one who needs answers!" I pout. Eric stifles another laugh.

Simon returns with a pair of glasses hanging around his neck, holding a notebook and some loose-leaf papers covered in unintelligible notes. "What are you doing, Eric? Don't interrogate her yet."

"Relax. I'm just testing the serum by asking her questions I already know the answers to."

"I could be tracking all of this data!" Simon throws his hands in the air.

"Don't worry, bud. I've got it all up here." Eric points to his temple with a confident nod to Simon.

The young scientist purses his lips. "Fine. You may continue." He turns to the monitor, adjusts some settings, and enthusiastically scribbles down some more chicken scratch.

Eric looks me in the eye and asks, "Are you attracted to me?" with a smirk.

"I guess," I say. Great. Well done, brain. Eric narrows his eyes. "To be honest," I add, "your smile is crooked, and it's been bugging me this entire time." Ah ha! Success.

He chuckles and flashes me a real grin this time. It truly is the most attractive smile I've ever seen on a man.

"I mean, that was super cute," I continue, totally unable to stop myself, "but it doesn't outweigh the fact that you drugged and kidnapped me."

Eric juts his jaw out, scowling.

"Tell me about it," I say. "Oh, and don't even get me started on your attitude, mister—"

"Alright, for God's sake." He clasps a hand over my mouth. I continue spouting nonsense into his palm like a deflating whoopie cushion.

Simon taps the screen. "That should do it." He places his spectacles on the bridge of his nose and turns to me and Eric, pen and notepad at the ready. "Is the truth serum working?"

"Unfortunately," Eric mutters.

Simon giggles. "Fantastic! Alright, let's get started—" he says, but he's interrupted by his phone ringing. He looks at the caller I.D. and puts it on speaker with a huff. "Director?"

The Director's shrill voice escapes from the phone. "What's going on? I received an alert that—"

"They drugged me, and now I'm paralyzed!" I spout, muffled by Eric's hand.

"It's just truth serum and muscle relaxant," says Eric.

"Eric, what are you doing there? And what do you need muscle relaxants for?" I didn't realize someone's voice could sound so tight.

"It's a safety precaution. Her body entered a state of convulsion as soon as she launched Project McGuffin," says Simon.

"What!" The Director yells. A beat. Then, "Take me off speaker."

Simon does as he's told, but it doesn't stop The Director's high-pitched shouting from being heard by everyone else in the room.

"You launched Project McGuffin without my approval?"

What is this McGuffin thing they all keep mentioning? Images of MacGyver pop into my head, but I'm pretty sure it's not that.

"Technically, Julie did, ma'am," Simon says. "She tried to escape and accidentally activated the launch button during the process—"

"She tried to escape?" She mutters, "I leave for one minute —" Pause. "What about the database? Did we lose our information?"

Simon and Eric share a worried look. "Let me check." Simon rushes to his desk. He puts the phone on speaker again while he searches his computer files. Eric crosses his arms and watches determinedly at the over-sized computer screen.

"I'm not sure yet." Simon gives Eric a strained look. Eric motions for him to hurry, and stage whispers, "Hang up the phone!"

"Er, there's no information in The McGuffin database," Simon says to the phone.

"You're telling me we just uploaded all our Top Secret information into a civilian's brain with no guarantee we can retrieve or remove it?"

"Yes." Simon nods his head at the phone.

Eric facepalms his forehead and then glares at me. As if this is my fault!

The Director goes quiet, and the faint sound of her watch beeping fills the background. Then she lets out a deep breath.

"Well, at least we have a backup," she says, more to herself than to Simon. Simon nods in agreement.

"Alright, here's what you're going to do," she continues. "You're going to find out whether the transfer worked. If so, you'll determine how to replicate Project McGuffin on a more suitable subject, and if it can't be done, I'm scrapping the entire thing." Simon bites his lip at the thought. "Understood?"

"Don't worry, Director. I'm going to perform a deep exploratory surgery in her cranial—"

"Surgery?" I screech. The heart rate monitor goes crazy.

"What's that noise? What's happening?" The Director demands. Simon rushes back over to the data monitor.

"Her cortisol levels are affecting the data." His gaze darts all over the monitor, taking in every stat, then he turns to me and shouts, "Stay calm, or you'll ruin everything!"

How very helpful.

"Don't tell me to stay calm!" I screech, my voice cracking. No way they're getting me under the scalpel. Damn these dead muscles! "Get me the hell out of here!"

Eric claps his hand over my mouth once more and yanks the phone from Simon's grasp with his free hand. "Don't worry, Director. I'll handle this. Go treat yourself to a nice manicure or something."

"Eric, you should be filing your—"

Eric ends the call and tosses the phone back to Simon, who fumbles to catch it. He finally gets a grip on the small device and drops it back in his lab coat pocket. This kid can't even catch a phone and he wants to perform surgery on me? I don't freaking think so.

Eric turns to me. "I'm going to take my hand off your mouth. When I do, you're going to hold your tongue. Got it?" He stares me down. I stare back.

"Fine," I say, but it comes out like "Phnmg." Eric gingerly removes his palm.

"First things first—you must calm down." Simon places a hand on my shoulder, but I can't flinch away.

"Don't touch me!" I shriek. Simon feverishly glances between the monitor and me.

"I knew it." Eric shakes his head at me. "I knew you wouldn't listen."

"Don't you have some kind of logs to take care of?" I hiss at him.

"And miss this? No way." He grins. It simultaneously turns me on and irks me to the core.

Simon pulls a chair up to the other side of the bed. I try to move my arms with all my might, but it only sparks another surge of pain that sends the monitor flatlining again. Is this how I'm going to die?

Nope, I think, as the beeping goes back to normal. I sigh.

Welp, that took all my remaining energy. "What do you want?" I ask with a weak voice.

Simon holds his pudgy hands up in the universal 'please stay calm, we're not going to hurt you' signal. "We need to perform some tests on your brain, preferably while the transfer is still fresh—"

"Look, if you want me to cooperate, you're going to have to answer some of my questions first," I say.

"We don't have time for this, Julie," Eric says. "Just trust us."

"Sure, says the guy who pushed me out of an airplane!" The monitor beeps faster. Eric rolls his eyes at me.

Simon jumps to attention, reaching for the readings on the screen with a plea in his expression. "My data!" he cries, then he recomposes himself.

"Alright. What do you want to know?" Simon asks.

"Who are you, and what do you want with me? Where is this place? What's Project McGuffin? What happened to my brain?" I stare them down, ready to finally get some answers.

"That's too many questions," Eric says.

Who knew there was a limit?

Simon purses his lips and whispers to Eric, as if I can't hear them right next to me, "It may be the only way to protect the data."

"Fine, but keep your answers short and to the point, Mr. Explainy," Eric 'whispers' back.

Simon turns back to me, a professional smile plastered on his face. "Hello." He holds out his hand. "My name is Simon Zedler."

I tell my hand to shake his, but it merely twitches. Simon abandons the gesture. Good start.

"I'm the Head Computer Scientist and Senior Analyst here at T.O.P.S.E.C.R.E.T."

"What's Top Secret?" I ask.

"T.O.P.S.E.C.R.E.T. is an undercover government organization devoted to protecting the United States from foreign and domestic threats," says Simon.

"So… you're spies." I let that sink in for a second.

"We're secret agents," Eric says.

"So, what, you do things like in Mission Impossible?"

"More like James Bond. I work alone," Eric says. There he goes again with the cheesy lines. I guess he really is a spy.

"Not technically," Simon corrects. "I help by delivering mission updates to Eric from The McGuffin and interpreting the information he obtains in the field. We're a team," he says with a smile. Eric screws up his lips at that. It appears he doesn't think so.

"Okay," I say. "What is a McGuffin?"

"The McGuffin," Eric corrects. "It's the single most powerful and all-knowing source of all T.O.P.S.E.C.R.E.T. private intel."

Right, because that sounds like a good plan. All your secrets in one place. Bravo.

"So, it's like a cloud-based filing system, or…?" I squint my eyes, expecting some sort of logical explanation to follow.

"It's a proprietary piece of technology that tells us who we're after and what the mission is, among other things," Simon says, matter of fact.

"Alright, and who tells The McGuffin what missions to hand out?" I ask.

"No one," says Simon.

"C'mon, Julie. You think a single person could know all the secrets of the world?" Eric snickers.

I narrow my eyes. "Then how does The McGuffin know?"

"It just does," Eric says. Simon nods.

"So, The McGuffin is an all-knowing source of secrets that randomly gives you missions to save the world?" They nod their heads. They're not kidding. "You just described a magic eight ball," I say.

"This isn't a joke, Julie," Eric says. "Do you think we'd waste our time with you if the world weren't at stake?"

So dramatic. "Look, even if I believed this crap, it still doesn't explain how I'm involved. What did you do to me?"

Simon perks up at this question. I get the sense he likes to explain things.

"About two years ago, I thought, 'Wouldn't it be great if instead of sending T.O.P.S.E.C.R.E.T. information to our field agents through easily interceptable means such as messengers, drop boxes, safe house locations, etcetera, etcetera, we could send the information directly to our agents' brains?'" His eyes light up and he stares at me expectantly.

Oh. This is where I'm supposed to look impressed. "Uh. Sure," I nod. "Sounds like a good idea." Simon beams at my approval and continues.

"I presented my idea to The Director, and she loved the efficiency of it. So that's when I began working—"

"Simon," Eric interrupts. "Just skip to the part about what happened to her brain."

"Wait, I want to hear everything," I stammer. Why does Eric

seem to know the direct route to under my skin? "Please, keep going."

"Right," Simon says, looking between Eric and me as we glare at each other. He clears his throat. "Well, once I felt the system was ready, I created a test 'message', about the same size as your standard T.O.P.S.E.C.R.E.T. case briefing."

"And how big is that exactly?" I ask.

"One hundred forty pages or so," Simon confirms. Jeez, nothing like preparing your field agents for work on-the-go. "I tested sending the message directly to the brains of all our top agents, Eric included, but none of them were able to receive the information successfully. Some agents died during the transfer, some agents were severely traumatized as a result of the foreign digital data, and some agents simply couldn't receive the data at all, like Eric, here." Eric looks away, his jaw hard.

"So, I placed my test message online to be discovered by whoever could trigger it. I programmed it to reveal itself whenever someone completed our 'career quiz' in a precise way, to ensure they'd be suitable at least for the fundamental level of testing. Hundreds of people got to the end of the test, but the only person to activate the data transfer was you."

"Wow…" I take a moment to let it all sink in. "I knew that wasn't a normal computer virus," I think aloud.

"Perhaps because it wasn't a virus," Simon corrects, pushing his glasses back up the bridge of his nose with his pudgy pinky finger. "We sent Eric to retrieve you so we could figure out why you were able to trigger the message and, hopefully, replicate the same response in one of our agents."

I furrow my brow. My muscles must be coming back. "So, you put a deadly virus online endangering the lives of innocent people?"

"Nonono, Julie," Simon says, hands going back up to shoo my worries away. "It wasn't a virus. It was a message. And it would only activate if, well let me try to explain in a way—"

"What Simon means to say," interrupts Eric, "is that it would only work if it could work. Understand?"

"Sure, I understand," I say. "You let me almost die from information overload and then waited for me to be on a freaking airplane before kidnapping me." Unbelievable.

"Apprehended," Eric corrects. If I could move my arm, I'd slap him again. But for now, I settle for an angry nostril flare.

"Now what? You're going to keep me prisoner and lobotomize my brain?"

Simon raises his hands again, urging me to calm down, but it only succeeds in annoying me further.

"We originally planned to perform easy, simple tests to become acquainted with your brain. Only after determining whether my initial message had successfully been received would we then continue on to more invasive techniques for more detailed analysis. But, well, you sort of skipped all that when you launched the entire contents of The McGuffin into your mind."

I close my eyes, blocking out their nosey faces for just a moment.

A computer virus that sends information into your brain. A spy sent to save me from a plane crash. Because I passed a Top Secret government agency's un-passable test.

This all seems entirely unreal.

Then again, I've always had a knack for acing tests.

"What happens now? Can you get this McGuffin out of my head and let me go home?"

Simon trots over to his giant flat-screen TV, referencing his intriguing mysterious data analytics as if the oscillating color and ticking number mean anything to me. "Ideally, I'd like to perform some tests as soon as possible while The McGuffin transfer is still fresh in your mind," he says, his fingers twitching with anticipation. "We have no idea how your brain has processed the information, or what kind of complications or dangers might arise without proper initial analysis."

"Dangers? Complications?" The heart rate machine makes a dramatic beep.

Simon waves his hands dismissively. As if that'll help. "Well, of course. As with any experiment, there's bound to be health risks, potentially life-threatening—" He stops at the sight of my horrified expression.

"Of course, this is all theoretical. It's just that, even we have no idea of the full extent of The McGuffin's knowledge. It's always been sort of a mystery to us, and now it's locked within your unique brain." He's practically seething at the mouth.

"If it was so damn dangerous, why would you leave a giant red launch button lying around?" I ask. Besides, how do they not know what this McGuffin thingy does if they designed the damn thing? At least, I'm assuming they made it. My God, what if it was sent from outer space? What if this McGuffin thing is sending me these crazy ideas right now?

Simon looks bewildered by the question, like it never occurred to him to not have a giant red LAUNCH button lying around. He opens his mouth to speak, but Eric hastily interrupts whatever he was going to say.

"Don't question T.O.P.S.E.C.R.E.T. methods, Julie," he says.

"Look, I don't want to be involved—"

"It's a little late for that," Eric says.

No shit, Sherlock.

"Please understand, Julie. You are very special." Simon looks at me with pleading eyes. I almost forget he wants to put me under the scalpel.

"Just, give me a second," I say, the gravity of the situation fully setting in. I'm pretty much stuck in this isolated secret place in the middle of who knows where with two guys who are more than capable of killing me, whether intentionally or not.

For someone who's irrationally afraid of needles and barely

gets out, I think this goes as some kind of record. Plus, despite everything, I'd like to know why I passed their test.

"Hello? Julie?" Simon waddles over and waves his hands in front of my eyes. Eric stands from his perch on the edge of my temporary bed and crosses his arms, staring me down with a contemplative look. I wonder what's going through his broody mind.

"You're not kidding," I say, incredulous.

"We never kid when it comes to The McGuffin," says Eric.

I struggle to sit up straight, intending to make these boys see just how serious I am. When I stop breathing heavily, I glower at them with my best businesswoman face. "Okay, let's get this straight," I say. "I want to know what's going on in my head, too, but you've got to understand something— I don't do needles."

Simon opens his mouth like he's going to protest. He turns to Eric, who shrugs. Simon sighs reluctantly. "I suppose that's doable," he mutters.

"Or scalpels," I add. "Or any kind of invasive surgical technique or bodily intrusion."

"That's going to make it extremely difficult—" Simon starts to say, but the fast beeping returns. He glances at the monitors again. "Fine—I welcome the challenge."

"And one other thing," I say. Simon presses his lips together, a tick starting up his jaw. "When we're done with your tests, and we figure out what's going on in my brain, you're going to take The McGuffin out of my head and let me go home."

"Well, we don't know how—" Simon starts, but Eric kicks him under my bed.

"Great idea," says Eric. "Do we have a deal?" Simon watches with an uncertain expression as Eric reaches his hand out to shake mine. I get the feeling they're not telling me the entire truth, but I suppose I can't do anything about it anyway.

My curiosity gets the better of me.

"Let's just get this over with." I manage to shakily raise my palm into Eric's grasp. He gives me one firm shake, not bothering to hold back a look of disgust as my cold, sweaty hand slides out of his and flops back down on the bed like a dead fish.

"Alright," I say. "Let's do this."

7 / TEST IS MY MIDDLE NAME

We're in a different room now, slightly larger with all kinds of exciting doodads lining the frosted glass walls on steel shelves. It's sort of like a recording booth for bands, except instead of cozy and warm and conducive to the creative flow, this place is sterile and cold and perfect for dissecting aliens.

"Now hold your left arm perpendicular to the floor. That's it," Simon says from behind his computer monitor.

He has me standing on one leg with practically every part of my body connected to more wires. My ass is still on full display because of this ridiculously useless paper hospital gown. I feel entirely naked. Eric watches with his mysterious, calculating eyes, arms crossed as he sits on the edge of Simon's giant metallic desk.

The floor is separated into fourths. One fourth is wood, one fourth is carpet, one fourth is tile, and the other quarter is a pool of water, covered by a plastic casing. I'm standing on the carpet part now, barefoot, and shaking like a scared wet dog.

"Now put your tongue behind your front two teeth and say 'Hippopotamus.'" Simon's voice echoes through the speakers in the room, ending with the audible click of the microphone button.

Ugh, I just did that. I swear half of these tasks are probably being whispered into Simon's ear by a certain smirking someone who just wants to watch me suffer. I've already been drenched in freezing cold water, blindfolded and subjected to concise, intense periods of no oxygen, exposed to chemicals for the purpose of "olfactory testing," forced to put my hand in mystery boxes for the sake of my "tactile response health", and asked to recite the alphabet backward to the tune of "Happy Birthday." Each time I let out a cry of pain, it seems to give Simon a burst of encouragement.

It's hardly reassuring.

As I stand here, hair still dripping from my most recent swim in the floor tub, I think about my parents. It's hardly fair. I'm being tortured and held prisoner while they're somewhere off the coast of Freeport getting drunk with a bunch of strangers. Thousands of smelly strangers stuck together in a floating box of germs.

On second thought, I'll take the torture. However, I wouldn't say no to a Pina Colada right about now.

But I have to wonder if my parents will even worry when they hear about the plane crash. If they hear about it.

Alright, stop being a drama queen, I tell myself. I'm just starting to freak out about the possibility that I won't ever be allowed to leave this place. Or that The Director will have Simon erase my memory. Or that, most likely, they'll just kill me.

Either way, I'd really like to put some pants on first.

"Perfect," Simon says. He releases the microphone button, leaving me to lip-read his and Eric's conversation behind soundproof glass. I strain my eyes, tracking every move Eric's luscious lips make. Simon smiles at whatever he's saying, then Eric looks right at me with a smirk. Microphone static fills the air, and Simon's voice follows.

"You may put your arm down now," he says. It flops to my

side, tingling with the pins and needles of no blood flow. "Now turn your attention to the floor. Do you see that line of tape there?" I nod. A line of red tape runs about twenty feet down the wood floor. "Please walk along it."

I take my first step, then the next, trying not to trip over the wires attached to my calf muscles. "I'm not drunk, you know. Is this even necessary?"

No response.

My toes tingle with each step. I'm still regaining feeling in my big toes and the inside of my lips, but for the most part, everything else is back to normal. It's been a while since I got here, and I'm honestly surprised I haven't been offered any water or snacks or bathroom breaks. It's a wonder I haven't peed my pants yet, or lack thereof.

"Can I get a bathroom break soon?" I reach the end of the tape. "Hello?" I'm talking to myself here.

"Turn around and walk back," Simon instructs. He hasn't said "please" this whole time.

"Ugh, fine," I say, carefully lifting each foot over the other's wires. They can definitely see my entire naked derriere as I walk back along the line. Maybe that's why Eric is snickering, or maybe it's the giant "LAUNCH" shaped welt on my bruised butt, but this constant string of mortifying events has pretty much desensitized me at this point.

"Stay on the line," Eric's voice comes through the speaker. I jump in surprise, almost losing my balance.

"Maybe I would if you'd stop interrupting me!" I shout back.

"Oh, and please lower your level of sass."

I roll my eyes and mutter through gritted teeth, "Pardon me for being a little upset about my current situation."

Eric presses the speak button again and a screeching sound pierces my ears before his voice fills the room. "You'd be surprised the kinds of weird crap Simon has to deal with, especially with past subjects purposely trying to tamper with Simon's research."

"Golly jee, why would anyone do that?" I ask sarcastically. It goes right over Eric's head.

"You know, competitors or foreign agents trying to infiltrate T.O.P.S.E.C.R.E.T., nab our experiments, and copy our data files. And there's always someone trying to steal The McGuffin. Truth serum is now standard procedure."

I finish my little walk and turn on my heel to face the guys. "Yikes," I mutter. "There's a whole spy world that I have absolutely no idea about." Hey, wait a minute. What if these guys aren't actually spies and are just a couple of loonies out in the middle of nowhere? I try to push the thought aside.

"We're just scratching the surface, babe," Eric says.

I give him an exasperated look, ignoring the fact that he called me babe. "Can we move on to the interesting part and find out why Project McGuffin worked for me and why it didn't work for Eric?" I ask. The last bit of the truth serum is still flowing through my body, and it's definitely to blame for my childish behavior. At least, that's what I'm telling myself.

Eric lowers his steely gaze at me in response to my comment. Do I detect a hint of jealousy? The thought pleases me. Though, I'm sure it's because of the drugs in my system. I'm never this petty. Or sassy. Or whiny.

Maybe this "McGuffin" has unleashed sides of me I never knew existed. Besides my competitive side, of course, which always comes out during academic decathlons and state-wide testing. I've only ever felt truly confident under the pressures of testing. Which is probably why I'm chock full of sass right now. Once it wears off, I'll be back to my worrywart self, I'm sure of it. I have my mother's genes to thank for that.

The sealed glass door swooshes open as Simon eagerly waddles in, scanning his trusty stack of notes with wide eyes. Eric follows, hands in pockets, a permanent smirk on his face.

"What now?" I ask.

"We're finished with the physical health testing," Simon states.

"And?"

"You passed. A plus," Eric jokes, but it seriously pleases me.

"Alright. One test down, one to go, right?" I ask Simon.

"If you're lucky," Eric mutters.

"Please take a seat over there." Simon gestures to a wall.

"Uh... where?"

"Oh! Silly me." He types a seemingly arbitrary pattern into the tile on the wall and suddenly it opens up, revealing an entirely different room cloaked in dim lighting. What a weird place. I heave all the wires around my ankles into a big pile at my chest.

As we walk closer, lights flicker on in the high ceiling above us to reveal a very stark, smooth white room. In the center lies a raised, circular part of the floor with pulsing blue lights emitting from beneath it. The circle slowly turns, bouncing light off the curvy, metallic-looking chair atop it.

"That's a chair?" I ask. "It looks more like a sculpture."

"Yes, it's quite beautiful, isn't it? My favorite T.O.P.S.E.C.R.E.T. asset, if you ask me." Simon puts a hand to his cheek and stares dreamily at it.

"What does it do?" I ask, slightly terrified of his possible answers.

"It does many things—"

"That we don't have time to discuss with you," Eric finishes, flicking a look at Simon. I let out an agitated huff.

"Let's just say, this thing can give life, and it can take life," Eric states, ominously. I stare at it, wondering how many ways it might kill me. I shudder.

"And you want me to sit in it?" I say.

Eric nods. "Standard procedure," he says with a wicked grin.

I should have guessed.

"Please take a seat." Simon gestures to the oddly shaped piece of equipment, still turning as the floor slowly spins beneath it. I awkwardly step onto the ledge, lose my balance, and trip into the weird seat, dropping all the wires to the floor. I let out a short, high-pitched shriek as my butt touches the cold metal.

"What are you looking for now?" I ask.

Neither of them answers me.

Simon pushes his hands against a white tile panel on the wall. A desk unfolds from a cutout behind the panel, complete with multiple monitors and loose-leaf papers strewn about, as if Simon had been working here all along and simply folded his desk into the wall when he was finished.

Eric presses against another panel, and a closet door opens. He pulls out two soft-looking rolling chairs and gets comfy in one of them, ready to watch the show as Simon submits me to a whole new slew of tests.

Simon grabs a small silver remote and taps a few buttons. The floor stops spinning, and a set of armrests emerge from the chair's sides. "Place your hands on the edges there," he instructs me from his desk. Then he presses another button, and a set of footpads emerges at the bottom of the chair. "Place your feet atop the scanners," he says, touching one more button. A helmet emerges from the top of the chair, smoothly setting into place just above my head. Colorful lights twinkle and soft beeps start up. Simon then pulls his rolling chair up near me and plops down, paper and pen at the ready. Eric scoots closer, as well.

"Explain when you first encountered my test message. Tell me everything about the experience," Simon says, "down to every detail." The bubbling enthusiasm underlying his words makes me feel excited about what's to come, temporarily dispelling my fear of undergoing the upcoming death-chair test. This shouldn't be too bad...

"Okay." I scrunch my face up, trying to remember it all. "I was sitting at my desk. In the kitchen. In my apartment. It's a small apartment. One bedroom, one bath, a small stove, and barely any room for preparing meals. Which, honestly, isn't too bad since I'm only usually cooking for one anyway—"

"Try to stay on point," says Eric, jiggling his leg impatiently. "Jesus, both of you," he mutters.

"Tell us what happened when the message appeared," Simon urges.

"I finished the test, and the screen turned black. Then a small white square popped onto the screen." Simon rapidly scrawls all this down in his notepad. "It started flashing. Then I felt like I was mesmerized by it. I don't remember what happened after that, except that it felt like I slammed into a brick wall."

Simon rolls back over to his computer and types up a few things. "Do you remember if you saw anything? Heard anything? Remember to hold the armrests," he adds.

His insistence on the armrests has me feeling hesitant, but I grip them tighter nonetheless and think back on the moment. Suddenly, the images come back to me. "I saw flashes of explosions and people, I think. But they were dark, like shadows, and there were weapons."

"What kind of weapons?" Eric asks.

"I don't know," I say. "I just blacked out. That's all I can remember."

Simon plucks a few seemingly random loose-leaf papers from his desk and sifts through their contents, then he clicks around on the screen. Eric walks over to his side. Together, they ponder the information on his monitor.

"What? What's happening?" I ask. The angle of the monitor makes his readings look like a bunch of scribbles to me.

"You interpreted the text as images," he says. "Very peculiar."

"What text? What was your message?"

"My message was the entire movie script for Mission Impossible Two," Simon says.

I stare back at him, brows furrowed. "You sent me a script?"

"Yes, it's about the same size as a standard T.O.P.S.E.C.R.E.T. mission brief, and I thought it was topical, seeing as we're secret agents and all." He smiles, proud of his little nerdy joke. "What's most impressive is you received the words correctly but interpreted the message as a combination of stand-out images. Your brain is quite unique."

"So she got the message, but she didn't know what it meant," Eric says, disappointed.

"I'm sorry—you said you sent me a movie script?" I ask again, but the question bounces right off their thick heads.

"This suggests her imagination is powerful, as well as her creativity," Simon explains to Eric. "The fact that Julie is interpreting text in other forms prompts a whole slew of befuddlements," he says, smiling from ear to ear, "seeing as the whole point of Project McGuffin is to deliver T.O.P.S.E.C.R.E.T. intel, unaltered, directly to an agent's brain."

"Maybe that's because she's not a field agent," Eric suggests. He stands, begins pacing around the strange chair, making my head spin. "If I could replicate her brain waves or something, maybe I could understand the messages."

Simon bursts into hearty laughter.

"What? Isn't that the whole point?" Eric asks.

"No one can replicate brain waves." Simon wipes a tear from his eyes. "Especially not from this brain."

"Why not?" Eric asks. He flexes his muscles in frustration.

"It's a very... unique brain."

"You keep using that word," I say. "What makes my brain different from the rest of your test subjects?" Saying the word makes me feel like a lab rat. Besides, didn't he mention something about this being potentially life-threatening? Suddenly, this doesn't feel like such a good idea. I really don't want an ear grown out of my back like that mouse, or something equally as strange.

"Yeah, why did she get the message and not me?" Eric's eyes flicker to me and back to Simon. He isn't sitting well with the idea that someone might be better than him at something.

This pleases me.

"In practically every field agent I tested, they each used the same or similar parts of their brains— the parts that have to do with physical exertion, instinctual reflexes, and emotional responses such as fear, excitement, and pride, etc." Simon turns in his swivel chair to face me.

"But with Julie," his eyes glimmer, "it seems there is far more activity occurring in the areas involving memory, projective imagination, and interpretation. Also, she's exhibiting more complex emotions such as," he looks at the monitor and continues, "wonder, anxiety, mortification, distress, dread, panic, terror, exhilaration, attraction, etc." Eric snickers at that last one. "And it's inspiring to see this high range of capability when it comes to apprehension and even physical ability."

"What are you saying? She's more capable?" Eric points to me as if I'm a potato, sounding incredulous.

"She's more… emotional. More honest. More open," says Simon.

"So, a woman," Eric states. "And obviously unfit for an agent." I roll my eyes.

"Perhaps, but possibly just right for Project McGuffin." The same giddy smile is plastered on Simon's pale, freckled face. I can practically feel the crackling energy coming off him every time he mentions The McGuffin or his readings. This kid is seriously freaking me out.

"You got all that from reading my palms?" I ask.

"Among a few other tests I performed while you were unconscious. The point is," Simon continues, seeing my worry at his last statement, "these are all surface-level readings. The chair will tell us even more."

"What about my physical reaction to the message? I passed out for a whole day," I say.

"And she was sweating like a pig on the plane ride. Not to mention acting like a total freak," adds Eric.

"You're one to talk," I jibe. "Eric's right, though. I was sweating a lot, and I felt like my head was splitting apart."

"Your physical response is slightly alarming. We wouldn't want our field agents to pass out on the job, but it's also much better in comparison to my previous test subject responses."

The image of the ear-backed lab mouse comes back to mind. "Uh… what happened to them?"

Simon ignores my question. "If all you experience is the sweats and slight nausea, I'd say it's a success."

"What about the full-body convulsions?" I ask.

"Yeah, she almost shook herself to death. That's not exactly ideal," adds Eric. He runs a hand through his hair and lets out an exasperated sigh. Someone's getting impatient over here, and he's not even the one being tested!

"That's right," Simon says. He taps his chin contemplatively, then stands from his desk and slowly circles me in the chair with his hands clasped behind his back. He tilts his head to inspect me from behind his spectacles, then stops every few moments to sniff my hair, my feet, flick my toe…

"Hey—" I start, but Eric shushes me.

"Oh!" Simon stops pacing and claps his hands with an enthusiastic little jump. "Perhaps your convulsions are a response to the test message because it was the first foreign data influx!"

"What about the second time?" I ask.

"It's possible you experienced such a strong physical response the second time because of the sheer amount of data." He smiles. "I mean, that was twenty-five terabytes of information. Digital information. Gone right to your brain!" He practically dances.

My palms sweat against the armrests. This does not bode well. "What's next?"

"Now, we're going to test whether The McGuffin information officially transferred to your mind." Simon hustles over to his desk, readjusts something on the monitor, then excitedly plops into his rolling chair again, scooting close to my side. "First, tell us everything you remember from the transfer."

I ignore the terrible sinking feeling that comes with the fact that this seems to be going nowhere, and instead tell myself that we're almost done. Just a few more questions and I'll be well on my way back home. With a huff and a shake of the head and a determined attitude, I get to explaining. I tell the two boys how, just after I accidentally pressed "LAUNCH" with my ass cheek, it was like overlapping images and clips and silhouettes and explosions and memories and violence and blueprints, and yadda yadda, all combining to form one master feeling of dread.

"Do you have any idea what it means?" asks Simon.

"Not exactly. It just felt like one bad nightmare."

Simon calculates something. He silently scoots back over to the computer and clicks around. Eric steps closer to me, silently assessing me from top to bottom. It's impossible to know what he's thinking behind those beautiful, dark hazel eyes. I hope he can't see too clearly through this paper dress. I turn my head away in an attempt to hide the blush forming on my cheeks.

"My readings suggest that The McGuffin did, indeed, transfer to your brain," Simon says. "But I wonder how or if we can access it."

Eric and I wait patiently for Simon to continue while he makes more scribbly notes, but he just sits down and stares at his papers, eyes dancing with ideas.

"What are you thinking now?" Eric asks.

"No one at T.O.P.S.E.C.R.E.T. knows the true extent of The McGuffin's knowledge, not even myself. Once created, The McGuffin sort of took on a sentience of its own." Great. An alien is making itself at home in my brain. "We don't know what we don't know, which is what makes this so difficult."

"There's no way to find out what's in my head?"

"Not based on our limited knowledge of The McGuffin," says Simon.

"That sounds like a bad thing," I say.

"Perhaps," Simon says, still looking like he's hopped up on a pound of Smarties candies.

"Then why are you happy about it?"

"Because there is so much we do not know!" He lets out a heartfelt giggle.

"That's not true." Eric scrubs his hand over his face. "We might not know everything The McGuffin hasn't told us, but we do know everything it has."

"Precisely!" Simon claps his hands together. "We can try to awaken The McGuffin by exposing Julie to information only The McGuffin would know from previously completed missions!"

Their burst of excitement is slightly alarming. "You're going to trigger me? I don't want to start convulsing again."

"I saved some muscle relaxant, just in case," says Eric. He pats his pocket reassuringly, but the fact he's kept it this whole time is disturbing. The idea of being trapped with two crazy people who think they're spies hits me again. Maybe they're actually some weird Doomsday preppers who got bored. I take a deep breath. Calm down, it's not likely. I hope.

"Lie with your back directly against the chair, Julie," Simon says. He presses another button on his chair remote. The helmet lowers onto my head and— ZZZZZZZZ! A surge of electricity jolts through my bones. I can't even scream it happens so fast.

Eric dashes to my side and unplugs the chair in one motion. We all stare at each other. Every hair on my body is singed. Is that what burnt hair smells like? Gross. I'm still breathing heavily.

"Oops, accidents happen," Simon says in a sing-songy manner. He stifles another giggle and rapidly scribbles more notes.

Accident my ass.

"Apparently, the chair was last used for an electrocution interrogation." I about pee myself at the mental image of death by electrocution. Dear God, what does this scientist boy do in his free time? "I—er, someone must have turned it off improperly…" He recomposes himself.

Eric readjusts a dial and plugs the chair back in. It boots up correctly this time, emitting a low hum.

"The good news is, it seems the electricity jogged your brain waves," says Simon. "According to my readings, they're more active."

"You think?" I cough. My hair sends a faint trail of smoke into the air. Why am I letting myself be subjected to this? Oh yeah, because I passed an unpassable test and I want to know why. Darn my curiosity.

"Eric, let's start by referencing some of the information The McGuffin had given you on your previous missions." Simon pulls his chair up again.

Eric nods. He thinks for a moment, then looks right in my eyes and says, "Cookie Monster," dead serious.

"I thought you said this wasn't a joke," I say.

"It isn't." Eric furrows his brow. "Did you feel anything when I said… Cookie Monster?" They both lean in.

"Not a thing. Except now I want some cookies." My stomach grumbles as if to prove it. "What are you talking about?"

"The McGuffin doesn't remember," Eric says to himself, sounding slightly offended.

"Remember what?" I demand.

"It's classified, Julie," he reminds me.

"Don't you think we're past that?"

Eric sets his jaw. "Fine. Cookie Monster was the name of an evil villain who wanted to get rid of all the obese people in the world, so he poisoned the top cookie-making factories to try to wipe out all the fatties." I raise an eyebrow. "Don't worry, I handled it."

"Fatties?" I frown.

Eric shrugs. "He wasn't a very PC Evil Villain."

"There's such a thing as evil villains?"

"Don't be naive," says Eric.

"Why, of course," says Simon. "But that's beside the point. Tell us about," he pauses for dramatic effect, "Omar the Czar."

Silence. I stare back at them. "Oh, was something supposed to happen? Sorry. I got nothing." Simon makes a note. Eric groans.

"Who was Omar the Czar?" I ask.

"A circus freak who wanted to take control of Russia. Don't fret," Eric says at my shocked expression. "I went undercover as a gymnast and took care of it. And returned The McGuffin to headquarters in record time." He smirks. I picture him in a leotard and the image is disturbingly intriguing.

"Isn't The McGuffin supposed to be, like, super top secret?" I ask.

"Oh yes, very," assures Simon.

"Then why do people keep stealing it?"

"It's what happens when you have the most important collection of classified intel in the world," Eric says, like duh.

"Let's get back on track, yes?" says Simon. I glance longingly at the giant AC ducts lining this high-ceilinged room. They remind me of my failed escape attempt earlier (oh how things were simpler before I tried to take matters into my own hands), and of the fact that we could seriously use some fresh air in here. It's getting musty. Or maybe that's just my anxiety-induced BO.

"Yes, let's get back to the questioning so I can get this thing out of my head and go home."

Eric shakes it off and zones in on me again. Simon sits poised with his pen at the ready.

"How about… Gizelle?" says Eric.

I milk their reactions just a bit before saying, "I got nothing."

"That didn't jog your mind? You didn't see anything about Antone's Drone, Gizelle?"

"Nada," I say.

"That was a big mission, as I recall," says Simon.

"Well, I sure as hell remember Gizelle," Eric says with a knowing grin.

Eew.

"Okay, next one," I say, shaking my head. This is like a very weird game of Jeopardy.

"What about… Limoncello?" Eric asks.

Nothing, once again. "Do I even want to know?"

Eric sighs and sits back in his wheelie chair. After a moment of silent temple massaging, he says, "How about… Greyson?"

"Wait a minute," I mutter. Greyson, Greyson, Greyson… the name sounds familiar. "Oh, Greyson!" I exclaim. They perk up at my response. "Wasn't he the guy you blew up after the plane crash?" I ask Eric.

"Yes, but… did The McGuffin tell you anything about Greyson's Daycare?" asks Eric.

These missions are sounding crazier and crazier. "No, I didn't know Greyson was a babysitter."

"These were all seriously intense, high profile missions," scoffs Eric. He starts pacing in a circle around the chair again. "I can't believe The McGuffin doesn't remember a single one of them. It's like they meant nothing to The McGuffin."

"I'm sure The McGuffin appreciates your hard work, Eric," assures Simon. Why are they talking about it like it's a person?

"Alright, let's move on to a different kind of test." Simon presses another invisible button on the chair remote. It maneuvers so I'm lying flat on my back and the helmet forms a dome over my face. It's a claustrophobic cave of twinkling LED colors and beeps. I wonder if this is what being in space feels like.

"I'm going to send you another message— don't worry, it'll be tiny." Simon's voice sounds muffled from outside the tiny helmet. "Especially in comparison to twenty-five terabytes." Metallic belts clamp shut around my waist, my wrists, and my ankles.

"What's happening?" I ask. "What are you doing?"

"That's just to protect you from yourself, should you start convulsing again." Simon dismisses it like it's nothing. "I'm going to send you a simple text message. One line. Ready?"

He types something and clicks a button.

I gasp, my back arches, and my heart stops for a moment as I receive a surge of colorful information.

I'm sitting in a musty old wooden house, almost like a barn, and there's a handful of people with me. We're wearing old clothes, like from the sixties, and everyone's laughing.

Suddenly, we're all floating, and the laughter turns creepy like it's slowed down.

Then I'm pouring a bright purple liquid into a giant silver spoon while images of an umbrella pop in and out of my vision. A bunch of dirty men dancing in piles of coal surround me. I see some tiny penguins and then BAM-- that's it.

I twitch until my heart comes back to life. I gulp down the air. My armpits pool with sweat, and a short-lived wave of nausea takes over, but then… that's all. The helmet recedes, and the chair returns to its semi-normal chair shape.

"What happened? What did you see?" Simon asks.

I take a moment to catch my breath, shaking the pain out of

my head. "Something weird was happening— laughter, I poured something purple, there were dirty men all dancing around me," I sputter.

"Is that really what a young woman should be dreaming about?" Eric teases. I ignore him.

"There was something else, but I can't…" My words fail me. "Give me that."

I grab Simon's pen and notepad and hastily start drawing the images I couldn't describe. I don't even know what I'm drawing until I'm done drawing it, driven by an intense need to get it out of my head. We all squint at my amateur scribbles.

"It looks like an umbrella," says Eric.

"Being held by a penguin," I add. "Oh, and that's coal." I point with the pen at my chicken scratch drawing.

"Fascinating!" Simon grabs the notepad from me. "This is absolutely intriguing. You said it was like a memory for you?"

I nod.

"Would you like to know what the message was?" he asks.

"Yes."

"Supercalifragilisticexpialidocious."

"Are you kidding me?" I say. "Why would you use that as the message? Why not an actual word? Or something like 'Hi my name is Simon', or 'Testing, one two three'?"

"Julie, you're missing the point," Simon corrects. "I sent you a single word, and your brain clearly knew it was a reference to Mary Poppins. However, you didn't interpret the text as text."

He's pacing now. His words grow louder with each new exciting thought. "Nor did you dream up anything specifically related to the word I sent. It all seemed to be references to other parts of the film. But your brain knew the correct film. Judging by my readings," he turns to his computer again, and I wonder about these magical readings, "it looks as though your brain referenced past feelings you had about the film, combined those feelings with the scenes you remembered most, and then played them for you like your own memories."

Simon claps his hands together again. I flinch.

"This is fascinating, indeed. Let's do another test."

"Wait—" I protest, but he's already set the chair into MRI brain scanning mode, and I'm back in the tiny claustrophobic head dome.

They test my brain on clips from Jurassic Park, Reagan's State of the Union Address, old television shows like I Love Lucy and Walker Texas Ranger, and even audio clips of Eric's mission recordings and Taylor Swift songs. Each time my mind does something different with the data.

Sometimes, I see myself doing things related to the content, like riding a T-Rex like a horse or shaking Reagan's hand, and other times I'm reading a book, and random words start floating through the air. With every message, my brain comes up with a different combination of memories and visuals, but it never touches on what the message actually is. The weirdest part is that I'm unable to retain half the information from these "visions" unless I draw it out before I lose it.

After a few more rounds of these makeshift tests, Simon lets me take a break. I massage my head. Eric walks to the corner of the room and stretches, does some push-ups, squats, faux boxing, generally being a nuisance, while Simon stares at his data. He's grinning like a fool, which means whatever the data is showing probably isn't conclusive in the slightest.

"What does it all mean, Simon?" asks Eric mid jumping jack. "Can you somehow copy this method over to my brain?"

Simon bobs his head up and down as he follows Eric's moving eyeline. "It means Julie's brain is unpredictable."

"But we know she is receiving the data," Eric reminds him, switching to lunges. If he's trying to impress me... damn it, it's working.

"Yes," Simon says, "but it's unreliable."

"And we still have no idea how to access The McGuffin," Eric realizes, stretching his biceps behind his back.

"Precisely," Simon says.

"So all this was a waste of time," I say.

"No! My goodness, no. This is fascinating and valuable information, indeed," says Simon. He gestures to his monitors. "I've established a connection to a person's brain through digital means and have successfully sent different types of messages to said brain. The most exciting part is that the subject— I mean, you—" he glances at me, "were able to receive the messages and relay back to me, well, not the message exactly…"

"Like she said, it was a waste of time," says Eric, finished with his aerobic exercises for now. "Just great."

"Well, I guess that's it," I say. "Time to take off the helmet, remove The McGuffin, and send me home. Right?" They look at me blankly. "Right?"

"What are you two saying?" Simon furrows his brow, shakes his head. "There's much more to be done. We can perform more tests, but this time we will ramp up the physical requirements—"

"I'm exhausted and starving, and I just want to go home. You said if it didn't work, you'd take The McGuffin out of my brain." I lie back down in the chair. "So c'mon, let's do that."

Simon squirms a bit. "If you insist."

"What's the problem?" I ask, figuring if Simon is squirming there really is something to be worried about.

"Who said there's a problem?" Simon nervously exchanges a look with Eric. I stare at them expectantly.

"I can technically remove The McGuffin from your brain," Simon states.

"Technically?"

He bites at his lower lip. "But not without it killing you."

My eyes dart between Simon's grimace and Eric's shocked expression.

"You're kidding," I say.

"We never joke about The McGuffin," Simon says once more.

That's right, I forgot The McGuffin is the holy grail. Something occurs to me.

"Did you know this the whole time?"

Simon wrings his hands. "Well..."

"Unbelievable," I say.

"I-I had a hunch, but I wasn't certain until the electrocution accident really sealed it in your brain."

"Accident! Yeah, right. You did this on purpose just so you can keep playing scientist." I slide off the freezing chair.

"The readings say so!" Simon sputters.

"Oh, well, if the readings say so," I mock, then I rip the wires off my body. "Looks like I'll be taking the damn McGuffin home with me then."

"No! You'll affect the readings—"

"What readings?" I stomp over to his computer. "It's just a bunch of squiggly lines and gibberish! Are they all-knowing as well?" The absurdity of the situation finally hits me. "How do you even know what they mean? What kind of scientist are you?"

"I'm the T.O.P.S.E.C.R.E.T. Computer Scientist," Simon says, shaking from the confrontation. "It's my job to know! I just know!"

"Oh sure, like The McGuffin just knows everything," I say.

"That's how things work here, Julie," Eric says. He puts his hand on my shoulder and pulls out the remaining muscle relaxant from his jacket pocket. "Calm down," he warns. I shove his hand from my shoulder and cross my arms, giving him the best "I hate you" expression I can muster. Once my blood pressure decreases, I reluctantly do as he says. Simon shakily clicks around on the screen.

"The readings," he starts, I flinch at the word, "tell me your pathways are totally sealed."

"What does that even mean? You're just making this up," I grumble.

Simon turns to me, suddenly serious. "I know what I'm saying, Julie. The McGuffin is stuck in your brain."

The three of us stand there for a moment, immersed in our own thoughts.

"So, what now? You're not going to kill me, are you?" The familiar tingling sensation of fear creeps up my spine.

"You're a liability," says Eric. "And this was a major waste of everyone's time. Unfortunately, we'll have to see what The Director wants to do with you next."

Something inside of me cracks. "Why can't I just go home?" I ask, dangerously close to breaking into tears.

"Because there are highly classified, terribly important and irreplaceable documents stuck in your brain," says Simon like I haven't been listening this whole time.

"Obviously, you can't go walking around with that information in your head," says Eric. "The fate of the country, the world, is in there." He assesses me as I stand there, arms crossed, wondering why I had to go and take that damn career quiz in the first place.

"Looks like you didn't pass the test, after all," Eric says. I hunch forward, totally disappointed in myself.

Simon looks longingly at his gibberish readings. "I suppose it's time for me to give The Director a call." He pulls his phone out.

"At least you have a backup, right?" I ask, remembering what The Director said in their last phone conversation.

Just then, a loud horn blares through the building. Flashing red lights replace the white fluorescent bulbs, and a recorded voice repeats, "CODE RED, CODE RED, CODE RED…."

Instinctively, I cover my ears from the deafening sound.

"It can't be!" Simon gasps. He hacks away at his keyboard in a worried flurry. "My God…" He stares in shock at whatever it is he's seeing.

"What's happening?" I yell.

"It's a Code Red!" confirms Eric.

Gee, I hadn't noticed. "What's a Code Red?"

Eric turns to me dramatically, wind blowing in his hair (where is the wind coming from?) and says, "The McGuffin backup has been hacked."

8 / CODE RED

Eric grabs my upper arm, pulling me along as Simon scurries behind us down the hallway. The alarm continues blaring, bouncing off the white-tiled walls, and I realize I'm traveling deeper into the heart of T.O.P.S.E.C.R.E.T. headquarters.

The walls rise high above us, turning into large clear windows that connect with the tiled ceiling. I witness the last few seconds of natural light beaming down into the cavernous hallway before metallic gates roll down behind them with a CLANG, shutting out the sunlight.

The bright white fluorescent lights turn red, accented by a flashing strobe. More metallic gates slide to the ground, sealing shut a seemingly random selection of rooms as we race past.

We squeeze through a hectic swarm of men and women (I assume they're other agents) dressed in all different kinds of gear. Some of them sport suits and dresses, while others are totally decked out in tactical fighting gear— black on black on black with bulletproof vests, guns, and knife handles sticking out of every pocket. A woman waddling around in scuba gear bumps into Eric. "'Scuse me, bub!" she says through her snorkel.

"Watch it, Denise!" Eric shouts back. He grabs my arm and

yanks me past another onslaught of agents scurrying about in skydiving parachutes, safari garb, hiking gear, you name it. The farther down the hall we get, the more interesting the outfits become until we reach an opening that appears to be the entrance to a lobby.

Large metallic signs hang from the ceiling, etched with the same thin, modern font as was on The McGuffin in the plane. The signs direct us to multiple different offshoots connecting to the main lobby. "Interrogation Rooms A through G," "Weapons Department," "Forensics and Analytics," "Chemical Warfare," "Tactical Training," "Simulation Decks 1-15."

This place feels like a busy international airport, full of worldly travelers running to make their flights, minus the deafening "CODE RED" alarm that paints the whole place red with chaos. It's overwhelming and energizing and mostly relieving because, as it would seem, Eric and Simon are not crazy kidnappers trying to grow an ear on my back. I only make out half of the labels before Eric jerks me around a corner into the "Hall of Elevators."

The tiled walls stretch on for what looks like a whole mile. Our footsteps echo off the reflective surfaces around us as we continue racing down the seemingly endless hallway. I wonder why they need so many elevators.

"CODE RED, CODE RED," the booming voice continues. We reach a wall between two elevators. Eric presses a panel in the tile. It flips over, revealing a hidden camera. He leans in, and a blue laser scans his eye. "Eric Shaw," he says. The laser turns green. "Access granted," the computer replies. To the right, an elevator door opens.

"Hurry," Eric says, and we all shuffle inside.

Eric pulls out a laminated card from his jacket pocket and scans it on a little black square in the wall. The elevator lurches downward.

"Where are we going? What's happening?" I say, trying to

catch my breath. The alarm repeats itself right when I open my mouth, drowning out my questions.

The elevator stops, and the metallic doors open, revealing what looks like a half-floor. We have to duck when we step out into the small room to not hit our heads on the low popcorn ceiling.

It looks like an office building from the eighties. Cheap carpet spreads the length of the floor, grossly lit by flickering fluorescent lighting. A half-full water cooler bubbles in the corner next to a side table with a fake plant collecting dust. A single metallic desk sits in the center, adorned with a small "T.O.P.S.E.C.R.E.T. DIRECTOR OF OPERATIONS" nameplate. I wonder why The Director of Operations would tuck herself in such a cramped space between floors.

We hurry toward her, all hunched over.

"Then get your best men on it and find—" the alarm cuts her off. "Did you hear me?" She has one hand in her free ear, blocking out the "CODE RED" voice, and the other holding a dusty rose-colored desk phone. "Just keep working until you track down the source." She hangs up the phone, then gives a little jump when she sees us approaching, hunched over like a bunch of Igors.

"What are you three doing here?" she yells over the alarm. "She shouldn't be in here!"

"The McGuffin Backup has been hacked!" shouts Eric, still holding my arm. I try to shimmy out of his tight grip, but he doesn't budge.

"Yes, I know!" she says, eyes narrowed and darting between the three of us. "Why did you bring her to me?" She nods in my direction.

"The McGuffin is stuck in her brain," says Eric.

"Well, get it out," The Director says.

Simon steps forward. "Uh, we can't do that, ma'am. Not without—" he glances at me and then stage whispers, "—killing her." He's wringing his hands again. The Director looks between the three of us, incredulous. "We came to ask what we should do with her, now that there's a Code Red and everything—"

Eric interrupts him, stepping in front of the two of us. He finally lets me out of his grip. "Director, you already know what to do. Send me after the hacker! We need to retrieve The Backup."

"That's exactly what I would do," she says, "if our team had any idea where the hacker came from, or where the data was transferred to. This hack is untraceable!" She rubs her temples, glaring at the ceiling as the alarm continues to remind us that we are, indeed, still experiencing a "CODE RED." "I'd say we should consult The McGuffin, but apparently that's not an option." They all turn to me.

I grimace. "What are you going to do with me?"

Eric takes another hunched step toward the edge of The Director's desk. "Clearly, she can't go walking around with all that information in her head."

"We must continue my testing!" says Simon. He scurries forward, wedging himself in the conversation. "I've only just scratched the surface—" he continues, and their arguing blends in with the cacophony of noises around us.

As they continue arguing about my fate, I notice something on The Director's computer screen: a bunch of little brown dots appear, forming a grid.

I'm drawn to it for some reason, highly intrigued by the little brown digital mouse that pops up in the corner. It follows the dots round and round until it reaches the center of the screen where a small piece of cheese awaits. I step closer to the screen, somehow pulled toward it like a magnet. The little mouse bites the cheese and then—BAM!

A white flash takes over my vision, leaving behind a silhouette of a rat with bared teeth. It vanishes as quickly as it appeared, replaced by a succession of rapidly flashing images of what look like handmade pieces of machinery; thick metal welded into an assortment of oddball household objects like fishing hooks, paper clips, and pens. More seemingly homemade doodads flash by, too fast for me to register what they are until a lacrosse helmet covered in different colored wires stands out from the rest. Straws and frayed copper jut out the edges of the mask, making it seem both like a child's plaything and a deadly device.

The images whirl away, and suddenly I'm looking up at a white sign with pink cursive words that spell out "Tout le Monde." The image is replaced by little cartoon planet Earth with every significant iconic building from around the world— the Eiffel Tower, the statue of liberty, the pyramids of Giza, the Great Wall, etc. — protruding all around it.

Earth disappears, and now I'm sitting in a small cafe with little pink napkins and curly metal seats, right next to a river. I smell butter and sugar, bring a cup of coffee to my lips, and realize with an odd tingling sensation at the back of my head that the blurry building in my peripheral vision is the Eiffel Tower. The memory-like clip swirls and disappears, replaced by the sight of a scrawny, bald, white man.

He's shrouded in shadows, nibbling on a piece of cheese in a mysterious, cold, eerie place that sends goosebumps down my spine. The rush of water fills my ears until white noise drowns everything out. The man's figure morphs into the shape of the rat silhouette from before, and a throaty, high-pitched laugh echoes between my ears. Then everything turns black.

I gasp for air and crash into the carpeted floor, already overcome by an onslaught of allergic convulsions. My twitching body knocks into The Director's desk. The computer screen dies down to blackness, leaving behind the symbol of a silhouetted rat baring its teeth— the same as the first image that just flashed in my mind.

Oh snap. I can feel the sweats coming on again. I take deep breaths, trying to make sense of it all.

Suddenly, the lights go back to normal. The incessant "CODE RED" voice ceases to exist, leaving our ears ringing.

"Jesus," Eric says, shaking a finger in his ear.

The Director notices me convulsing on the floor. "Christ!" She jumps in her seat. "What's wrong with her? What just happened?"

Eric leans over the edge of her desk, acknowledging my new position on the floor. "She convulses when a message has been sent to her brain." He waves it off like I'm just a drama queen. "Can we get back to the more pressing issue at hand? We need to find The Backup."

Simon gasps. "You're right, Eric!"

"I know," Eric says. "I'll head to the Bahamas first. I have a feeling it's in the Bahamas."

Simon shakes his head. "No—you're right that a message was sent to her brain." Simon visibly fights down the urge to do a happy dance. "But from who?"

The Director lightly touches my forehead with her cold, bony fingers, then quickly recoils as if from the sizzling surface of a hot stove.

"If you didn't send it, Simon, who did?" The Director asks.

"Perhaps it was The McGuffin," he squeals excitedly. They all turn to me. "What did you see, Julie? What was the message?"

Stars still dancing in my vision and unable to speak just yet, I shake my head.

The Director fills a glass of water and hands it to me, along with a blanket from her bottom drawer. Who keeps blankets in their drawers? I carefully drape it over my shoulders and hug it close, comforted by its scratchy warmth. I didn't even realize I was shaking.

"Poor girl," The Director mutters. Eric makes a pfft sound at her comment, and she tells him to get off her desk. The three others stand awkwardly over me, waiting for my account of the vision.

I take a deep breath and recount everything, even down to the pink napkins and the cold, creepiness of the little bald man's laughs. They listen to every word. When I'm done, they cross their arms, put their hands on their hips, and scratch their chins, silently assessing my story.

"The McGuffin was talking to you," Simon says in wonder. He turns to The Director and Eric. "Maybe it knows we require its help and is trying to communicate."

My stomach chooses this moment to growl like a hungry kitchen garbage disposal. Oh, something inside me is trying to communicate, alright. But I'm not so sure it's The McGuffin.

"What triggers these visions?" The Director asks, clasping her hands together on her desk. I notice her fingernails are bitten. Probably from dealing with Simon and Eric on the regular.

"We don't know exactly," Simon says.

"Care to elaborate?"

"We tried a few methods, but couldn't access anything from The McGuffin's historical logs, though we successfully activated it by sending messages of our own. She tends to interpret text as images."

She arches an eyebrow. "You mean to tell me, you have exactly zero conclusive data on what you've done?"

"Something must have triggered it," Eric says, blatantly ignoring her accusation. He stares at me as if he can intimidate The McGuffin into cooperating.

I absentmindedly look at the computer. The silhouetted rat is still there, taunting me with its bared teeth. "That did," I say, nodding to the desktop. Everyone looks at the creepy rat. "I know it."

"I hadn't even noticed," The Director says. She wheels her chair closer to the screen. "What is that symbol?" She taps the screen with her bitten nail, spreading germs without a care and adding to my growing anxiety. I bite my lip in an attempt to remain calm. "We must have encountered it before. Eric, do you remember it?"

He squints at it for a moment, then shakes his head. "No, I've never seen this before. I haven't been on any missions related to this image."

Another moment passes. I can practically hear everyone's gears turning. The Director removes her grey suit blazer and sits back in her chair, crossing her arms and looking off into the distance contemplatively. Tiny circles of dark purple spread from the underarms of her shirt, accentuating the bags under her eyes. She needs a nap more than I do.

"Too bad we can't just ask The McGuffin what it said," says Eric. He shakes his head at me like it's my fault. Then I remember, it technically is.

"But it did tell her something," Simon says, back to his enthusiastic self.

"Looks like Project McGuffin does work, after all." The Director gives Simon a nod of approval. He smiles proudly.

"But it doesn't mean anything," Eric interrupts their little moment. "We still can't understand the message, and I don't know where to go to find the bad guy."

"You said you saw the Eiffel tower in your vision, right?" The Director looks at me expectantly.

"Yes, I think so." I nod. "But it was blurry. Now I'm second-guessing it."

"There's no room for second-guessing," she says.

My shoulders grow heavy with pressure. The Director's intent gaze tells me this is no joke. Something massive is at stake here, and I'm right in the middle of it.

What have I gotten myself into?

"Then... yes, I did see the Eiffel tower."

"If The McGuffin really is speaking to us, I think our hacker might be in Paris," she determines.

"We don't know that for sure," says Eric, frustrated. "It could be the Bahamas."

"We do know one thing," Simon says with knowing eyes. We all look at him. "Julie definitely can't go home now."

The Director sighs. "You're right. At least not until we retrieve The McGuffin backup hard drive."

"Damn." Eric kicks the floor like a child.

"What do you mean? Why not?" I ask, but a knowing dread has already started creeping up my spine.

"You can't leave because," Simon stifles an excited giggle, "The McGuffin needs you in the field."

9 / T.O.P.S.E.C.R.E.T

I sit quietly on the floor, still reeling from the influx of information, while Eric, The Director, and Simon argue about my fate.

It's the strangest feeling. I've always been in control of my life, executing my plan, making headway toward the next stage in my carefully mapped out academic life. Now I'm just a pawn in these strangers' incredibly dangerous game, still in need of some pants.

What scares me more than the fact that they keep forgetting I'm a human, as opposed to Simon's lab rat, is that it's terrifyingly clear they don't have a plan.

"What are you saying, Simon?" The Director asks, her voice cracking from dehydration. She's leaned over her desk, resting her head in her hand, eyes glossy with exhaustion. Her frizzy hair forms a halo around her head, and the purple bags beneath her eyes have deepened since earlier.

Simon has spent the last twenty minutes catching her up on all his findings from our tests earlier, but she, like me, still hasn't entirely accepted the reality of the situation. I'm their new McGuffin, and there's nothing The Director can do about it.

Unless she's willing to let Simon put me under the scalpel,

but I've been silently praying for that suggestion to not come up. I wonder if I click my heels together three times and say, "There's no place like home," if I might magically end up back at my apartment, safe and in my comfort zone with a pile of assignments in front of me.

I'm embarrassed to say it doesn't. And by the way everyone's looking at me, they're embarrassed for me too.

Her phone continues ringing on her desk, but she lets it go, adding to the claustrophobic atmosphere of her half-floor office space. "You can't possibly expect me to send a civilian into the field? My God." She shakes the thought out of her head.

"I don't see how we have any other options," Simon states, referring to the stack of notes in his arms. "My readings couldn't be clearer." He flips his stack of colorful charts and incomprehensible squiggly lines around to face The Director. I silently curse his all-knowing readings. "The McGuffin speaks to Julie, but only when it is activated, if you will, by certain triggers. What constitutes a trigger is still unclear, but text and images seem to work. This is why Julie needs to go into the field with Eric, in order to make herself available to any future triggers."

The Director's eyes glaze over at the realization that Simon's right.

I watch with an odd combination of sleep-deprived weariness and adrenaline-fueled fear as they all asses my clammy, frazzled figure still crouched in the corner. Eric shakes his head. The Director purses her lips. Simon looks into my eyes and it catches me off guard. I can feel he's looking at me for the first time and not The McGuffin. He's just a teenager, but his blue peepers hold a knowing gaze, the kind of gaze that I've only ever shared with my hundred-and-two-year-old grandpa. I wonder what his curious mind sees in me. What scientific possibilities are formulating in him right now?

"Hell no," says Eric. He shakes his head at The Director, but it has no effect on her steely gaze. "I know exactly what you're going to say, and I won't do it."

"And what am I going to say?" she asks.

"C'mon Penelope. I'm not a babysitter," he whines. She raises an eyebrow at him. "You already sent me after her once and look what happened," he continues, gesturing to me as one would a dog peeing on a carpet.

"I don't like the idea any more than you do, but Simon's right. It's our only option," she says with a shrug.

"Ooh!" Simon puts a finger to the air, like he's formulating an idea. "Who knows what kind of effects sending her into the field will have on her mind! Not to mention her bodily responses..."

Finally, someone addresses my physical health.

"What if she convulses mid-trigger again, and the transfer explodes her brain?" Eric says.

I involuntarily shiver at the terrifying mental image, balking at Eric with a petrified face. He continues on, ignoring the silent waves of fear emanating off me. "My point is, Julie will be nothing but dead weight. I'm not going to risk my life following ambiguous clues from an unstable source," he says. Yet he's been perfectly fine relying on The McGuffin's mystical powers this entire time.

"Listen, both of you," she says. She holds her open palms in front of her as if to block their remarks. "Thank you for sharing your concerns, but it's clear what needs to happen. Julie is currently our only source of information regarding the whereabouts of the stolen Backup. Therefore, she will join you, Eric." She gives him a stern look. "You'll head on a mission to retrieve the backup in case Julie is triggered by any other unexpected connections to The McGuffin."

Eric groans.

"Any questions?" she asks, testing him.

I raise my hand. "I have one," I say, my voice scratchy and

weak. Everyone turns to me, startled. It's incredible how quickly these people forget I'm right there in the room with them.

"What about the whole, 'This is your mission, should you choose to accept it' thing?"

"That's Mission Impossible, Julie," Simon says, stacking his papers together neatly. "That was just my test message. Remember?"

"And this is T.O.P.S.E.C.R.E.T. Where our agents obey orders without question," The Director says, giving each of us a separate pointed look.

"Does this mean I'm an agent now?" I ask.

"No." Eric's shaking his head vehemently. "No, definitely not."

The Director sighs. "I suppose so, but only temporarily. Your purpose is to accompany Eric in case anything triggers another message from The McGuffin. Once you retrieve The Backup and return it to headquarters, we'll remove The McGuffin from your brain, wipe your memory of your time here at T.O.P.S.E.C.R.E.T., and send you home."

Wipe my memory? I'm not sure if I like the sound of permanently forgetting a few days of my life. I guess that'd make me just like all the other twenty-something's who're getting black out drunk this week for Spring Break. It's probably best to leave any trace of this traumatizing experience in the trashcan, anyway.

"But we can't remove The McGuffin!" says Simon. The Director stares straight ahead, resigning herself. He quickly adds, "Er, because it'll kill Julie."

"While they're gone, you're going to figure out how to remove it. Without killing Julie. Understood?" He nods almost imperceptibly.

"Eric, take Julie to get prepped," she orders.

"It's not too late to change your mind, Penelope," Eric says.

The Director looks to the popcorn ceiling and says, "Why must you give me these problems?" She massages her temples.

"At least you're not T.O.P.S.E.C.R.E.T.'s best agent being demoted to a babysitter," Eric mutters.

"Who said you're our top agent?" The Director asks.

"Who else could it be?"

"Maybe it's Agent Fifty-Six."

Eric sucks in a breath. "I don't see what's so great about Agent Fifty-Six."

"Agent Fifty-Six never gives me sass. Agent Fifty-Six goes in and out and gets it done without a problem. Agent Fifty-Six delivers mission logs on time." He waves away her comments.

"There is no Agent Fifty-Six, and you know it."

The Director sets her bottom jaw with dead eyes.

"Excuse me?" I raise a finger. They all turn to me. "Do I have to go?" I ask, barely a whisper.

"Were you not just listening?" Eric jumps off the desk and turns to me. "The fate of the world is at stake because of you." Eric stares me down. "You started this mess, and you're going to help me clean it up."

"Me!" I shriek. "I'm not the one who put a highly dangerous and incredibly secret government test in an online quiz!"

"Yeah, but you took the quiz."

"Yeah, but you put it there."

"Technically Simon did," Eric clarifies. Simon smiles sheepishly, writing something else down on his papers. "Also, you're the one who launched Project McGuffin, Julie, which is the main concern here."

"Only because your vents aren't good for shit and you leave LAUNCH buttons lying around!"

"Stop questioning our methods!" Eric snaps.

"Alright, alright, settle down," The Director says. "Julie, please work with us here. This situation isn't exactly ideal for any of us."

Sigh. I guess this is what I deserve for panicking and turning to an online quiz for comfort in the first place.

"Can I at least call my parents?" Any excuse to not go just yet.

Eric gives The Director an annoyed glance. Then he raises his hands as if to say, "I'm not going to deal with this. You handle it."

"Julie, you cannot share any of this information with anyone outside of T.O.P.S.E.C.R.E.T. Even if—when you go home. Is that clear?"

I catch my breath. If? Hot tears silently well in my eyes when I realize just how alone I really am.

"It has to be this way. I'm sorry," she adds somberly.

It seems my only two options are to go with Eric and die in "the field," or stay with Simon and be stuck with needles, treated like a lab rat and killed in the pursuit of knowledge. Jeez, since when did my future become so grim?

At least with Eric, I'll get to see Paris.

"I'll help you, Eric," I say with resolve.

"I don't need any more help from you," he mutters.

I bite my bottom lip. What else could go wrong?

10 / THE PRINCE OF WEAPONS

I'm allowed a brief potty break and handed a granola bar before Eric leads me to the Weapons Department.

On the way out of The Director's office, I ask if I can change out of my breezy patient dress into something more fitting for a field agent. For the sake of time, The Director makes Eric give me a pair of his clothes, and now we're both wearing Eric's skinny jeans, black lace-up combat boots, and black short-sleeved shirts. The boxers bunch up around my waist in Eric's skinny jeans, which are still a size and a half too big on me.

Nothing like a thick wedgie to start a T.O.P.S.E.C.R.E.T. mission. At least Eric's man jeans have amazingly useful pockets. I can fit my entire forearms in these things! I fling Eric a sideways glance as he leads us down the hall, my arms down to my elbows in the little pants pouches. Guys are so spoiled.

I peek at our passing reflections as we walk back through the Hall of Elevators. Eric and I look like a couple of twinsies, as my mother would say. Simon jogs to keep up with our long legs.

"I'd really like to perform a few more small tests before you leave," Simon says, struggling to balance all his papers in his hands as we round another corner.

"There's no time, Simon. The McGuffin needs us." Eric is

stone-faced, focused on the mission ahead. Simon huffs.

"At least let me say goodbye, then." He jumps in front of me, forcing me to a halt.

"Uh, you heard Eric. No time for any more experiments," I say, not too eager for a last-minute needle stab. I eye him suspiciously as he shoves a chubby hand in his pants pocket.

"I just want to say that I'm so very pleased you decided to take my career quiz, Julie." He beams up at me like a proud younger brother.

"Er, you're welcome," I say, slightly disarmed by his puppy dog face. Simon opens his arms and awkwardly pulls me into a hug. He pats me on the back, then yanks a hair from my head with surprising force.

I let out a yelp, massaging the spot as Simon holds a pair of tweezers in front of his bespectacled eyes.

Seriously?

He giggles and runs off without looking back.

That's just great.

On our walk to the Weapons Department, Eric tells me we're to be outfitted with the most advanced tools and weaponry for our mission, hand-crafted by none other than "George Simple." He doesn't elaborate any more than that, but the way Eric says George's name makes me think he must be a prince of weapons.

We round the corner into a giant, cavernous metallic warehouse, where George himself awaits us. He's tall, lean, as beautiful as a sculpture, and walks with one foot directly in front of the other like he's on a runway. His short silver hair stands to spiky perfection, contrasting starkly with his smooth, caramel skin and electric blue eyes. He carries an aura of fabulous that matches his high-chinned saunter as he approaches us, arms wide as if he's welcoming us to his palace.

Yep, definitely a prince.

Eric puts his hand out. "Hey, George, nice to—" George goes

right for a dramatic cheek kiss, grabbing Eric by the arms like an enthusiastic auntie.

"Eric! I've been waiting for you, dear. Welcome to my humble abode." He gestures around him at his outstanding collection of weapons. It's not a humble abode by any means.

The warehouse is enormous—miles and miles of weapons stacked on shelves and organized by purpose: "Maiming," "Lethal," "Taunting," "Escaping," and that's just the first few rows near me. There's an entire block of aisles across the way, the size of a football field, dedicated to "Firearms" alone ("Rifles," "Submachine Guns," "Sniper Rifles," to name a few). They have "Aircraft," "Anti-Aircraft," "Flamethrowers," "Martial Arts Weapons," "Swords," "Rockets," "Torpedoes," "Missiles," "Practice Weapons"... the list goes on and on.

"The Director informed me of your mission to Paris." George ticks his tongue. "The city of love. Lucky, lucky you." He winks, giving Eric's biceps another quick squeeze of affection.

"Actually, it's the city of lights." My voice echoes in the cavernous space. George turns to me with a dramatic rise in his perfectly manicured eyebrow. "The city of love is Venice, Italy." I only know this because I wrote a paper comparing the two cities in middle school.

"And who are you?" George asks, head tilted in a dramatic show of appraisal.

"I'm Julie. Richardson." He assesses me from top to bottom with his sharp eyes. Then he looks to Eric for an explanation.

"She's a temporary agent. Supposed to help me recover The Backup." He shrugs.

"She's... your partner?" George asks, a noticeable rise in his voice. He eyes me suspiciously. "But you work alone, saving the world in a solo, sexy manner."

"It's only temporary." Eric gives me a side glance.

I fake a smile and shove my hand in George's bubble, a forced attempt at civility. He carefully shakes it twice with the limpest grip I've ever felt before dropping my hand like a pair of dirty underwear.

He turns right back to Eric. "You'll have to share my newest batch of weapons, then. I wasn't expecting a tag along." He eyes me again.

I get it, I'm not wanted! Did it ever occur to these people I don't want to be here either? Sheesh.

"Neither was I, but duty calls. Let's get right to it." Eric takes a determined step forward. George lights up once again.

"A man who takes charge. I love it!"

I roll my eyes.

"Show me what you've got, George," Eric says.

"Aye aye, captain." George playfully salutes with a sharp turn of his heel. The two men head down the center aisle of the warehouse, voices echoing off the walls. I hurry after them feeling like a third wheel.

"I took your notes from the last assignment very seriously," George continues. He makes a sharp left turn down an aisle of giant submarine torpedoes. Each one is shaped slightly different than the one before, but they all share the same feel— metallic, simplistic, smooth, and shiny.

"About the weight?" Eric asks. "It wasn't an issue of stamina." His eyes quickly flit back to me. "It just would have been nice to have something a bit more… travel-sized."

"Yes, yes, of course." George makes another sharp turn, and now we're walking past rows and rows of high-tech archery equipment. All kinds of arrows (flaming, poisoned, explosive, piercing, pheromone, you name it) sit perfectly organized atop an ongoing shelf of what I assume are bows. They're all so pointy and aggressive-looking that it's hard to tell.

"I came up with something genius if I do say so myself." George shakes his head excitedly. "No one will have any idea the difference between your arsenal and a brand-new stack of office supplies." He winks and turns another corner, revealing an office behind glass walls situated in the middle of the warehouse. Behind the office extends what appears to be a long, concrete shooting range.

It looks like the New York loft of a high-profile fashion designer, if the designer were putting together weapons of mass destruction on a catwalk of death.

He swings open the large glass door for Eric to follow. Eric steps after George and lets the massive glass door swing shut behind him, right as I walk into it with a loud "BONG."

Jerks.

I follow them to a large silver table, on top of which an assortment of twenty or so identical looking pens sit about two inches apart from each other on display.

"They're completely undetectable in metal scanners or x-rays. They're compact, light, travel-sized," George says that last one with a wink at Eric, "and each is activated by a single click of the button at the top." He taps a code onto the table, revealing a hidden touch-screen keypad that lights up with each touch of his fingers. A moment later, a row of target dummies pops up from a hidden compartment in the floor, about a hundred yards down the shooting range. George picks one of his pens up for display and points it at the large red circle on the center dummy's chest. "Just aim and click." He demonstrates.

A red laser beam shoots out of the tiny pen with a powerful "ZZZZZ" sound and completely saws off the dummy's head in a swift motion, like a finger swiping a coconut in half during a game of Fruit Ninja.

George clicks the pen again to disable the laser and places it back on the table. He grabs a second, identical pen from the opposite side of the table. "This one's my favorite," he says with a grin. "Would you like to do the honors?" He hands the pen to Eric with a bow.

Eric grabs the pen and points it like a gun, one eye shut as he aims for the second dummy. He clicks the top button and BAM!

A giant metallic arrow erupts from the end, shooting straight for the dummy's head. It rips right through the thick, Jell-O-like material leaving a gaping hole in the middle, singed around the edge.

"Nice!" Eric laughs like a little boy with a new Nerf Gun. George frowns.

"Actually, that's not the one I thought it was. Where are you?" He carefully inspects each pen until he grabs the one he wants. "Aha! This one's my favorite." He clicks and throws, ducking slightly. The pen lands twenty yards away with a soft clatter against the concrete ground. We stare, waiting a few moments.

"What's it supposed to—"

A giant ball of orange light explodes in front of us, engulfing the entire firing range in flames.

"Oooh, baby," Eric says, eyes dancing with the reflection of the pen's flames in front of him. George sucks in some air and claps enthusiastically.

I clear my throat. "I have a question." They turn to me, once again reminded of my presence. "How are you supposed to tell these things apart? They look exactly the same." George presses his lips together firmly, probably preventing a sassy remark from coming out.

"There's a small engraving at the bottom, see?" He holds one up, the light reflecting off the smooth surface. "GH for grappling hook, AR for assault rifle," he picks them up and points, but I can't make out any letters, "PSN for poison, PN for Pen," he says like it's so obvious.

"You made one a normal pen?" I ask. He scoffs at me.

"My God, no." He looks to Eric as if for assistance. Eric just shrugs. "None of these are," he struggles to get the word out, "ordinary weapons. The ink in this one is laced with a chemical that disintegrates the surface it's written on within minutes." He states it proudly.

"So then, what's the point of writing anything with it?" I ask. George is taken aback.

"Jules, sometimes in the highly classified world of T.O.P.S.E.C.R.E.T. assignments, agents need to write things down." He steps toward me. "We can't risk our super-secret notes falling into the wrong hands. So, we destroy them." I want to ask him what the whole point of writing them down in the first place would be, but they're already moving on.

"Is there a power down sequence?" asks Eric.

"Nope. When you're finished with a pen, just do with it the same thing you do with your women," George says, leaning forward on the table and placing his chin in his palm. He bites the tip of his pinky finger. Eric doesn't seem to notice George's seductive efforts.

"Just leave 'em," Eric says with a nod.

"You betcha," says George.

"Wait, you leave these dangerous weapons lying around for someone else to pick up?" I ask, incredulous.

George lets out a curt laugh. "Listen, Julia-"

"Julie," I interrupt. He ignores me.

"Once an agent uses a weapon, he can't use the same weapon again. It's just not done. Imagine if The Cookie Monster were to fight Eric again, and he used the same weapon against him?" They burst into laughter. "What would The Cookie Monster think?"

"Considering the fact that you leave your weapons lying around, the Cookie Monster would have already stolen Eric's T.O.P.S.E.C.R.E.T. weapon and would most likely be using it against him." I raise my eyebrows in a silent challenge. The two men stare at me like I'm an imbecile.

"An agent wouldn't be caught dead using the same weapon twice. It's just not professional," George states. He turns to Eric and he nods, confirming it.

"I thought you said you 'decimated' The Cookie Monster,

Eric?"

"I did. You're missing the point," he says.

"Which is?"

"Don't worry about it," Eric waves his hand. "Just leave the weapons and the fighting and… just leave everything to me. Okay? I'll handle it." He pats my shoulder patronizingly.

I shrug in response. "So, just to be clear, of this entire warehouse of weapons, we're going to use a bunch of pens to save the day?"

"Not just pens!" George cries.

"I know they're not just pens." Eric places a hand on George's shoulder. "I know. It's okay," Eric comforts George, who dramatically places his head on Eric's shoulder, smiling at me as if he's won the battle. I don't even bother trying to hide my grimace.

I notice something small and shiny hanging on the wall. "What's that?" I ask. George follows my gaze.

"That's a fanny pack. I was experimenting with different kinds of pockets and—" I don't hear anything else he says, for I've become entranced by the beautiful little sack of pockets.

I love pockets. And fanny packs. Any way to get out of carrying a big, clunky purse. I absolutely can't resist a functional pocket. If I try on a dress and it has pockets, I buy the dress. Regardless if it looks good on me. It's just so hard to find women's clothing with pockets big enough to be useful, ya know?

But fanny packs are super useful, albeit super ugly. This one, though… my eyes glimmer in the presence of the fanny pack. It's like a ray of sunshine.

"Uh, you like it?" asks George. I realize I've already put it around my waist. It fits perfectly and feels like someone's hugging me. A bit of warmth spreads through my body as a result of this much-needed dose of comfort. "There are so many pockets!"

"Yeah, that's what I was just saying."

"Can I use it?" I ask.

"I guess. It's just a fanny pack," George says, confused by my enthusiasm for a granny-purse.

"It's not a weapon," Eric says.

"You handle the weapons. I'll handle the fanny pack," I say, transferring my Lactaid tablets from Eric's deep pockets to the fanny pack. It was my only requirement before heading out into the field that I be equipped with at least one package of Lactaid. That, and a quick self-defense lesson, but Eric insisted we didn't have the time. The McGuffin is counting on us. Yadda yadda.

At least they had the Lactaid, and I'm grateful for the single two-pack of crushed tablets The Director found in her desk drawer. I'll take what I can get.

"Perfect!" I say with a final zip of the fanny pack.

It's the little things, it really is.

"Is that everything?" Eric asks.

"Yes, sir," George confirms, handing him a small silver bag filled with identical silver pens. "They're yours," he says, with eyes that say, "and so am I."

"Sweet." Eric shoves the tiny bag into his black backpack. "Thanks, George. See you on the flip side." He salutes, and George winks back.

"Thanks for the fanny pack," I say, overwhelmingly pleased with my discovery. Maybe this trip won't be so bad after all.

"It doesn't match your outfit," George says in a disapproving tone.

His attitude can't get to me because-- I have a fanny pack!

"Alright, let's get out of here," Eric says. He salutes, and George blows him a kiss.

"Ta-ta!"

I smile and wave once at George. He rolls his eyes, gives a huff, and turns on his heel, disappearing into the many rows and rows of T.O.P.S.E.C.R.E.T. weapons.

11 / THE NOT-SO-SAFE HOUSE

As we make our way up the escalator to the T.O.P.S.E.C.R.E.T. Hangar, I stop.

"Wait," I say.

Eric closes his eyes. "What now?"

"What about communications? How will we talk to each other? What if we get split up?" I ask, reality creeping up my spine, ruining my fanny pack revere.

Eric pulls out a cell phone with an unimpressed look.

"Oh," I say, somewhat disappointed. I was expecting we'd use an earpiece with a secret microphone, or perhaps a phone-pen.

"We use the cell phone to communicate with Simon. We use these to communicate with each other," Eric pulls out two tiny earpieces. Ha! I go to grab one, but he snatches it away. "Not yet, I'm right next to you." He shakes his head.

We step off the escalator onto an open concrete floor, packed with all sorts of aviation machines, leading out to a single runway. We pass by a row of helicopters (black, silver, red, white, all decked out with weaponry), an entire section of jets (passenger planes, stealth bombers, propeller planes with those banana feet fit for water landings), and drones varying from the size of a cell phone to the size of a two-story building.

Eventually, we reach a handful of identical sleek white small cabin planes.

"Ooh, pretty." I reach out to touch the wing and Eric slaps my hand away.

"No touchy."

He presses his hand to the side of the plane's body, and a green handprint is left in his wake.

"Eric Shaw," a buttery female voice says. "Welcome aboard." The outline of a door forms next to the handprint. It folds out, revealing a staircase leading into the jet.

Eric smirks at my shocked expression. "Let's go," he says, walking up the steps.

Getting into the plane proves more difficult than I'd imagined. How hard is it to walk up a short flight of steps, anyway? I take my first step and start twitching at the very recent memory of my last experience on an airplane. It's not something I'd like to relive. I grit my teeth and take two steps at a time.

The interior of the small plane is sleek and sophisticated. Lightly colored curtains frame each window, two sets of four large bucket seats face each other across glossy mahogany tables, and toward the back of the plane, limousine-style booths hug the wall, leaving room for the snack and liquor bar in the center. The shiny dark centerpiece is flanked on each side by two bathrooms.

The warm, welcoming aura does nothing to calm my nerves. I plop into one of the big, comfy leather seats, shakily searching for a seatbelt. When I can't find one, my heart stops. Eric throws his duffel bag on one of the seats across the aisle from me and plops his feet up on the table.

"Nice, isn't she?" He runs his fingers across the dark wood trim on the wall.

"Where's the seatbelt?" I ask, my voice cracking.

"There aren't any seatbelts on this plane." He watches,

amused, as a look of fear grows on my face. "Just dig for it in the crease," he adds, pointing to my side.

I shove my hand in between the seat cushions, but I can't find any seatbelts. I let out a whimper. Eric groans and takes his feet off the table. Before I know it, he's leaning over me, one hand propped up against the seat by my head and the other gently placing my searching hand aside. His touch is electric. I silently curse my hormonal responses, chalking it up to The McGuffin's eclectic assortment of effects on me.

Eric pulls a seatbelt from nowhere and clasps it shut on my lap with an audible click. He smirks, and his minty scent fills my head as he stops just inches from my face as he murmurs, "Better?"

I roll my eyes. He shrugs, then swaggers over to the liquor bar as the plane engine starts. I don't remember seeing a pilot enter the cockpit.

"Uh, who's flying the plane?" I whip my head around to the front of the plane. The sliding mahogany door is open, revealing a beautifully polished cockpit with two seats and a whole lot of buttons, but no pilots. The engine starts, and we roll onto the tarmac. I gasp.

"No one's flying the plane!" I cry. Eric silently pours himself a scotch. I watch, bewildered, as the plane smoothly gains speed down the runway. I'm pretty sure my mouth is still hanging open as we gently lift into the atmosphere. We must be somewhere in Colorado or Utah, with all the beautiful mountains below us. Did Eric drag me here from the middle of the California desert? If he did, how long did it take? And what day is it? Shit. I didn't even think about that. Has anyone noticed I'm gone? I try not to hyperventilate and stupidly glance out the window.

The mountains are replaced with fluffy white clouds, and it makes me think about my parents. I wonder what my mom would think if she were on a plane piloted by no one. She'd probably have a heart attack on the spot, I realize with an amused smile. Good ol' Mom. I wonder if my parents have thought about me once while on their vacation. Probably not.

I stare out the window in thought, remembering my childhood bedroom back in Beechmont, Florida. Will I ever see those childish mermaid decorations again? Or the cuckoo clock Grandma gave us in the kitchen? A tear threatens to run down my cheek. I wipe it away before it gets the chance, and decide to say something before Eric notices.

"Is it on autopilot or something?" I ask, prepared for a smart-ass response from Eric. Instead, he drops an ice cube in his maple-colored alcoholic beverage and casually sits across from me, an amused smile tugging at the corner of his mouth.

"It's the P.I.L.O.T.," he says. Then he clarifies, "Pretty Intuitive Lift-Off Technology." I nod my head, not relieved in the slightest. He takes a small sip of his drink, letting out a satisfied sigh.

It's quiet for a moment.

"Wait, what do you mean by 'pretty' intuitive?" I ask. "Is that pretty as in 'not so accurate' or as in... you know, pretty?"

He eyes me and swishes his drink, enjoying how much his silence irks me. My eyes do a somersault of their own volition.

"Are you sure it's smart to be drinking before a mission?" I nod at his beverage.

"I'm gonna need all the booze I can get if I'm going to make it out alive with you." He swirls the ice in his glass and raises it to his lips. All I heard in that sentence was "make out with you" and now I'm blushing.

"Need a sip?" He smirks. I cross my arms.

"No, thank you." I search the side of my seat with my fingers until I find a small metal button protruding from the leather. I press it back, and my seat slowly reclines into a flat position. I let out a sigh, suddenly very tired.

"You're not going to sleep now, are you?" Eric feigns displeasure. "Who am I going to talk to for the next ten hours?"

"Talk to the P.I.L.O.T," I say. Something occurs to me. "Hey, what does T.O.P.S.E.C.R.E.T. stand for, anyway?"

"Topmost Operatives Performing Secretive Espionage Charades Remedying Evildoer Tactics," he says with another sip. "T.O.P.S.E.C.R.E.T."

Of course.

The life-threatening events of the last however-many hours catch up to me all at once, and I'm out in a wink.

* * *

Before I know it, an obnoxious horn wakes me up. I jump a foot in the air, hitting my head on the ceiling of a low sports car. My heart pounds erratically while I take in my completely different surroundings. Where am I? What happened to the plane? I'm sitting in the passenger seat of a Lamborghini, hugged by sporty leather seats emitting the smell of new leather. To my left, Eric watches amused as I groggily wake up. "Where are we?" I ask.

"The Safe House," he answers. He pushes his door open (or, rather, up, as this car apparently works like the Batmobile).

We're greeted by an onslaught of car horns. Eric ignores them, grabbing his duffel bag from the trunk of the car. I wipe the drool off my chin and follow his lead. As soon as my feet hit the pavement, the fresh, humid air of the night tingles my ankles, sending a wave of pleasant goosebumps up my legs. I stand, taking a deep breath of the delicious air. Is that... freshly baked bread? I turn around, following my nose, and realize we're parked on the curb of a bustling French street. Cars speed past in a flurry of lights and high-pitched horns. I take it all in with my jaw hanging open.

We're in Paris, France! Who would have guessed that Julie Richardson, the germophobe hermit crab of a nerd, would find herself on the streets of Paris at just twenty-two years old? Definitely not me.

I search the skies for the Eiffel tower, but all I see is the beautiful night above me, stars twinkling down as if to say, "Welcome, Julie." It's quite a magical moment.

Until a moped flies past, splashing muddy water all over me from head to toe. An attractive young couple walks past, entertained by my misfortune. I wave at them, accidentally splattering some of the gross water on the girl. She lets out a disgusted cry, and they hurry on.

From across the street, Eric waves me over. He's standing in a glow of golden light coming from a sparkling hotel lobby behind him. Beautiful pillars rise high above the ground, telling all passersby that this here is one fancy fine establishment. French flags wave in the slight breeze beneath an astronomical clock and a marble-carved sign that says, "Le Maison Sûr." In English— "The Safe House."

It's definitely not what I expected a safe house to look like. Then again, what do I know?

I grab my bag from the trunk. After a few moments, the traffic opens up, and I dart across the street, fueled by a sudden surge of hope.

Maybe this mission won't be so bad, after all.

12 / CRÈME BRÛLÉE

"This isn't exactly low profile," I say, taking in our new home base. Eric checked us into the topmost floor of the hotel. And I mean the entire story.

The whole place is decked out in gaudy furniture, decorative wallpaper, thick fancy carpets, and sconces filled with warm-colored lightbulbs that light the open floor-plan with a flickering light that mimics candles. It feels like only a matter of time before Queen Victoria herself walks through the door to hand us extra pillows.

Eric takes his shoes off and jumps on the sprawling bed, spilling fluffy pillows on the floor and crinkling the shiny quilted duvet. Is there a size bigger than King? If there is, that's how big this bed is. Man, I can't wait to rinse off and fall asleep in that giant mound of fluffy goodness—

"I call dibs," Eric says.

"Excuse me?" I cock my hip to the side, my drenched oversized man-pants squeaking with the movement. "What about giving the lady the bed?"

"Only people who have saved the world get to sleep in this bed. There's a nice comfy couch over there." He points behind me to an awkwardly shaped loveseat that looks like it's as hard as a rock. I roll my eyes at him. I'll claim the bed while he's using the restroom, I tell myself.

My stomach growls, reminding me how starving I am. "Is there a room service menu?"

He pulls one out of the drawer and throws a heavy binder to me. It lands at my feet, and a few pages fly out. I glare at him, then flip through.

It's entirely in French. "Fromage" and "crème" pop out at me in practically every item description. Is there seriously nothing dairy-free? I check my little fanny pack for Lactaid. Whew, still there. But I really only like to use them for emergencies, like in the many cases where I order something strictly without butter or cheese, but the meal comes back tasting a little too good. That's when you know there's dairy.

I order a plain salad (sans fromage) and a small fruit bowl for myself, and a sixteen-ounce juicy ribeye meal with green juice and a bowl of fries upon Eric's request. The heavily accented room service man tells me it'll be another hour at least before we get our food, so I decide to head for the bathroom to get cleaned up.

Walking into the marble-floored bathroom is like walking into a whole new world. Everything twinkles with opulence, from the golden-stitched towels hanging on the wall to the crown molding that lines the entire space. There's a bathtub on the right, accompanied by fancy decorative soaps and even rose petals in a glass jar. For what, I don't know.

Next to the tub is a steam shower in the corner of the room with glass walls from floor to ceiling. Multiple gold shower heads protrude from the ceiling and even the back wall, and a touchpad hangs on the door by the handle. Across from the shower/tub combo is a double sink countertop with brightly lit mirrors and French labeled perfume bottles stacked in the center.

Holy snap! I doubt even Queen Victoria was living like this back in her day.

I decide to test out the steam shower first. Let me tell you, hot water has never felt so good in my entire life. I let it wash over me, taking with it the grime of travel and all (most) of my fears for the mission. However, after a few deep breaths of water I decide I'd rather not drown in the shower, thankyouverymuch.

Once I'm squeaky clean, I hop over to the tub for some grime-free soaking and a relaxing view of the city below me. With the window slightly ajar, the cars driving by and the general ambiance of the city sounds like the ocean. If I close my eyes it almost feels like I'm back at home in Beechmont, Florida.

I take a deep breath, trying to enjoy the sudden calmness around me. But with a mind that doesn't stop and genes that defer to worrying, pretty soon the bubbles feel like they're in my stomach when they should be in the tub. I pour a bottle of "les bulles" around me and let the suds build while I rationalize myself through the nerves.

Thinking about the positives always puts things in perspective for me. There's no room for doubt. No room for fear. No room for second-guessing, I tell myself, remembering what The Director had said. Not if I'm going to be facing off against some kind of evildoer with the world's most selfish spy.

I roll my eyes at the thought of Eric. Okay, positives.

Positive number one: I'm in Paris. Like, Paris, Paris. Even if it's under terrifying circumstances, at least there's a chance I'll see the Eiffel tower. Oh, can I see it now? I open the window a bit farther, craning my neck as far as it'll go without revealing my naked body to any passersby (not that anyone would be floating around twenty floors above the street, but this is a whole other country so you never know). With a sigh I plop back into the water. That's a negative for the Eiffel Tower sighting.

Positive number two: I'm technically staying the night with a super attractive man in a super fancy hotel in a super romantic city. If I pretend Eric isn't a super selfish jerk, I can almost convince myself this is awesome.

Positive number three: Eric is supposedly the world's best secret agent. At least, he thinks he's T.O.P.S.E.C.R.E.T.'s best agent. I'm going to interpret that as a positive and say I'm in the best hands I could be in. Besides my own.

Positive number four: It's only temporary that I'm the world's McGuffin and that I have to work with Eric. Pretty soon, we'll retrieve The Backup, and everything will go back to normal.

If I say it enough, maybe I'll start to believe it.

I step out of the tub and dry off with the thickest, most jumbo towel I've ever used in my life. It's warm, too! Why is it warm? Is that a towel heater? Ohmygawd, this place is too cool.

Finishing my nightly routine, I flip my wet hair up in a towel and put on the comfy bathrobe hanging by the door. Queen Victoria, step aside.

When I walk back into the bedroom, Eric is cranking open one of the windows, wearing what looks like a pair of silky black pajama pants. With no shirt. I bite my lip at the sight of his perfectly chiseled body. Is it a requirement to be this handsome as a spy? His bicep flexes with the final crank of the handle. He hears me clip-clap into the room with my hotel slippers and takes in my dewy appearance.

"I like the new look," he says. I realize this is actually the first time he's seen me not looking like a hot mess. I try to take the twisted towel off my head and swing my hair like a mermaid, but it just gets caught, and the sopping cloth drops to the floor with a plop.

"Er, thanks," I say. Eric keeps watching me, and I can feel the blush spread down my neck. "It, uh, feels good to be clean." I'm trying to fill in the awkward silence, here, buddy! I avert my eyes from his unyielding gaze and notice he's left the bed wide open.

This is my chance.

I jump onto the bed, spreading my body out to take up as much of the space as possible.

"Are you trying to seduce me?" he says. I know he's joking, but his devilish grin takes me off guard. I cross my legs under my robe, suddenly hyper-aware of my lack of clothing. What was I thinking? I'm such a child.

He jumps on the bed and crawls toward me. My heart races. What is he doing? I scoot backward, as far away from him as I can while still claiming the majority of the bed for myself. He leans in close. Close enough to kiss me. Is he going to kiss me? My breath catches as he slides a hand behind my back…

And pushes me off the bed. I fall to the floor with a clatter, tangled up in my over-sized robe. I scoff at him. "I can't believe you just did that!"

"I called dibs," he says with a wicked grin. A wicked cute grin. Damn it.

Just then, the doorbell rings. "You going to get that?" I ask.

"And leave my territory vulnerable for another attack by the half-naked lady?" I blush. "Not a chance, babe," he says, crossing his legs and flipping through a French yachting magazine. I let out a huff and stomp out of the bedroom and into the foyer. I'm a fool if I let my hormones affect my actions. Shake it off, Julie.

A few angsty strides later, I swing the front door open in a huff and start at the sight of a full cart of food. "Oh, snap! I mean, merci," I gush excitedly. I usher the room service butler inside, but he just stands in the hallway, unmoving.

"Oh, right. Uh," I think back on my years of AP French. "Bienvenue. S'il vous plait entrer." I gesture with my arm for him to enter, pleased at my proper inflection. I have a pretty good accent if I do say so myself.

Wordlessly, the butler pushes the cart of food forward. It's a multilayered wooden cart, draped with a white tablecloth that reaches the floor, protecting the food from getting cold on the lower shelf. He pushes the cart into the room and forces it over the thick ornate carpet, rattling the silverware resting atop the bright white tablecloth. It's the only sound in the room, besides Eric flipping the pages of his yachting magazine and the distant rush of Parisian traffic.

Even hunched over, the butler looks like a pretty big guy. His muscles bulge beneath the short sleeves of the standard white uniform he's wearing. And his skin is covered in nasty purple and green bruises. One of his eyes is sporting a dreadful shiner, which appears to have been hastily covered up by a home-made eyepatch. Yikes, he must do boxing in his free time.

Silently, the man removes the silver dome over Eric's ribeye, letting the mouthwatering aroma of steak fill the suite.

"Yesss," Eric says from his perch on the bed. I can hear him rustling the sheets, excitedly slamming the magazine shut. "It's about time!"

Manners have taught me better than to stare, but something about this behemoth of a waiter is not right. I narrow my eyes, watching suspiciously as he continues to reveal each dish on the top tray.

It's not until he locks the door behind him, stands to his full height, gives me a menacing grin and reveals teeth in dire need of some floss and a good mouth wash, that I realize who the waiter really is.

Greyson.

AKA Blondie.

But how can that be? There's no way he survived that plane crash! I can still see Greyson's figure erupting into flames, falling behind a mountaintop, never to be seen again.

Or so I thought.

His nasty teeth send a shiver down my spine that paralyzes me right there in front of him.

"What's taking so long?" Eric says as he rounds the corner into the entryway.

Greyson's ears perk up like a hound dog when he sees Eric.

I stand in shock, unable to react as the giant henchman heaves a fifty-pound bazooka from under the table and rests it on his shoulder.

"Bon appetite," he says with an icy smirk, pointing the weapon right at me.

13 / WHAT'S HAPPENNING?!

Greyson presses a button on the side of the gun and bends his knees, bracing for impact. But instead of KABOOM, the bazooka makes a delicate beeping sound.

"Aww hell," Greyson gravelly voice scrapes out. He stands straight and lowers the weapon from his shoulder, flicking a tiny switch before returning to his firing position.

"Julie, get down!" Eric yells. He rushes at Greyson, shoving the food cart to his side and right into my gut. I collapse on the floor as plates of delicious food rain down. A steak knife stabs the wooden floor just beside my head with a loud THWACK!

Through my stringy wet hair, now covered in Eric's Crème Brulee, I watch as Eric flies through the air and smacks into Greyson, knocking the bazooka out of Greyson's hand. It slides across the room, scraping the stained hardwood floor.

Eric lands a punch right in Greyson's chin, but the man barely flinches. Eric smacks him in the neck, the groin, the side, and every single pressure point a person could have in a flurry of motions so fast that even Jackie Chan would be impressed.

Greyson just stands there and takes it like a brick wall, laughing that creepy laugh, his deep voice reverberating through the room.

In one forceful movement, Greyson grabs Eric by the neck with his meaty paw and raises him off the ground. Eric wriggles and kicks, but to no avail.

Eek, I remember what that felt like. Not fun.

I hastily grab the nearest plate fragment off the floor and haul it at Greyson.

But my aim is just a little bit off.

The sharp piece of plate smacks Eric in the side of the head, breaking into a bunch of smaller pieces just over his eye.

"Agh!" he gargles. Greyson tightens his grip while laughing at him.

Crap.

Greyson throws Eric into the wall. The ornate mirror in the entrance foyer shatters and falls to the ground with Eric as he gasps for air.

I frantically search for anything to help the situation.

The knife! I pull the steak knife from the ground next to me and scramble to my feet. This time I don't rely on my aim. Instead, I ram it right into Greyson's side. The sharp blade bends against his body like it's made of plastic.

Is this giant made of bricks?!

Eric raises his legs and locks Greyson in a chokehold around his thighs.

"You just couldn't stay dead, could you? You had to come back for more," Eric says through gritted teeth. Greyson lets out a roar, and I jump out of the way just as Eric unleashes another round of karate moves on the beast.

They attack each other in a twister of punches and kicks and grunts and groans. The two men clash into every ornate, expensive thing in the entire suite. The vase, the curtains, the tables, the flowers, the mirrors— all destroyed by the giant wrecking ball bulldozing the whole place apart.

Eric rips the fancy curtains off the wall and wraps them around Greyson's head with a triumphant, "Ha!", but Greyson picks him up like a twig and sends Eric flying into the glass chandelier above the bed. It rains beautiful tiny shards of glass above him and all over the floor.

Greyson grabs the bedside table, raising it high above his head. He steps toward Eric, crunching the tiny shards of glass into silvery dust beneath his immense weight. In one fluid motion, he heaves the heavy drawer system down on top of Eric.

Probably, I should do something.

I grab the nearest thing that isn't destroyed— a heavy-looking table lamp— and run into the bedroom with it held high above my head. My floppy over-sized slippers lose their grip on the glassy powder covering the floor, and I slide across the room. Right into Greyson.

Using my momentum, I swing the thing at the back of his giant head. It bursts on impact (score!), but Greyson barely twitches. Jeez, this guy is barely human! He turns to me, snarling like a feral dog.

Crap.

I notice a tattoo on the side of his neck. It looks similar to the silhouetted mouse from the computer virus.

Within seconds of laying eyes on it, the oppressive sensation rushes at me. I grimace. Though I'm not eager for what's about to strike, it's the whole reason I'm here.

I hold my breath and let the onslaught of convulsions take over as colorful, foreign images race through my mind in a flash of light and emotions.

Speak to me, McGuffin!

I'm transported to someplace wet and dim. Rushing water fills the background from somewhere in the not so far distance. The cobblestone walls flicker with candlelight. I take a tentative step forward, my foot splashing in a thin layer of water. Silhouetted figures dance on the walls of a long tunnel in front of me. Cries of pain echo down my way, making my stomach lurch.

Is this some kind of medieval torture chamber?

The image transforms into a room with cheap wallpaper and a sink that looks like it hasn't been given a good wash in a few years. As I turn on the faucet, the wall transforms into a secret tunnel. I take a step forward and fall into the dark rabbit hole. Then I land crisscross-applesauce in front of a pedestal, on top of which sits a tiny USB drive. Lights shine down on it from everywhere, and the whole room turns to gold before another flash of white takes over.

A moment later, I'm transported back into our suite at "Le Maison Sur." Grunting finds its way to my ears, and I bolt upright to see Eric in the middle of another twister of fight moves with Greyson.

He seems like he's got this handled.

Breathing heavily, I try to trap the images in my head while the convulsions slow down to random twitches.

Paper.

Pen.

I need to write this down before I forget.

Eric watches from the corner of his eye as I scramble across the floor toward his duffel bag. I rifle through his things, surprised at the amount of underwear he decided to bring (and somewhat relieved I'm not the only one who overpacks on the essentials).

"Where are all the pens?" I shout, shaking the contents of his bag onto the bed. Mostly underwear falls out.

"In the pen bag!" Eric says, dodging a punch. He makes Greyson's movements look like slow motion.

The reflective surface of the silver pen bag catches my eye from Eric's heap of underwear. "Yes!" I rip it open, and pens fly across the bed, mixing with Eric's delicates. I grab the pen closest to me, click the clicker to start writing on my palm, but there's no ink.

"Oh, come on—" I start, cut off by a FLASH! And a BANG!

An explosion of light floods the entire suite with blinding brightness. A solid two seconds go by before everything returns to normal.

"Julie!" Eric yells. I blink away the remaining brightness in my eyes. He's rubbing his eyes while Greyson inspects his hands as if he's seeing them for the first time. "What the hell are you doing!"

"I thought it was a normal pen!" I yell back, but I don't think he hears me over Greyson's battle cry.

Greyson launches another attack on Eric, who is now fighting temporary blindness and an abominable beast. Greyson grabs him in another chokehold.

Eric sputters out, "Hurry up and do something, Julie!"

I grab another pen, shake off Eric's silky drawers, and point the tip at Greyson. I sure hope it's something useful and not another flash grenade. I click the little clicker, and a tiny red dart flies out, stabbing Eric right in the ass.

Crap!

Eric lets out a yelp. "Julie!" he gurgles.

"Sorry!" I yell, already grabbing another pen and clicking the clicker. Nothing happens at first. I inspect the tool and notice the hotel logo scrawled in cursive on the side of a black pen.

It's the hotel pen—an actual pen!

I frantically scribble some notes on the inside of my arm. When I'm done, I look up to find Eric passed out, and Greyson headed right for me.

I scramble to my feet, totally unprepared and underdressed, as he lunges for me. I duck and slide between his legs, surprised at my own agility.

Search the room for a weapon, any weapon, I think. I curse myself for leaving the bag of pens behind. Greyson is already halfway to me. I decide to go for the shock factor and jump on him.

I put my foot on the ledge of the open window and leap on

Greyson's face. He claws at me, but I hold on tight and wrap my arms around his torso.

Now what?!

Greyson twists his enormous body around and smacks me into the wall, hard. All the breath in my lungs lets out in one quick grunt. My grip loosens, but damn it if I'm going to let go.

I re-grip right as he smacks into the wall again, snatching around back at my waist with his giant heavy hands. He gathers a big chunk of my robe in his hand and yanks me to the ground, hard. I clamber to get away, flailing my arms around desperately to catch hold of something to pull myself away faster.

My fingers catch on something substantial and metallic.

The bazooka.

I heave it onto my shoulder, bucking at the weight. The giant weapon is pointed straight at Greyson. He freezes in his tracks.

"You don't have the guts to pull that trigger, girl," he growls.

"Where's The McGuffin Backup," I demand with a shaky voice. Greyson bursts into laughter.

"I said," I raise my voice, willing it to stay level, "where's The Back—"

My sweaty finger slips, accidentally squeezing the trigger. The giant bazooka bullet flies across the room in a fiery explosion, right out the window, setting the drapes ablaze. The force sends me to the ground, knocking the gun out of my hand.

Shit!

Greyson grabs me by the arm, dragging me toward the window like the dead weight that I am. He swings my body above his head.

Just as he's about to throw me out the window, my entire body stiffens up like a wooden plank. I lose all sensation in my limbs. Greyson drops me unexpectedly, but when I hit the ground, I don't feel a thing.

What the heck?

Greyson looks down at me, his savage face twisted in a look

of raw confusion. Hey man, don't look at me. I have no idea what's happening, either!

The flames are growing higher now, engulfing the entire drape and spreading to the wall.

Am I dying? Is that why I can't move? Have I already died, and my vision is the last working bodily function to go?

Greyson bends down to grab me again, but I burst into a fit of convulsions and twitches. My leg juts out, tripping Greyson right out the window!

A few moments pass until my body stops twitching. I'm flooded with feeling again, now privy to the giant bruise on my entire side.

The heck just happened?

I pop my head out the window to see how far of a fall Greyson must have had (we're a good twenty floors up), but he's nowhere to be seen.

Where did he go? Did I imagine it? What is it with this guy who can burst into flames and hit a mountain and still come back with gusto? Are flames and falls his thing, or what?

A loud BANG hits the wooden door to the suite.

"Monsieur! Mademoiselle! Laissez nous entrer!" someone's muffled voice worriedly cries to us in French. "Est-ce que tu vas bien?"

Great, now security is here. That door is going to come down any second!

"Uhhh... Ca va bien!" I say, attempting to sound calm. With flames engulfing half the suite, Eric out cold, and hotel security threatening to burst down the door, I'm anything but.

We have to get out of here. Fast.

I dart back to the bed, searching through the pens strewn about. I inspect the tiny engravings one after another, throwing them aside until I find the one with an engraving that I'm hoping means Wake Up Gas and not Wacky Unhelpful Gadget.

I hold the pen under Eric's nose and click the button. A jet stream of water shoots out, right up his nose and spraying him all over the face.

Oops!

The water stream runs out as quickly as it started. I inspect the inscription a little closer this time to find that, according to George, WUG stands for Water Utility Gun. Go figure.

Eric snaps back to life in a dramatic show of shock, choking and gargling.

"Damn it, Julie!" It's the first thing he says. He whips his head around to take in the wall of flames behind us. "Holy shit!"

"We have to get out of here!" I say.

"What did you do?!"

The door to the suite CRACKS as the French crew continues to force their way in. Eric spins around, nostrils flared. I grimace.

"What now?" I ask. He grabs the empty bag of pens, noticing our stock has considerably lessened. "How many damn weapons did you waste?"

"Just get us out of here!" I yell. He rushes to the other side of the room, the one facing away from the street and not on fire, and forces the window open. Sirens wail in the distance.

Oh boy.

Eric grabs a pen and, without even looking to check what it does, he clicks the button. A giant grappling hook explodes out of the small tip, sinking its teeth into the side of the building just above us. Eric yanks me close to him and grips me tight.

"Hold on to me," he says. I realize we're about to jump from the building. A thought suddenly occurs.

"One second!" I rush over to my things, pulling them away from the flames and searching through my pile of dirty clothes until I find my trusty fanny pack, still full of Lactaid.

Whew. That would have really sucked.

I snatch all the pens I can find from the bed and shove them into the fanny pack before darting back over to Eric. When I wrap my arms around his muscular torso, I can feel every ripple in his beautifully toned body.

"Ready now, princess?" he asks.

I roll my eyes. "Just go!"

He grabs my waist, and together we jump out the window just as the hotel staff burst through the door. We rappel down the side of the building.

I don't even question how Eric can hold our weight in the awkward grip of the tiny pen, or how Greyson managed to survive twice, or why I randomly became paralyzed.

I'm just glad to be alive and (somewhat) safe in Eric's arms.

14 / TOTAL RECALL

We drop to the ground just around the corner from the hotel entrance as a group of emergency responders skid to a stop in the street, blocking traffic from both directions.

The French sirens sound distinctly different from American ones, a higher-pitched, faster-paced "eee-aaaa" that somehow matches the throaty accent of the nation rather than the slow and daunting "weeee-wooooo" of American police sirens. I mentally add that to my ongoing internal list of useless interesting facts.

Eric claps his hands in front of my face. "Julie! Focus." He retracts the thick wire back into the pen rappel before throwing it into an old drain near us on the sidewalk.

"What are you doing?" I ask. "That's a perfectly good pen rappel! What if we need to use it again?"

"Spies never use the same tool twice, remember?" He flashes a quick glance over his shoulder at the frantic onslaught of paramedics and firefighters rushing into the building. Above us, flames lick the edges of the windowpane, threatening to spread to the outside of the building. All the commotion draws a crowd of onlookers across the street. Their numbers are growing by the second.

"We need to get out of here," he says, his voice low and urgent. He's really good at stating the most obvious things at the most obvious times. I idly wonder if that's something all spies have to be good at. "Let's go." He grabs my arm and tugs me down the sidewalk.

"Wait!" I pull my arm out of his grasp, and the sleeve of my robe falls down my shoulder, revealing bare skin. My arm pebbles up as soon as it's exposed to the fresh night air. I tug the sleeve back on with a shiver.

"Julie, we don't have time for one of your temper tantrums." He notices an armed guard around the corner of the building and quickly presses himself against me, flattening us against the wall. The guard doesn't see us, too focused on the flames now trailing up to the roof. The guard says something into his walkie talkie and bursts through the side entrance to the building.

Eric lets out a sigh, his breath somehow still as fresh as a mint leaf, and I'm acutely aware of his rock-hard body pressed against mine. Thank god I'm not a guy or he'd know exactly how I feel, considering we're so close. I hold my breath, just in case it smells like empty stomach. He looks me in the eyes, and, for the briefest of moments, I feel lightheaded. Perhaps it's because the scrape above his eye is starting to ooze. Or maybe because I'm starving. Definitely not because Eric's warm body is still pressed against mine.

"That was a close call," he says, still inches from my face. I nod, agreeing with him, but currently unable to speak for fear that my voice might come out sounding like a squeaky toy.

"BBBBRRRRIIIINNNGGGGG!" The cell phone vibrates in my fanny pack, sending a shock-wave through my entire body. I fumble through the fanny pack pockets to find it.

"It's Simon!" I urgently whisper. Eric pulls me into the nearest shadow as I answer the call, putting it on speakerphone. I hastily turn the volume down low. "Simon," I whisper. "Is that you?" Eric rolls his eyes at me and points to the screen, which clearly states, "Simon Zedler."

"Yes! You sound alive," he says, sounding immensely relieved. "How did my test go? Do you have anything measurable to report?" I hear the distinct clicking of his trusty note-taking pen in the background.

Eric and I look to each other with furrowed brows. "What are you talking about? What test?" he asks. I think back into the past hour. Then it dawns on me.

"Oh my GOD!" I shout. Eric clasps his hand over my mouth, shoving me further behind the building into its cloak of shadows.

"Did it work?" Simon's excited voice rings out from the phone speakers. "I tried tapping into your central nervous system to manipulate your convulsive reflexes. I thought perhaps it might help you stay calm in case of another message from," he pauses for effect, or perhaps respect, "The McGuffin." I slap Eric's arm. He reluctantly lets me go, giving me a wide-eyed, pursed-lip warning face.

"Simon! You almost got me KILLED," I stage-whisper angrily.

"What do you mean? According to my readings—"

"You paralyzed me in the absolute worst possible moment, and I almost died because of it," I state, barely controlling my voice.

"Ooh, very interesting." His pen meets paper in the very audible sounds of scribbling. Before I can scold him some more, another line is added to the call, and a familiar voice enters the conversation.

"Simon, what have I told you about communicating this way?" The Director says.

"You said cell phones were okay," Simon says, his voice rising in defense.

"I mean regarding Julie's testing." She sounds just as exasperated as she did when we were back at headquarters. I wonder if she's managed to get her blood pressure down. God knows I haven't.

Eric paces back and forth in the tiny shadowed area in front of me, checking around the corner every few seconds. "We don't have time for this," he says. His eyes flash in all directions, looking for an escape route. His gaze catches on a small alleyway a few blocks down the street. "You'll have to walk and talk." He grabs my arm again, this time extra firmly, and looks me in the eye as he says, "Think you can handle that?" I give him a pointed look, but he waits for an official confirmation. I nod, and he tugs me down a thin path down the backside of the hotel.

"Give us an update, Eric. What's your status?" The Director says.

"We're currently… on the move," Eric says.

"As in tracking a target, I hope?" The Director asks.

"Not exactly," Eric says, giving me some sass over his shoulder as we continue onto a nearby street, sticking close to the shadows. Sirens fill the air, but the wailing slowly grows distant as we head away from the crime scene.

"Are those sirens?" The Director's voice raises an octave. "I said low profile, Eric!"

We're still barefoot and wearing pajamas. Well, in my case, just a robe. Low profile for sure. I shake my head at the situation. "Greyson attacked us when we ordered room service, and I saw something—"

"Room service? Where were you?"

Eric interrupts me before I can speak.

"You're ignoring the larger picture, Penelope. Greyson attacked Julie. But don't worry, I handled it," he says.

"That's what you said about Greyson the first time, but apparently he's still not taken care of."

Eric sets his jaw. "Well, he looks like hell."

"How so?" Simon asks. A couple rushes past us, pointing toward the burning hotel. We slow down, turning our faces away until they're a safe distance from us, then pick up the pace again.

"He was bruised all over, and he had this really nasty looking eyepatch." I grimace at the mental sight of it, imagining how he might have applied the clunky contraption to himself. Eek. "But he still managed to kick our asses," I add.

Eric turns to me, attitude twisting his features. "About that—were you trying to help the bad guy?" I give him a questioning look. "You nearly got me killed and managed to set The Safe House on fire," he emphasizes, with a hint of remorse for his favorite five-star hangout.

"The Safe House?" The Director takes a deep breath. "Don't tell me you managed to set fire to a five-star hotel." Another round of sirens fills the air, as if on cue. I can practically hear her mentally face-palming herself. "Dear God, what is going on?"

"What's going on is that I should be doing this alone," Eric says toward the phone. The Director sighs. "Remind me why you thought it was a good idea to bring an uninformed, inexperienced college kid on this mission?" The sass is strong with this one.

"Because I had another vision!" I shout, but the cobblestone walls deaden the echo halfway down the alleyway. It's like Simon and The Director are here with us, and I can feel them turn to me as Simon claps his hands with a gasp.

"What was it? What did you see?" He's practically a panting puppy.

"I wrote it all down," I say, tugging at the sleeve beneath Eric's grip. He lets go, and I pull up my sleeve, revealing a jumbled mess of ink. "Nice work, iron-grip!" I shoot him a glare.

"What did The McGuffin tell you, Julie?" The Director asks.

"Hang on a sec." I squint my eyes closed, ignoring the stressful pounding of my heart as I tell my brain to pull up the images from before like a mental filing system. I'm surprised to find they come back to me like white on rice. Thank God for my photographic memory. No need for taking notes, as it turns out. Looks like the first couple of times shock got the better of me.

I tell them all about the candle-lit chambers, the secret tunnel, and the tiny USB drive in great detail.

"Simon, did you get all that?" The Director asks. The sounds of him scribbling confirm it.

"Yes, Director. All of it," he says.

"Let's cross-reference past missions, see if we can't find anything useful for their hunt for The Backup. And Julie," she pauses. I lean closer to the phone.

"Yes?"

"Good work."

I feel a smile forming on my lips, and the familiar feeling of achievement tingles my spine.

"Thanks, Director," I say. Eric narrows his eyes. Jealousy, perhaps?

The Director's pager pings. "I have to go," she says with another sigh. "Just, find The Backup and get back to headquarters without blowing up another building, please?" she whines. "And Simon—no more remote testing."

"No promises," Eric says.

"What's that? You're breaking up—" Simon fumbles with the phone and then his line goes dead.

The Director groans. "Over and out." Click.

Eric and I appraise each other, standing there in the alleyway in our pajamas, barefoot, wild-eyed.

"Eyes up here, babe," Eric says. I realize I'm staring at his chiseled chest. The corner of his frown turns upwards into a smug smile. Ugh.

Eric marches forward, his feet splashing in a puddle.

"Ack," he grumbles, kicking the water off and trudging on. I follow behind him.

We approach the end of the alleyway to see the sun rising above the city, casting a beautiful orange glow over everything, making the moment feel like a dream. The two of us stop walking to take in the rare peaceful moment. Are we really standing here in Paris? Did we really just catch a five-star hotel on fire? Is the world seriously resting on our shoulders?

My stomach grumbles loud enough for both of us to hear it, breaking the moment and proving, with a surprisingly intense sharp pain, that this is, indeed, reality.

"I'm hungry too," he says.

"Where should we go now?" He looks me up and down, not even trying to hide his grimace.

"We can't go anywhere looking like this," he says. I nod.

"Right. New clothes first. Food later." Something occurs to me. "Wait, how are we going to get new clothes? Everything besides my fanny pack, a few pens, and my Lactaid is still back in the room." Burnt to a crisp by now.

"Not everything." He gives me a knowing smirk, then whips something from out of nowhere, holding his hand out to me as if presenting a golden ticket. In fact, that's exactly what it looks like. A small, plastic golden rectangle.

"A credit card?" I ask.

"The T.O.P.S.E.C.R.E.T. company credit card. A spy's most valuable weapon," he says with a smirk.

The Director's going to kill us.

15 / NOT YOUR GRANDMA'S PANTIES

Who knew a pair of women's jeans could be so comforting?

I step in front of the mirror in one of the less expensive shops at Le Bon Marche, essentially a giant multiplex of shops here in Paris' most popular Left-Bank department store. Eric insists we shop here, despite the multitude of tourists and possible McGuffin triggers, because "quality is what counts." That, and he has a golden credit card burning a hole in his pocket.

Nevertheless, my uptight, frugal mind just won't let me take advantage of the situation. I keep things simple, ditching my sweat-soaked, dirt-covered, over-sized robe for a pair of slightly bell-bottomed jeans that just kiss the ground, some unfamiliar-to-me designer sneakers, and the least expensive-looking black t-shirt I can find amongst all the name brands.

The disheveled, malnourished look seems to work for me. My shoulder-length dark brown hair, which is usually tightly wound in a frizzy bun on top of my head, has fallen in unpredictable waves that accentuate my natural frizzy curls. My stomach is flat (which I'm attributing to the last few days of unintentional fasting and not the black shirt that apparently hugs me in all the right places). My lips are a dark shade of red

(AKA chapped), giving me a, dare I say, sexy vibe that feels totally foreign.

Oh, and apparently, all the underwear in Paris is made for naughty purposes. I'm walking around sporting a secret pair of silky lingerie that tests my already poor poker face. If I put half as much effort into my appearance as I do my schoolwork, I might manage to look somewhat feminine for a change.

Another bout of cold, nervous sweat seeps into the shirt beneath my armpits, and I'm reminded just how unfeminine I really am. I roll my eyes at the fleeting moment of confidence. Welp, at least you're wearing black, I tell myself.

"You ready?" Eric bangs on the changing room door.

"Just a second," I say, slipping the little earpiece into place. Eric says we don't need them yet, but it's so small and I really don't want to lose it in the streets of Paris. I can barely feel the thing inside me, and now I'm wondering if I'll lose it in my ear canal instead.

I fasten the fanny pack around my waist. Surprisingly, it adds another layer of "cool" to my ensemble. Alright, I'll take it.

"Hurry up, Julie. We need to analyze your vision," he says, knocking again. I swing the door open mid-knock, and Eric's knocking fist stops just short of punching me in the face. He looks almost apologetic for a moment until his mouth forms into an amused grin. He appraises my disheveled look from top to bottom. "My, my. You clean up well."

"Thanks, you too," I say, nodding at his own ensemble. He's wearing almost the same thing as he was when we met on the plane— a white shirt, designer jeans meant to look distressed on purpose, and black boots. He's switched out his leather jacket and opted for a light, slim-cut blazer. The thin layer of stubble growing on his face gives him a rugged look that reminds me I'm wearing lingerie. I duck past him, trying to hide my blush.

"Can we eat now? I'm starving," I say, changing the subject.

I can feel his eyes on my hips as I lead us to the cashier. "Yeah, me too," he murmurs.

He whips out his gold T.O.P.S.E.C.R.E.T. card like it's a switchblade. I idly wonder why such a Top-Secret government agency even bothers trying to stay covert when they plaster their name all over their toys. The spy world doesn't make any sense.

After Eric pays for our clothes, which come out to a whopping three-thousand-seventy-five dollars (what are these underwear made of--diamonds?), we head back to the ground level of the shopping center. He wants to eat at a fancy, expensive French restaurant that specializes in creme brulee (AKA actual poison for my lactose-intolerant stomach). I manage to convince him to head outside of this multiplex of chandeliers and fancy pants in exchange for an outdoor location where we can discuss the details of our mission out of ear range from all the tourists.

As soon as we step outside, the fresh air and beautiful scenery give me a rejuvenating wave of energy. I take a deep breath, trying to memorize what this place looks and feels like before we have to head right back into mission mode, but Eric immediately sets off down the street to our right. I quicken my pace to catch up.

"Do you know where you're going?" I ask.

"This way." He nods forward.

Is he always this helpful?

We're heading down the sidewalk toward a busy intersection with more tourists and cars, which means more attention. The congestion ahead makes my stomach squeeze tight. I don't want all of Paris' eyes on me in the case of another convulsion session.

"Can't we go someplace less crowded?"

He gives me a side glance. "Do you want food or not?"

"Yes, but we also need to figure out what we're doing next

and…" A large group of tourists waddles past us with their cameras out, threatening to push us off the sidewalk. We shove our way through, ducking under their flashing onslaught of photographs. Once they're out of earshot, I continue in a hushed voice, "I don't think everyone here needs to know all the details of our plan."

"What plan?" Eric walks right across the street without even looking both ways. I double-check there's no oncoming cars and dart after him.

"Exactly. We need a plan," I say.

"We'll make a plan. After I get a Monte Cristo." He continues marching forward. Something glittering catches my eye between two buildings on our left. I backtrack and realize it's a body of water, reflecting the sunlight.

"Oh, snap! The Seine!" I practically jump. Eric turns around.

"What about it?" he says.

"I've never seen it before. It looks so pretty," I say, squinting my eyes to get a better view of it from in between the buildings.

"You can't see it very well from here," Eric says, taking a few steps nearer to look over my shoulder. I'm acutely aware of his presence as he leans closer, almost touching my back.

"Yeah, but it's still pretty," I say, eyes almost entirely shut from squinting. "We should keep going." I blink and get back on track. No time to waste. As I step past him, Eric grabs my arm. I turn to him with narrowed eyes. "What?"

"Let's go this way," he says, heading back to the intersection.

"I don't understand, I thought the food was that way?" I gesture behind us.

Eric leads us around the corner until we're on the opposite side of the buildings, facing the Seine straight on. The constantly moving water reflects the blueness of the sky on its glittering surface. It's just as beautiful as I always imagined.

"Wow." It escapes my lips as a whisper.

"Come on, let's go eat," he says with a smile as bright as the Seine.

"Do you know a place by the water?" I ask.

"No, but we'll find one," he says as he continues down the sidewalk. I realize he has no idea where he's going, but it doesn't seem that way. He marches on like he owns the place, his shoulders square and his head held high.

If I were a spy, I'm not sure I could handle the uncertainty. The fact that we're still aimlessly wandering around without a plan only adds to the growing stress ball in my stomach. How does Eric do it?

I follow silently, but a few steps farther and something tugs at my stomach. Intuition, if you will. I stop walking and Eric eyes me suspiciously.

"What now?"

"Actually, I think we should go this way." I point over my shoulder.

He puts his hands in the air like, "I give up," and gestures for me to lead the way. So I do. I've no idea where this sense of direction is coming from, but pretty soon we're walking up a set of stairs onto a new street, just along the bank of the river. It's way more low-key, populated with small flower shops and a few tiny cafes. Much better. A sense of calm washes over me.

"Hey, look." Eric points to a small cafe across the street with a pink awning. It says, "Tout le Monde." I gasp.

"That's the cafe from my vision!" I stare open mouthed. Holy snap. "The McGuffin must have led us here." A creepy thought, but slightly comforting nonetheless.

"Let's check it out." Eric strides forward once more, not even hesitating.

"Wait!" I tug on his sleeve like a child. My shoulders nervously creep up to my ears. He looks back at me expectantly.

"What if the creepy man from my vision is there?" My

thoughts return to the eerie silhouetted figure laughing maniacally.

"Then it means we're getting closer to The Backup. Come on." Eric hurries across the street without waiting for me. My breath hitches. The familiar pang of worry and stress tightens all my insides into a knot. I focus on my breathing once more, trying to stay calm in case The McGuffin has something else to tell me.

What if I get another vision, but this time I don't wake up? What if the bad guy is in there and he kills us? What if I forget how to say, "no cheese, please," in French, and the waiter accidentally kills me anyway?

So many things could go wrong.

But people are counting on you, I remind myself. The world is counting on you, and you're the only one who can do this.

I try to convince myself it's just like any school project. And with any school project, I always give it my all. Have I ever actually wanted to write essays on Queen Elizabeth or do calculus homework for hours on end? Hell no. But I get it done because that's what I'm good at. Getting shit done. So, get in there and get it done!

I nod vigorously, silently encouraging myself with this inner dialog.

An old man sitting on the curb with a baguette and a stick of salami stares at me, the epitome of my stereotypical mental image of France. I give him a sheepish smile, and he rips another bite of meat off the stick.

I take it as a sign that I'm ready. Let's do this.

16 / TOUT LE MONDE

As I step closer to "Tout le Monde," sounds of silverware clinking and casual chatter fill the immediate atmosphere.

I'm stepping into a tourist's French dream, a bubble of pink napkins, swirling metallic chairs with matching tables—the classic "French" look in every "French" restaurant in America. Multiple older couples wearing clunky white shoes and too much sunblock sit across from each other, clinking glasses and taking in the general splendor of the Seine. The smell of frying oils, baked goods, and the unmistakable smell of butter intoxicate my olfactory senses, tricking my stomach into thinking I might have ingested something I shouldn't have.

I shake it off and search the place for Eric. He's already sitting at a table in the corner with a view of the Seine. Little tour boats slowly make their way down the river. I observe the beautiful scenery as I take my seat opposite him, placing my cheap, pink, paper napkin on my lap. Besides the cheesy decor, this place would be the perfect spot to relax and take a breather, to plan what museum to check out next or what bakery to try for a taste of Paris's famous French macarons. That's no doubt what all the other tourists are up to, with their giant maps all spread out and their digital cameras flashing every now and then.

But not us. Not the only two people here on business.

I ignore the urge to join the tourists and take a million photos. Instead, I get right back to work.

"Did you find anything?" My voice is low, secretive. I'm hunched over the table in a conspiratorial stance. If my voice doesn't give away that we're hiding something, my posture surely does. Eric stifles a laugh.

"Not a thing," he says, low enough so only I can hear. "I inspected the bathroom and the kitchen and did background checks on all the waiters." He smirks at my look of astonishment.

"That was a quick sweep."

"Besides the hokey decor, this place is clean." He nods at the general ambiance of the restaurant.

I look around once more, noticing the dirt swept into the corners of the restaurant, all the grime caked between the cracking tiles on the floor. I wouldn't exactly call this place "clean." The entire restaurant looks like it could use a good once-over with some Clorox wipes. I grimace.

"Are you sure The Backup wasn't, like, hiding in a pot or something back there?" I ask.

Eric raises an unimpressed eyebrow at me. "You're kidding, right?"

I slump my shoulders because I honestly wasn't. A part of me really did think it'd be as easy as walking in, grabbing The Backup, and getting the heck out of Dodge. Maybe Eric would have to punch the small, evil bald man on the way out, but I was hoping that'd be it.

How naive of me to think things would really be that simple.

"We need to trigger The McGuffin again." Eric flips to the back page of his menu and whips it in front of my face, so the restaurant logo (the globe with all the little world relics standing around it) is staring right at me. I remember it from the vision, but the sight of it does nothing to my mind.

I slowly push the menu down with my hand, revealing my eyes staring right into Eric's. He looks expectantly back at me.

"It didn't work," I say.

"Damn it. How about this?" He grabs at the pink napkin on the table and holds it up for me.

"Nope."

"This?" He grabs the saltshaker.

I shake my head.

He continues to shove every table item in my face. When I fail to convulse uncontrollably at the sight of any of them, Eric resorts to pointing out all the tourists, employees, and eventually even the individual tiles on the floor.

"Nothing's working, okay! Stop pressing me like a button." I lean back in my chair with a heavy sigh.

He jiggles his leg under the table impatiently. "You said this was the place from your vision, right?"

"Yes, Eric, but nothing else is triggering another message. I can't control it."

"Okay then, let's recap what we know for certain," he says, resting his forearms on the table.

I tick off each fact on my fingers as I go along. "We know Greyson fell to his death from a twenty-story building," I say, then I remember his large body disappearing mysteriously out the window of "Le Maison Sur."

"No, we don't." Eric reads my mind. "If you don't see them die, assume they're still alive." It sounds like a mantra he repeats to himself. I nod. Seems like a reasonable rule. For once.

"Henchmen are like insects, Julie," Eric elaborates, "and Greyson's a cockroach." Eric says the last part with obvious disdain. "The brute always manages to weasel his way back into the picture, usually by the hand of a new employer looking for some thick skin and an even thicker skull." His gaze wanders as if he recalls an unpleasant memory. Or maybe a bunch of memories. I wonder how many times Greyson has dropped into Eric's life, unannounced.

"Then we can probably guess he's working for our bad guy," I say, interrupting his thoughts.

"You're probably right." I perk up at the statement. "But I'd say we're dealing with an Evil Villain, not just your run-of-the-mill bad guy."

"What's the difference?" I ask, ignoring the ridiculousness of it all. I mean, seriously. An evil villain?

Then again, we are following clues given to use in the form of mysterious messages from the magic eight ball in my brain.

I better start taking notes.

"Bad guys are just screwed up people trying to make their own lives easier, usually at the expense of others." He states it like a dictionary definition, something I should know. "Evil Villains are like..." He searches for the best definition. "You ever seen a superhero movie?"

I give him a look like, "duh."

"Well, Evil Villains are like the maniacal enemies in super-hero movies. They usually have one goal in mind and will stop at nothing until they get what they want, regardless of the destruction and death and pain they leave in their wake." He chuckles darkly at a thought he has. "The ironic part is, half of them think they're doing it for the greater good." He shakes his head at the memory of all the bad guys he's thwarted. Or were they Evil Villains?

"Do you think our bald man is a Bad Guy or an Evil Villain?" I ask.

"What do you think?" He doesn't say it with an attitude, he's just curious. Am I really listening to him? Am I taking this as seriously as he is?

I decide I am.

"If I had to guess, I'd say he's an Evil Villain. Something in my gut tells me so."

"Me, too." Eric nods. "So, we're dealing with an Evil Villain and a henchman that won't die." We sit in silence, thinking over everything.

"How did Greyson know we were at The Safe House?" I ask, trying to ignore the memory of setting a five-star hotel aflame.

"I was thinking the same thing. You mentioned the tattoo on Greyson's neck matched the one from the computer virus?" He looks into my eyes for the answer, as if the deeper he looks, the easier it'll be for him to see what The McGuffin showed me.

"Yes. It was like a silhouetted mouse."

He thinks for a moment, absentmindedly staring out at the Seine. "Maybe The McGuffin is somehow tied to The Backup, and it's sending the Evil Villain information of our whereabouts." I make a horrified face. "Or," he continues, not too eager to see me flip out, "Maybe Greyson put a tracker on you." Not sure how that's a more favorable alternative. Eric eyes me up and down. "I should have given you a pat-down," he says with a smirk.

Yeah, like my half-naked hospital gown was hiding anything important.

Eric's self-satisfied grin makes me want to punch him, but the thought of him giving me a "pat down" makes me blush. I change the subject.

"So, that's it," I say. "That's all we know. And we don't even really know any of it for sure."

He slumps back in his chair. "God, I hate being in the dark," he says. At least we have one thing in common.

Just then, a pretty waitress approaches us with two champagne flutes. She flashes Eric a beautiful white smile. Her platinum blond hair is pulled back in a clean ponytail that bounces with each step.

"Bonjour, monsieur." She smiles, placing a tall champagne

glass delicately on top of a square napkin in front of Eric. "Le jour est joli, n'est-ce pas?" I don't even have to think twice about it. My years of AP French studies all come back to me at once, and it's like she's speaking English. "Pretty day, isn't it?" she says.

"Yes, you are," Eric responds with a wink. (Seriously? That didn't even make grammatical sense.) The girl giggles as she places a second glass in front of me. She pops a cork from a bottle of cold alcohol, pouring bubbling pink liquid in Eric's glass only.

"Thank you, beautiful," says Eric. The waitress beams with rose-colored cheeks and places the bottle in a cold bucket of ice. Then she heads back to the kitchen with her tray, giving Eric another glance over her shoulder and sashaying her hips extra voluptuously. The whole thing is totally overdone, but I can't help but feel a little envious at her confidence. Then I realize she didn't bring us any water.

"Do people in France not need to drink water? How are we supposed to stay hydrated?"

Eric reaches his champagne flute out to me, ignoring my questions. "Cheers," he says.

"Cheers to what? We're at a dead-end, and we don't even have a plan."

He sighs and puts his glass on the table. "Here's the 'plan,' Julie..." He leans forward. "The way I see it, we're in the right place, according to your vision, so all we can do now is wait until The McGuffin gives us another clue. Until then, I think I deserve a glass of champagne." He leans back in his chair.

He does have a point. But still, "How can you relax when the fate of the world, as you put it, is resting on our shoulders?"

"Technically, the world is resting on your shoulders."

"Gee, that really helps put things into perspective," I say. The sarcasm rolls off him.

"Then think of it this way," he says, "we can't help it if the last place The McGuffin led us to was here." He gestures to the Seine behind us.

Admiring the Seine, though beautiful, only reminds me of how much I can't relax and adds another layer to the giant ball of nerves growing in my stomach. Why couldn't I have gone to some beach to get drunk for Spring Break like all the typical twenty-two-year-olds of the world? They're probably all sitting in a pool somewhere, sipping on Margaritas with tiny toothpick umbrellas, flirting with each other, and enjoying their taste of the world outside of school. And I'm sitting here all worried about the fact that I'm sharing a lovely view with a handsome spy.

Eric notices my scrunched-up face and crumpled over posture.

"Julie?"

I look up at him, drawn out of my depressing reverie. For the first time ever, he's looking at me with genuine concern. Probably he's just worried about his McGuffin.

"You need to relax." He fills my glass of champagne and hands it to me. I reluctantly take it.

"Simon did say cortisol affects The McGuffin," I murmur.

"Exactly. Just leave everything to me. All you have to do is tag along, tell me your visions, and stay out of my way. That's all."

He makes it sound too easy.

Nothing is that simple.

But his eyes encourage me to take a sip and surrender to the situation. After a moment of serious deliberation, I decide there's a good chance I'll end up dead by the end of this. Might as well enjoy a sip of champagne while I'm still alive.

"Sounds easy enough," I say, and clink my glass against his in a triumphant moment of "screw you" to my stress ball.

Except I clink a little too hard, sending the fizzy pink liquid all over the table in an explosion of glass shards.

"Ow!" Eric shakes his hand, a thin line of red forming on the inside of his hand between his pointer finger and his thumb where the glass cut him. I grimace, champagne running down the side of the table and right onto my crotch.

So, this is what happens when I try to relax.

17 / A BUTTERY BETRAYAL

"Let's try this again," Eric says. He pours a fresh bottle of bubbly pink liquid into two "glasses," this time made of plastic.

"Really, I'm fine." I press my lips together, not too eager to cause another scene.

"You've got to hydrate somehow." I wonder if he realizes that alcohol totally does the opposite of hydrating a person. "When in Rome," he insists, then hands me a fresh cup of bubbly.

"We're in Paris," I correct, reaching for the bubbly, but he smoothly pulls it out of my reach before I can take hold. I purse my lips.

"It's an expression." He swirls the drink in the glass and extends it back to me, saying, "You gotta promise to at least try to enjoy it."

"Only if you promise to at least try to come up with a plan," I counter.

Our waitress returns with a glass of room temperature water, a tray of cheese, and three super thin slices of salami with what looks like mold growing on them. The "cheese plate," minus the cheese, that I ordered. She smirks, knowing she's deprived me of any sufficient supply of nutrients.

Before I can ask for anything different, she tells Eric to enjoy his Monte Cristo sandwich and is already off to take another patron's order.

Eric watches my vexed expression with an odd sort of grin.

"What?" I grump. He doesn't answer, and I pout. "Let's just come up with a plan already. Sound good?"

He thinks about it for a moment, looking at me with an expression I haven't seen on him before. It's like he's actually seeing me, sitting right there in front of him, for the first time. And for the first time, it doesn't look like he's annoyed or amused as if by a circus freak. He doesn't have a dark smirk on his face or a secretive look behind his eyes. He's just looking at me as I am, with a genuine smile.

It's even more attractive than his sexy half-grin.

"Deal," he says.

I grab the glass from his outstretched hand, gently brushing against his fingertips. It's barely anything, I know, but the touch sends electric waves through my body. Hopefully, he can't tell that my heart rate hiked up a notch. I clear my throat, forcing myself to return my focus on the goal at hand— relaxing.

"Deal," I say, this time very carefully clinking glasses with him. Nothing breaks, and I let out a breath I didn't realize I was holding. We raise our glasses to our lips at the same time, and I let the pink, bubbling liquid crawl it's way slowly toward my lips.

Through his glass, I can see the biggest smirk on Eric's face as he watches me take my time. I roll my eyes and take a sip.

The bubbles pop gently against my mouth, and I savor the sweet taste as it travels down my throat. Nicole would be so proud of me. I imagine if she were witnessing this moment, she'd burst into a fit of girly giggles. She'd be so shocked to know I'm in Paris right now. Sharing a glass of champagne with a guy that she'd say, "tops the hottie charts." I feel a satisfied smile spreading on my face. I decide I'm allowed to enjoy this moment.

"Look at you," Eric says, but he isn't sarcastic.

"What? I've had alcohol before," I say, quick to defend myself. The truth is, I've had a few glasses of wine here and there, but I've never tried champagne before.

I don't tell him that, though.

"Could have fooled me." He laughs, and it's a lovely sound. Immediately, I feel my shoulders release, falling a good two inches from where they usually sit hunched over. I let out another deep breath and take a large sip of champagne. It tastes good. Is this what enjoying yourself feels like?

"You do that a lot, you know that?" Eric takes a bite of his sandwich.

"What? Drinking alcohol?" I furrow my brow, trying to remember a single time I've had a sip of alcohol in front of him in the last day and a half.

"No," he says through a full mouth. "The sighing. The hunched over plotting. The worrying." He takes another large bite, chewing thoughtfully. "You look much better when you're not stressed."

His comment takes me off guard. I don't even think he meant it as a compliment, but nevertheless, I realize he's right, and it makes me smile more. Maybe I should try relaxing more often.

I feel rebellious just thinking it.

Eric pours some more champagne in my now empty glass. I take another small sip, and my stomach rumbles loud enough for both of us to hear it.

"Aren't you going to eat something?" He gestures to the plate of rotten meat and cheesy cheese. The sight of it makes me gag in my mouth.

"I'm alright," I say, but my stomach grumbles even louder this time, betraying me.

Eric sighs. "Here, have some of this," he rips off a piece of the sandwich and hands it to me. I ignore the germs and take it in my hand, ravenously overcome by what feels like a month's worth of starvation. I let out a moan of delight as my taste buds explode.

"Mmmm, this is so good," I mumble through a full mouth. Eric laughs at me and raises the remaining two bites of his sandwich in the air in a silent salute. I do the same, affirming the mutual deliciousness of the moment, before finishing off my remaining bite.

Man, that was good. Much better than any of the sandwiches I ever order. "What was that made of?" I wonder aloud. For such a cheesy restaurant, that was one quality sandwich.

"Ham, white bread, mayonnaise..." Eric ticks off each ingredient with his buttery fingers, then licks each one clean.

Wait.

Why are his fingers buttery?

An ice-cold surge of panic shoots through my veins. I glance at my own glistening fingertips, a knot forming in my stomach as the horrible realization sets in.

"...salt and pepper, eggs, usually a bit of paprika," he continues, and I wince because I know it's coming, "some Gouda cheese and a dash of milk," Eric says with a final satisfied suck of his thumb.

Uh oh.

Eric doesn't notice my ashen face or the horrified look in my eyes when he adds, "Oh, and butter. Lots of butter in the pan." He nods, driving the nail home.

Dear God.

Three dairy ingredients?!

I fight the urge to throw up. I can't believe I actually enjoyed consuming the unholy trinity of dairy. Eric finally notices the nausea taking over my features.

"What's wrong?" he asks, genuinely concerned about my wellbeing for the first time since I met him.

"Butt- butt- butter," I finally sputter out, shaking my head in denial. If I weren't so scared of the coming aftermath, I'd slap him for poisoning me with les produits laitiers!

He furrows his brow, then sneaks suspicious glances all around us. "Did you get another vision?" he whispers, suddenly serious. His obliviousness of the situation angers me.

"No, you idiot!" I shout, prepared to berate him, but instead, I clutch my stomach as an onslaught of cramps takes hold of my intestines. Sweat finds its way to all my nooks and crannies. I'm grimacing, clenching my teeth as tight as I am my ass.

I need to find a bathroom.

Eric watches from across the table, shocked and totally unable to help as the full effects of lactose intolerance set in.

"What's happening?" He awkwardly pats my shoulder in an attempt to calm me down, but all I'm thinking about is how I could have let this happen in the first place. I mentally bash my head into a wall, then run through my remaining options, any escapes from the terrible oncoming situation I might still have.

But I know very well that there are no other options.

It's too late. The dairy has already gotten into my system. My only hope lies in the hands of my trusty Lactaid pills.

A ray of hope shines through me when I remember the emergency tablets hiding in my fanny pack.

I shake Eric's hand off my shoulder and quickly unzip the bag on my belt, searching with shaky hands for my little chalky saviors, my only salvation from an excruciating day spent in the bathroom. But with three different levels of dairy poisoning, each with their own method of destruction, I know it'll be more like an entire week of intestinal distress.

Which is not part of the plan.

"Where are they?" I shriek, not finding any pills. People are starting to stare.

"Julie, chill out and tell me what's wrong," Eric says through gritted teeth, his temporary concern replaced with frustration.

I gasp.

"What?" he says, edging forward to get a better view of whatever I'm doing on my side of the table.

I pull out a two-pack of Lactaid tablets, but the paper has already been ripped and the pills taken from their little homes. All that's left is a thin layer of fine white powder resting at the bottom of my fanny pack.

The way Eric sucks in a breath tells me he's somehow guilty. I look up at him with wild eyes.

"What did you do?" I hiss.

"Who says I did anything?" he whispers feverishly.

I lower my voice to match his, shaking the empty paper casing in front of him in an accusatory manner. "Eric, tell me the truth," I say, then I take a deep, shaky breath because I really don't want to know the answer to what I'm about to ask him. "Did you use the last of my Lactaid?"

He stares back at me for a second. Then he says, "Even for a normal stomach, a Monte Cristo is a lot of dairy to handle." I stare, dumbfounded, as he somehow manages to defend himself. "You should have packed more." He shrugs.

How did he even get them? I've had the fanny pack on the entire time!

Fire burns in my throat. Smoke comes out of my ears. I reach a level of hatred I've never felt in my entire life.

"What the hell is wrong with you!" I throw the paper at his face, my voice rising. "First, you poison me, and then you take my antidote?!"

Now everyone is staring. A woman loudly whispers "poison" worriedly. Someone nearby pulls out their phone, hopeful that they might be filming the internet's next viral sensation.

"What else was I supposed to do?"

I scoff. "Think about someone other than yourself, perhaps?"

"I gave you half of my Monte Cristo," he says as if it holds the same significance as donating a kidney.

"Unbelievable," I mutter. Another pang of pain seizes my lower intestines.

It's here.

A male waiter approaches us, asking if there's a problem. Before Eric can de-escalate the situation, I blurt, "Where's the bathroom?"

The waiter shakes his head at my English.

"Les toilettes!" I shout at him.

He points near the kitchen, and I make a dash for it, hoping I haven't already ruined my very first pair of lingerie.

18 / GETTING TO THE BOTTOM OF IT

I'm not sure if an hour has passed or if I blacked out, and it's already the next day. I just know I want this to end.

As I sit in the disgusting bathroom in my tiny stall, knees touching the grime-covered door in front of me, I make a mental note not to ever trust Eric again.

I mean, seriously? If I can't trust him with a damn sandwich, how in the world am I supposed to trust him with my life?

Another bolt of pain lurches through my intestines, and I worry that I'll be stuck in here until the restaurant closes.

But nothing happens. I let out a sigh of relief and resume worrying about more important things, like how I'm going to face Eric again without scratching his eyes out. Or how we're supposed to figure out where The McGuffin wants us to go next. And why it wanted us to come to this tourist trap of a café in the first place.

Sitting here on the toilet, I feel stuck. Physically and mentally. What's the plan? We desperately need a plan.

I keep wracking my brain for answers, but none come. I even ask The McGuffin to talk to me, goading it to come out from hiding in the deepest recesses of my mind. But after a few minutes of talking to myself, I realize the damn thing is not going to answer me.

It was worth a shot, at least.

Another few minutes go by without any more intestinal issues, so I decide it's time to get up. I'll probably be fine long enough to make it to the next bathroom.

Assuming Eric knows where we're going next.

Or that Eric hasn't ditched me.

I roll my eyes at the genuine possibility, absentmindedly reaching for the toilet paper. My heart sinks when I see it.

There's no toilet paper.

You've got to be kidding me.

I ask God why he intends to torture me so. But then I think better of complaining to Mr. Almighty and instead, choose a more thankful approach. After all, I am somehow still alive after everything that's happened, and it's definitely no thanks to Eric.

Being thankful turns out to be a good idea.

As if sent by an angel, a woman walks into the bathroom just then. Her heels click-clack as she takes a few steps further into the small restroom area, but she stops short after a moment, probably noticing the less-than feminine smell in here.

Sorry.

She decides to brave the noxious gas and take a seat in the stall next to me. Her door swings open and a pair of five-inch high red heels click-clacks into view beneath the divider. The woman takes a seat and lets a pair of leopard print silk panties fall to her ankles. Does everyone here wear lingerie all the time?

Her shoes look shiny and brand new, but the skin on her feet look wrinkly and old, revealing blue veins spreading just beneath the thin surface of her skin.

Is she an elderly woman? The thought strikes me as odd. Surely heels that slick would be dangerous for an old woman, right? Or maybe French women don't let age affect their fashion choices, regardless of the safety hazards. Something about lingerie and wrinkles just doesn't seem right. My stomach tightens at the off-putting combination.

The woman flushes, and I realize I may have missed my opportunity. I blurt out some of my under-practiced French vocabulary and ask her for an extra square.

After a terrifying moment of hesitation (during which I briefly wonder what would happen if I have to get Eric in here to help me), the woman hands me a wad of toilet paper. When I grab it from her, I notice her nails are long and painted the same red as her heels. Her fingers reveal more of that semi-translucent skin. I quickly look away, trying not to overthink about her veins, and make sure to say thank you very much.

I take care of business and awkwardly maneuver my lanky body out of the cramped stall, hopefully leaving behind me the only lactose-intolerant episode of this trip.

We wash our hands at the same time. The woman really is an old lady. She has wrinkly skin all over, and her wiry red hair is pulled back into a gentle ponytail at the nape of her neck. She's wearing a tight floral dress that hugs her lumpy body all over.

Interesting fashion choice, but who am I to judge?

I nod at her politely, thanking her again. She tells me it's not a problem, "De rien," and we wash our hands in silence. I sing Happy Birthday in my head (the proper amount of time for efficiently washing hands), idly noticing the wallpaper in the bathroom. The thin material and repetitive pattern seem familiar for some reason, but I can't put my finger on it. I keep sudsing my hands next to the old lady, silently pondering where I've seen that pattern before.

The song comes to an end in my head, and when I reach to turn off the faucet, my hand stops short at the sight of the grimy handle. This sink, I think. Where have I seen this sink before?

The old lady notices my hesitation and gives me a concerned look. I decide I'm just over-thinking things. It's familiar because I've been in this damn bathroom too long! I turn off the water and head for the door, eager to leave this gross place, but the old woman stops me.

She holds out a hand, her red nails reflecting the light from the ceiling.

"Excuse me," I say, a creepy feeling emerging from deep inside. The old lady reaches into her purse. My breath catches. Is she another assassin? I prepare for her to pull out a gun, but instead, she pulls out a tiny bottle of perfume.

She holds it out to me in a gesture that says, "Would you like some?"

I let out a breath, surprised that my initial thoughts were so dark. Of course, this old lady isn't an assassin! I need to get back to my normal life.

"That's very sweet, but no, thank you," I tell her. "Non, merci," I correct myself in French. She gives me a look that says, "Honey, you need it."

One sniff of the air in here, and I know she's right.

"Okay, fine." I put my hands out, ready for a quick spritz on the inner wrists. Instead, she sprays a little bit right in front of my face.

It smells flowery, like a combination of all the perfumes you'd find in a Victoria's Secret store. I cough once from the closeness of the spray. "Thanks so much, madame." I curtsy and head for the door.

"No! Merde." The old lady searches in her bag, muttering something in French. I turn around and ask her if she needs help with something.

"Mauvais parfum," she says. (Wrong perfume.)

"Oh, that's alright, I liked the first one. Thanks again—"

She pulls out another perfume bottle and quickly spritzes chemicals in my face once more.

I sneeze and blink the sting away, fighting off tears from the strength of the concoction. It smells worse than the bathroom. What is that, acid?

"Thank you," I choke out, heading right for the door. But the next step I take sends the room spinning. "Whoa," I stumble forward, grabbing hold of the trashcan for support.

A second later, I fall to the ground, wincing at the thought of all those germs on my back.

What did you do to me? I ask, but the old woman can't hear me because I didn't say anything. I can't speak, and I can't move as the woman reaches toward the sink and turns the hot water handle. It's not until the bathroom wall falls out from behind me, revealing a secret staircase, do I realize why this place feels so familiar.

The grimy sink, the cheap wallpaper, the secret tunnel—it's all from my vision!

I sharply inhale in a brief moment of excitement when I realize we're on the right path— the one The McGuffin has sent us on. I can't wait to tell Eric and the team that we've made progress!

But then the frail old woman grips me with hands as strong as a UFC fighter and hoists me over her shoulder. Her heels click-clack as she takes me one step at a time further down the secret path into another unknown place. My eyes droop, and the last thing I see is the trap door slowly sealing itself behind us.

And then I pass out.

Again.

19 / INTO THE DUNGEON

The sound of whimpering wakes me up.

I roll to my side, still groggy from the old woman's perfume, and push myself upright. The ground is cold and wet on my hands. I blink away the blurriness until I can see clearly. The space that lays before me is dimly lit, but as my eyes adjust, I can make out more of the details.

I'm lying in some kind of caged cell on a stone floor. The metal bars all around me look rusty and old like they've been growing mold and rotting away for over a hundred years. Something that sounds like white noise fills my head, but as I focus on it, I realize it's the sound of rushing water in the distance. A lot of it. Makeshift lamps made of filament bulbs and what looks like tennis ball baskets hang five feet apart from each other on the stone walls. They dangle in the hallway from small black wires tacked to the cracks between the cobblestones in the domed ceiling.

Where am I?

I stand up, wiping my hands on my jeans, which are streaked with whatever nasty germs and other gross accumulation of crap the grimy floor has collected over the years. And I'm assuming plenty of years have gone by. This place feels like an ancient dungeon, complete with the sad moaning of tortured souls. Wait a minute, I'm not imagining that sound. Where is it coming from?

I squint and take another, more pointed, look around, and that's when it hits me. The sad, soft whining, the random shrieks of fear and pain, the insane bits of laughing that drift my way down the dimly lit hallway— I'm in prison.

What kind of prison? I have no idea. But it's definitely not an ordinary prison. And judging by the wails of pain, I'd say it might even be a torture chamber or something creepy like that.

There's a man in the cell to my right. He's moaning and crouched over in the center of his cage.

"Psst— hey," I whisper. He flinches, but it might just be part of his consistent trembling. "Hello?" I snap my fingers, but he doesn't turn around. "Where are we?" I continue, hoping he can hear me and is just choosing to ignore me. "What is this place?"

The man wails and turns toward me in a brilliant show of bright light. I shield my eyes from the blinding illumination. His horribly sorrowful sobs pierce my ears.

After a moment, he crouches forward again, and the light begins to flicker. I peer through my fingers to see the man pawing at his glowing eyes— which are an incandescent blue— and realize his eyelids are closed. The light being emitted from his eyeballs is so bright he can't even contain it with his own eyelids.

While I stand there, trying to comprehend what I see with an open mouth, the man brings his mitten-covered hands to his face in an attempt to hide his eyes. Fraying silver duct tape wrapped around the bottom of his gloves fastens them to his wrists.

What happened to him? Why is he here? How long has he been here?

A sudden rattling to my left calls my attention. I whip around to find an Asian-looking woman cradling herself and rocking back and forth in the center of her cell. I lean closer to the bars that separate us. The woman's beautiful porcelain face is smeared with dirt, and her straight black hair is plastered to her temples and neck with sweat. Every few seconds, she goes from panting and sweating and licking her lips to rocking back and forth, shivering with goosebumps and a chattering jaw.

I try to grab her attention as well, but her eyes are glazed over. She's focused on something in an entirely other world.

These poor people.

I step closer to the edge of my cell, facing the hallway to get a better look at my surroundings. It looks like all the cells are occupied by people. Each one of them has been physically deformed in some way or another. The cell across from me is holding a large fish tank, but whatever is inside is way too large to be a fish.

Someone down the hall bursts into a fit of insane laughter, perfect for a movie about The Joker.

But we're not in a movie. And I'm definitely not Batman.

I need to get out of here.

Okay, first things first. Where is "here"?

I calm my breathing and take another purposeful look around. The floor is wet and cold, the wrought-iron bars are crusty with rust and mold, sounds seem to echo, water rushes in the distance, and everything seems to be covered in a fine layer of mist. We must be somewhere underground. Sewers? Eww. Not a nice thought. Moving on. How to get out? That's the question.

I decide to treat this like any old Nancy Drew PC game puzzle. It can't be that hard to find a way out, can it? But I'm not so easily tricked by my own brain. I know this is no ordinary puzzle. I was kidnapped and dragged down a hidden tunnel by an old woman with unnatural strength. I shiver.

Where is Eric? Has he even noticed that I'm gone? How long have I been out? Oh crap. I don't even know. This is definitely not good. How in the world is Eric going to find me? I remember the flirty waitress and realize Eric has probably not even noticed my absence. Wait. What if the waitress was sent to distract him? I rub my forehead. Ugh. This is getting complicated.

I roll my eyes at the thought of him. He stole my Lactaid and sent me to the bathroom in the first place. Technically this is all his fault. The warm feeling of anger surges through my body, heating me up and fueling my adrenaline.

I'd better assume Eric isn't coming for me. Which means I'm on my own now.

I gulp down the coming onslaught of terror and anxiety. I recount the words of The Director, "There's no room for doubt." It's time to take action.

I reach for my fanny pack— there must be a laser cutter pen or a lock hacking pen or something to get me out of this cage— but my fanny pack is gone. The old lady must have taken it! Oh, snap. Now they not only have my favorite fanny pack, but they also have T.O.P.S.E.C.R.E.T. weaponry!

Shoot.

Despite the genuine possibility of contracting tetanus, and the somewhat ridiculous possibility of this rusty door being electrified, I grip the bars of the cell, shaking with purpose and a whole new reason to get out of here.

Bad idea.

My whole body is thrown across the cell in a bolt of electricity. I smack into the back wall, get hit with another surge of electricity and land face-first into the gross puddle in the center of my cell.

OUCH.

I groan, adding to the orchestra of pain. The horrible smell of burnt hair fills my nostrils. I push myself back up with numb hands and a back that's sure to bruise for weeks to come. Assuming I'm alive for that long. I force myself to move, stepping toward the cell door for a re-assessment. Upon inspection, I notice a keypad on the outside of the cell, humming with the buzz of electricity.

I should have looked more closely before.

The familiar sound of click-clacking heels echoes down the hall.

The old lady.

She's whistling poorly, pulling someone on a gurney into an empty cell at the other end of the hall. Blood seeps from white bandages wrapped around the person's head.

I hold my breath, trying not to make any sudden movements. It doesn't look like the person is alive until the body adds yet another moan to the cacophony of wails among us.

Dear God. What is the old lady doing to all these people? What is she going to do to me?

It's like she can hear my thoughts.

She turns on her out-of-character high heels and heads down the hall— toward me! Quickly, I think of all the ways this could go down. In every scenario, I end up dead, which isn't very encouraging. I gulp down my fears and grip my hands into tight fists, hoping my first punch will be a good one. She's only a few feet away now. I'm sure she's coming toward me. She has to have seen me by now.

Just as she reaches the Asian woman's cell, all the lights go out with a loud ZZZZZZZZZ, leaving all of us in complete darkness.

"Merde," the woman curses, her raspy voice a reminder of just how old she really is.

Did all the electricity go out? I think about opening the cell door and making a run for it while Mrs. Old Lady is distracted, but with my clumsy track record I decide it's probably best not to do anything too rash. Yet. Instead, I'll just nudge the door open ever so slightly so it doesn't connect. Then wait and see.

Her heels click-clack past me to the other side of the tunnel.

She fumbles around with something metallic until it makes a loud SWITCH sound, but nothing happens.

She sighs. More fumbling.

FFFFTTT! A tiny match lights a small circle at the end of the tunnel, and then POOF! A much larger circle of light is formed when the little flame spreads onto a torch, revealing another set of stairs I hadn't noticed before. They're heading up.

The way out.

CCCRRRRKKK— something staticky fills the air.

"Chantal!" a grumpy, high-pitched voice says through a walkie talkie.

The old woman answers, "Yes, Doctor, I know."

"Fix it!"

They're speaking in French with heavy accents.

"The breaker's down. Looks like they finally turned our power off."

A beat.

"Damn it, I'm in the middle of working with subject three thirty-three." Beat. "Get down here. And bring with you more HCurrent. I've used a whole cannister already. And I need your steady hands."

Steady hands? If this wrinkly old lady has steadier hands than the doctor, then I really don't want to get called in for a check-up.

"Only if we get to use my steady hands for pleasure."

"Do you have no boundaries, woman?"

"That's why you love me."

Uck! I stifle a gag.

"Hurry."

"Copy that."

The old woman puts her walkie talkie back on her waist and starts walking down the hallway, holding her torch high and ignoring the whimpering sounds of suffering from each prisoner she walks by.

I duck when she gets close to me. Hopefully, she doesn't remember I'm here or see the cage door is slightly of its latch. She hesitates for a moment, just in front of my cell.

Uh oh.

Right when I think she's about to bust into my cage and drag me downstairs, she turns to the cell in front of me. The one with the fish tank. She eyes her reflection, fluffs up her hair, and puckers her lips, kissing the air with a loud smooching sound. I wonder if she even notices the twitching humanoid figure behind the glass.

Then she turns on her heel and saunters toward the opposite staircase she came in from— the one that heads down.

I wait until I can no longer hear her footsteps before letting out the breath I've been holding. I need to get out of here before I become subject three thirty-four!

Cautiously, I step forward, careful of any remaining electrical currents that might still be alive within the rusty iron cell gate. Even with an inch of space between the latch and the handle, it might still connect. I crane my head and arch my body in a weird position to try to get another glimpse at the keypad on the door.

The little red dot is now totally black. I reach my hand out and quickly pat the iron, just in case it wants to zap me across the room again.

Nothing happens.

Whew! This is my chance to get out of here. I grab hold of the gate with both hands and push as hard as I can. The gate doesn't budge a centimeter. I take another deep breath, plant my feet on the cold, wet ground and push harder, this time with as much of my core as I can. Still nothing.

Damn it! I shake the fence angrily, and it pulls toward me as effortlessly as a swinging saloon door on a Western movie set.

Pull not push. What an idiot!

I pull the door toward me. It creaks as loud as a screaming banshee.

My pulse pounds in my ears. I glance around at my fellow inmates, but surprisingly none of them heard. Or maybe they did, but they're just unable to show it. These poor people, being tortured like this. Why? Who is The Doctor? What is he up to?

Never mind that.

To make things as quick and painless as possible, I yank the door toward me in one smooth motion, so the creaking only lasts a second or two. Then I step into the hallway.

It feels colder in the open airway. A chill that has nothing to do with the temperature pebbles down my back. I head toward the staircase leading up, as I assume that one will lead back out to civilization.

A few of the other inmates watch me with scrunched up faces of confusion. Shoot, how could I forget about them? I race to the closest cell. A blonde little girl wearing a Scooby-Doo T-shirt, not more than eight years old, looks up at me with sad eyes. The image breaks my heart.

"Shh." I hold a finger to my lips as I quietly approach her cell. "Don't worry, I'm here to help—" But as I reach for her cell, the little girl pounces toward me with an ear-shattering screech. She scratches my arm with sharp fingernails on hands shaped like bird talons. I recoil from the contact and cradle my bleeding arm, wincing at the sound. What the heck?!

The other inmates stir, moving closer to their doors to see what's causing all the raucous. "I told you, I'm not going to hurt you—" I start, but the girl screeches again, yelling at me in some sort of animalistic language. She bounds to the other side of her cell with one hop and clamps onto the crisscrossed cell bars connecting her to a neighboring inmate. Now she's screaming at the rest of them from her perch and the other prisoners start whimpering and crying and making little noises of their own.

This is not good.

"Keep your voice down!" I whisper loudly, but it's pretty clear the little girl wants nothing to do with me. And to be honest, it feels like she's spreading rumors about me to the other inmates, because now they're all giving me the evil eye. My heart rate hikes at the thought that I could be attacked by these people (can they even still be called people?) before the old lady even has a chance to torture me.

As much as I hate to admit it, I think these prisoners are past the point of saving.

After a quick promise to the inmates that I'll have T.O.P.S.E.C.R.E.T. HQ send help for them later, I grab the torch hanging on the wall (a lot heavier than it looks) and dart up the steps two at a time. It's a risky move, especially now that I'm handling a stick of fire, but I figure there's no time to waste.

Then something stops me.

This place was in my vision. A vision that The McGuffin sent me, which means The Backup is here. It has to be.

And there's no way Eric will find the secret passage. He probably ordered another round of champagne to split with the waitress. I roll my eyes, something I realize is turning into a knee-jerk physical response to the mere thought of Eric.

I guess it really is up to me to find The Backup. Without it, I'm The McGuffin, and there's no way I'll be able to return to my normal life. I think about that phrase for a second, "normal life," and all the images that go with it. Mom's chicken soup, my lazy hometown beach city, walking along the ocean's shore with nothing better to do and not a care in the world…

It seems so unrealistic now, and somehow the idea of lying on the couch at home feels a little wrong. How can anyone lie on their sofa when bad guys are capturing people and doing who knows what to them?

It makes me angry. Would The Backup have been stolen regardless if I'd become The McGuffin? Would The McGuffin have sent Eric to this place to retrieve it regardless of me getting involved?

There's no use wondering because I'm here now, and I have a job to do.

The dancing flames of the torch illuminate the stairwell heading towards the surface, a final reminder that it could be my only way out of here alive. I square my shoulders and turn around, heading back across the eerie hallway quickly. Before I change my mind. And before the bird girl discovers her cage isn't locked anymore.

Only half a second's hesitation takes hold of me before I head down, further into the Evil Villain's lair.

20 / OUT SNOOPING, CALL BACK LATER

The narrow winding cobblestone steps lead deeper underground. I move slowly, trying not to make too much noise with my footsteps, holding my torch a foot in front of me. I really hope the old lady didn't hear all the raucous earlier. Maybe I should have gone back and found Eric before coming down here all by myself? I press my lips together in silent disapproval of myself. Oh well, too late for well-made plans and all that.

The bottom of the stairwell opens up into an ample dome-shaped cavernous space, ripe with the pungent smell of sewage. Holding back a gag, I pinch my nose for support. The pathway continues forward, turning into a narrow bridge slick with water from the pounding waterfall of sewage to the left.

It doesn't look like there are any other paths, so I reluctantly step forward onto the bridge of poo.

Halfway across the bridge, a river of sewage snakes its way down a cobblestone sidewalk and out of sight into the darkness. Tied to a heavy-looking rock just at the edge of the obscurity floats a silver deck boat, minus the overhead covering.

Without slipping, I manage to make it to the end of the

bridge, where my torch illuminates another rusted iron gate like the ones in the dungeon (that's what I've decided to call it).

The handle sits next to a button pad identical to the one from my cell. And just like the one from my cell, this one looks like it's lost its electrical charge, too. The power outage must have unlocked everything— it's probably best to hurry before the power returns, I tell myself.

Yet I can't seem to make myself grab hold of the crap-covered handle. I take a deep breath, pull my sleeve over my hand, and quickly pull open the door, trying to avoid as much fecal matter on my hands as possible.

The gate leads to a long, dark chamber, luckily with no sewage waterfalls (though, my nose wouldn't know the difference based on smell alone). I step forward, right into a foot of slimy liquid. I yelp, dropping my torch into the liquid with a significant sizzle. Holding my breath and praying the sound didn't make its way to the old lady and the doctor, I take a step back onto the cobblestone sidewalk behind me.

Crap! That's precisely what I stepped in. A small little stream of crap. I try not to throw up in my mouth.

My eyes adjust to the darkness, and soon I can see a dim fluorescent light coming from the end of the hallway. Occasionally, a shadow flicks by.

I'm not alone.

A sick feeling grows in my stomach, and I try not to think about dying down here in this creepy sewage hellhole.

Sticking to the sidewalk, I keep my hands on the bumpy wall behind me, sidestepping toward the light and careful not to splash in the center stream. My thumb slides across a bump in the stones. I scrutinize it, my eyes once again adjusting to the intense darkness, and I realize it's a plaque.

If my French is correct, it says, "Water Breath." There's a dome-shaped cutout in the stone wall just behind it, so I peer inside.

A giant fish tank sits in the center of the small cutout. It's very similar to the one that was across from my jail cell earlier, but half the size. Lining the walls are black filing cabinets, topped with piles and piles of books. I step closer to read the titles. They're all in French, of course, but the general theme seems to be fishing. Behind the tank sits a desk with a very outdated desktop computer attached to a bundle of wires leading out of the room.

This little domed room seems like an office of sorts.

A loud ZZZ echoes down the hall. Above, a fluorescent light flickers on and off, blinding me temporarily. Must have been another power surge. I get the feeling I should hurry up with my snooping.

I step back out into the hallway again, head toward the end of the tunnel, and pass by another cutout.

The plaque on the entrance to the room reads "No Electrocute." Probably not that exactly, but it's what I interpret the French as. A medium-sized rubber box with electrodes extending from it sits on a tire in the middle of the otherwise empty room, save for the piles of French books on electrocution that line the walls. Yeah, definitely not "no" electrocute.

I step back out into the hallway, thinking about what these clues could mean. My eyes adjust to the darkness a bit more, and that's when I notice multiple other domed cutouts in the hallway.

Snap! The Backup could be in any one of them.

Time to take this snooping thing seriously.

I peer into each of the domed offices as I make my way toward the end of the tunnel, taking in as much as I can and storing it for future reference, just in case I do make it out alive.

The next little domed room is called "Animals." It contains miniature cages full of different kinds of creatures, mostly moths, lizards, rats, and dead birds. Multiple cages are empty, and my heart drops when I notice a hamster wheel, unmoving in solitude.

The office after that is labeled, "X-Ray Vision." Inside are tons of x-rays of what looks like arms with multiple bones extending from a single joint, hands with too many fingers, and a handful of human bone structures that don't look very human to me. More books on bones, growth, eyesight, and night vision. But no Backup.

I pass another room called "Regrowth" full of images and, you guessed it, more books on anatomy and the human body. Hand scrawled notes on the epidermis, boxes of shed skin from both snakes, and what is labeled as "human." I shiver and move on.

I keep moving, past multiple domed offices labeled "Fire Expel," "Weather Control," "Sickness Dispel," "Mind Influence," and "Take Flight." Glancing in each room, it appears the one thing they have in common are the stacks of books and the old computers connected to some sort of shared power source. And a lack of T.O.P.S.E.C.R.E.T. Backups.

The second to last room in the hallway is larger than the others. It's full to the brim with piles of clothes, tools, backpacks, and other random kinds of junk. Upon closer inspection, it appears a lot of this stuff seems to be handmade tools put together from technological devices throughout the last ten years. iPods connected to floppy disks, metal helmets welded to kitchen supplies, wires protruding from things I doubt conduct electricity.

What's even more bothersome than the mismatched tools is that none of them appear to be labeled. They're all thrown into hills of more crap (thankfully not the human kind). Perhaps they are discarded experiments. But what about all the clothes and backpacks?

Something glitters in the flicker of fluorescent light down the hall. I step closer—it's a silver T.O.P.S.E.C.R.E.T. pen!

It's sitting on top of a pile of soiled clothes, alongside another silver T.O.P.S.E.C.R.E.T. pen and my T.O.P.S.E.C.R.E.T. cell phone. What is our stuff doing here? Did the old lady take it from me when she knocked me out, and then drop it in a collective pile of crap? I find myself feeling slightly offended that she'd consider anything of mine to be "crap," especially considering her fashion choices.

I check the signal on the phone—none. There will be no calling Eric or Simon for help.

Shoot.

How many pens did I have to begin with? Did the old lady steal any? Has she realized they belong to T.O.P.S.E.C.R.E.T.?

But there's another question that bothers me more than the rest.

Where is my fanny pack?

Do not cry, I tell myself. It's here somewhere, and so is The Backup. Stay focused, Julie!

I shove the two pens and the cell phone into my jean pockets and continue on to the next area. The shuffling sounds of footsteps and muttering echo toward me, growing louder as I near the end of the hallway.

The last hallway cutout is square-shaped and contains a bunch of books, a scanner, and what looks like some kind of computer engine, but there's no monitor. I use my phone's flashlight to scan the area, and it seems like your typical "office." Manila folders overflowing with loose-leaf papers sit on top of the cabinet, which is missing a few drawers. Twenty or so piles of books, DVDs, and even old cassette tapes sit on the desk.

Briefly scanning, I manage to make out a few of the French book titles: "How to Instill Fear in Others While Maintaining Respect," "The Evil Villain's Guide to a Balanced Life," and "How to Succeed in Evil Without Really Trying." There are DVDs and even old cassette tapes about "The Art of Persuasion," "When to Run and When to Fight," "How to Stay Strong, Mentally and

Physically," "Flight and Aviation— Helicopter Edition." There are even cookbooks and high-school chemistry books.

Whoever this Evil Villain is, he's loaded with all sorts of information. I've got to give it to him, he's done his homework. I briefly wonder whether I'd make a good Evil Villain, given my propensity for studying. I shake the thought off. Focus, Julie. Save the world.

I check over my shoulder to make sure the coast is clear before looking through the pile of manila folders. I find photos from inside real human bodies, lined up next to cell counts and different stats. These subjects were apparently being tracked as they entered different stages of experimentation. I flip through more and more of these case files until I recognize the Asian girl who was in the cage next to me.

"Cellular Regulation for Extreme Temperatures." I flashback to her body with the goosebumps and then the sweating. The file contains information about a doohickey that you stick in someone's chest. I can't quite make out the French scrawl, but it seems to be an effort to regulate the temperature in extreme conditions.

I realize the people in the dungeon aren't just prisoners, they're lab rats.

My morbid curiosity propels me to keep digging. Photos of people with gills, people with exploded eyeballs, people with giant bags under their eyes and veins popping out of their heads. Each file is labeled a failure.

I turn away, sick to my stomach. I need to get out of here before this creepy man turns me into another one of his unsuccessful experiments.

As I head for the exit, I trip on something— the missing filing cabinets (damn disorganization)— and make a loud crash as I stumble onto the floor. My tumble sends a pile of books scraping across the stone ground. Crap. I quickly re-assemble them (unable to leave a mess in my wake) and head for the hallway. As I do, I step on a small black journal on the sidewalk. Shoot, I missed one.

I reach down to pick it up and notice an old piece of paper protruding from the journal. A heavy feeling in my gut tells me it's significant.

My heart races. Someone yells an unintelligible curse from around the corner, and I recognize the clacking of Chantal's footsteps heading my way.

Without thinking, I dart into the hallway, grab the journal, jump over the stream of poop, and race into one of the domed cutouts on the other side of the alleyway.

Whew!

It takes a ton of energy to calm my breathing, but I manage to do it while Chantal races past. She places a pair of sunglasses on her face (why sunglasses in this dark tunnel?) and then taps a button on the side.

The high-pitched whine of battery-operated mechanics initiates a green light in her glasses. She sniffs the humid air like a search dog and takes a step forward, right into the little stream of sewer water.

"Ack!" She shakes her soaked heel and continues forward, muttering something I can't quite make out.

I wait for her to pass with bated breath. Luckily, she keeps her eyes on the other side of the hallway. When she's out of sight, I angle the black journal toward the dim light at the end of the hall and flip through the pages.

The thing that stands out most is a large black sheet of paper — like one of those cheap bookmarks you get at the Scholastic book fair. Except this one doesn't have smiling faces or encouraging phrases.

It's entirely black, save for a logo in the center— an image of green snakes all slithering in between each other, intertwined and hissing, forming the shape of a sphere. The moment I see this image, I half expect to be triggered by The McGuffin. After all, it seems the sort of mysterious thing that might send an international database of secrets into a frenzy.

But the only thing that's triggered in me is a massive sense of dread.

Whatever this symbol means, it can't be good. Perhaps The McGuffin hasn't been exposed to this symbol before. I flip the bookmark over. The back is entirely black, except for a single line of text that matches the green of the snake symbol. It reads, "You're invited."

For whatever reason, I decide to fold the paper and slip it into my pocket. Then, I quietly flip through the pages of the journal, knowing full well that Chantal is still sniffing for me somewhere in these dark tunnels, and if her nose is anywhere as strong as her muscles, it doesn't look too good for me.

The interior flap of the journal says, "This book belongs to:" and on the dotted line is a tiny signature stating, "Dr. Souris." Seems a little odd for an Evil Villain to call himself "Dr. Mouse." Then again, he did choose the sewers as his hiding spot.

My eyes quickly scan each page as I flip through the tiny black notebook. The pages begin as an accumulation of little scribbled doodles that all seem to be of the inner workings of mechanical devices, paired with phrases like "increase flux capacity" and "reverse polarity." However, not a single page mentions anything about The McGuffin or T.O.P.S.E.C.R.E.T.

As I continue through the pages, they become more and more populated with paragraphs of scribbled text. My quickly scanning eyes pick up bits of familiar French vocabulary, but Dr. Souris' scrawl is so messy I can't make anything out. I flip another page, almost deciding this is a waste of time before the next journal entry catches my eye.

It's three lines of text are written in a much less hasty scrawl, and I can actually read the heading.

"An Invitation to the Rest of My Life"

"It has finally come! My golden opportunity to impress The N.E.S.T. is here, and I shall not waste it. I am already formulating an army of possibilities in my mind. I must get to work if I am to become a Python."

Okay, so he's big on snake talk. Must be a Slytherin. I read on...

"Initial Subjects"

"Eager to begin experimentation with my new batch of subjects. The cafe provides a perfect abduction location, as I am not seen, and the subjects are rarely prepared for a fight. Tourists turned out to be an interesting and varied selection, perfect for preliminary testing. Off to a great start. I have begun administering small doses of strength serum into a frail woman with similar muscular makeup to my own. If this results in the outcome I anticipate, my chances of winning the competition increase tenfold. Must initiate simultaneous testing to be ready by deadline. Hopefully, the woman will prove to be a helpful assistant."

That explains Chantal, then.

"Complications Arise"

"Money, time, and subjects. Three things I am in desperate need of! Not one of my subjects has responded positively. Half of the subjects have died, and the other half are either insane or unresponsive. Time is still running out. N.E.S.T. has complicated things immensely with their latest update. There is nothing but problems on the horizon. If I cannot make this work, I fear this chance may be lost to me."

"First Successes"

"Today marks the first successful execution of my strength serum. The old woman has responded positively. She almost succeeded in ripping my arm off, which might have worried me if it weren't an accident. The woman calls herself Chantal and is surprisingly eager to please me. However, I attribute this to her spiking hormone levels— an unexpected result of the serum, but hardly an issue. More promising is subject three thirty-three.

Though horribly disfigured and terribly close to death, he has continued to adapt to each upgrade I administer. I can test multiple updates at once without a loss of brain functionality. Though, I don't believe there was much of that to begin with."

Something about that last entry makes me think of Greyson. I shiver at the possibility that he could still be out there somewhere, or more likely down here somewhere. Shake it off, Julie.

"Time is Running Out"

"I've used all my funds in creating these experiments. I must find a solution to my problem before I lose power. If only I were already a member of The N.E.S.T. I wish I didn't have to waste time proving myself through such barbaric a system. I must hold on to the dream— when I become a Python, my problems will dissolve, and I will have access to all the laboratory equipment and testing subjects I could ever want. I must not fail.

Should it come to it, I would even use my last resort."

The rest of the pages are empty. I close the book, my mind racing with an entirely new batch of questions. What's The N.E.S.T., and what is their competition for? Why didn't Dr. Souris mention anything about The McGuffin or The Backup?

Re-examining the last entry, it becomes apparent the

numbers are dates, and the previous entry is marked March 12th— two days before Spring Break. Maybe that's when he got the brilliant idea to hack The Backup. But how would stealing The McGuffin help him with his horrific science experiments?

My thoughts are cut short by the loud BUZZING and RINGING of my cell phone! My heart rate hikes and my breath cuts short as I fumble for the phone in my pocket, it's ring echoing through the tunnels.

There's no way Chantal didn't hear that.

I pull the phone out of the pack, its LED screen blinding me momentarily, to see Simon Zedler's name. How in the world did he manage to get signal down here? I answer in a hushed tone, trying to hide the brightness of the screen by hunching over against the wall.

"Simon! I'm so glad to hear from you, you have to help me! I'm—"

"Julie! You'll never believe what I discovered! After our last mishap at The Safe House, I got to thinking about alternative methods—"

"Simon? Simon!" He can't hear me.

"—and, well, without boring you with all my science talk, let's just say I've been monitoring your brain patterns remotely, and I've discovered you have a capacity for even more information than that which The McGuffin contains!" He lets out a childlike giggle, revealing his actual age, which is perhaps even more frightening than all his science talk. A teenager holds my fate in his hands.

Then again, I've got the world's fate in mine.

Guess I shouldn't be one to judge.

He pauses for a moment. "Julie? Julie, are you there?"

"Simon? Hello!"

"It seems the signal is poor. Where are you now?"

"I'm underground somewhere— you have to tell Eric—"

"Since you can't hear me, I'll just tell you not to be alarmed. I'm fully confident this next test will be a success."

Oh no.

"Please, not another test!"

"You did say not to use needles!"

"Send help! There are prisoners down here and some kind of evil experimentation—"

From out of the shadows, a wrinkly, bony hand snatches my wrist, and long red nails dig into my skin.

"Found you, little mouse," the raspy old woman's voice grates my ears. She rips my phone out of my hand and crumples it in her iron grip like the whole thing was made of dust. Her wicked grin is extra off-putting in the dim green glow of her night vision goggles as she says, "You're in trouble."

I about pee myself.

21 / OH RATS!

Chantal leads me down the wet tunnel toward the flickering white light. Her grip is so firm I can feel my heartbeat in her hand. I decide, instead, to focus on the fact that my shoes are now soaked in sewage.

A shadow flickers across the wall, followed by a scream of pain that sends my stomach up to my throat. Chantal doesn't slow down. She pushes and yanks me toward the end of the tunnel. As we approach the room at the end, the floor turns to a short stairwell into a much larger domed cutout.

The room is lit with construction lamps— the kind you'd use to light the street fillers at three in the morning. There are two on opposite sides of the room, each illuminating two different people being experimented on. One is a young, dark-skinned man struggling beneath leather restraints strapped to what looks like a torn-up dentist's chair. The other is someone I was hoping I would never see again.

He lies motionless on a grimy hospital bed soiled in blood stains and other unknown greasy substances. Where he once sported a shiner, he's now wearing a metallic eyepatch, twitching each time the unique accessory sparks from the wires precariously connected to it. Huh. There's some sort of appendage fused to his eyepatch—what looks like the barrel of a gun, or perhaps a laser.

Here's hoping I don't have to find out.

The cheaply made bed groans under Greyson's weight as his massive muscles give a whole-bodied shudder.

Oh, snap.

My gaze is averted by the other subject's screams. The young man's wails are tortured and pained. It's so unnerving, I almost don't notice the petite scientist scurrying around him, plugging things in and adjusting dials on the sparking electrical equipment surrounding the young man.

Piles and piles of books, along with scanned images and computer screens from every era litter the desks surrounding the subject. The tiny scientist is wearing a white lab coat, turned sepia from years of stains from liquids I don't want to know about. He has patches of thin, wiry white hair (so white it's almost translucent) that fall past his shoulders.

When he turns to adjust something on a computer screen that looks to be from the '70s, I notice the same silhouetted mouse symbol sewn onto his breast pocket that I saw on Greyson. The same logo that was left on The Director's computer screen after the T.O.P.S.E.C.R.E.T. McGuffin backup was hacked.

At that moment, it all makes sense. The symbol of a rat, the laboratory in the sewers, the horrible experiments, and the self-evident name… the small scientist man is Dr. Souris. And he's an Evil Villain.

Another agonizing scream confirms my suspicions, and I'm jolted back into the present, entirely convinced that Dr. Souris is the one who stole The Backup, and my only chance at returning to my old life.

I don't like him.

"Do not fail me now!" he yells, his voice surprisingly low for such a small fellow. He bangs the side of the computer and watches as the screen makes twitching movements.

"Agh!" The young man makes a pained gurgling sound. I want to reach out and help him somehow, but I can't even pull my hands from Chantal's grasp. I feel utterly useless as I stand here watching the suffering continue before me. I try to let the young man know he's not alone, that I'm here with him and I know this is terrible, but I don't think he can even see me for he's in so much pain. Sadness tugs my heart into my stomach.

Dr. Souris whirls on his subject and watches intently, revealing oversized thick-rimmed glasses that magnify his eyes like an anime character.

Chantal doesn't seem to be affected by the horror show in front of us. She continues to push me toward the stage of flickering lights. The poor man screams once more before his eyes melt, and his ears erupt with smoke.

The computer screen blinks with a red error code and a soft chiming that doesn't match the situation at all.

"Merde!" Dr. Souris curses and throws his gloved hands in the air.

The man lies limp in his chair as his liquid eyeballs run down his face. What kind of world are we living in?!

I bend over and puke, right onto Chantal's red heels.

"Uck!" She shakes me violently, almost snapping my neck. "Doctor, I discovered this one snooping in the tunnels," she says, with an extra push to finish her sentence.

"Eh," Dr. Souris waves her off and trudges over to the computer with the error. "Why did you bring her to me? There is no time for another. Get rid of her."

He exits the program and pulls up a different screen. This one looks like a very long list of names and numbers, but the numbers are continually changing, like a password detection program.

Dr. Souris pulls out a small glass box covered in smudges

and dirt and grime, and within the box sits a tiny black USB. The short thumb drive is plugged into a circular power source that's connected to the ancient computer.

The Backup.

Though it isn't surrounded in golden light and sitting on a pedestal like in my vision, I know this is precisely what I'm here for. Perhaps the golden light was The McGuffin's way of telling me this is important, Julie. Either way, it's here, and I must steal it back.

"I thought you would like the pleasure of dropping this one over the railing," she says, attempting to make her raspy voice sound smooth like butter.

Dr. Souris stops his motions. His eyes flicker over his shoulder to Chantal, contemplating her offer.

"I know how you love to watch them scream," she says. The thought of falling off that poop-covered bridge and into the pounding sewer brings a strangled whimper to my throat.

This time the doctor turns all the way around, sporting a grin that seems to stretch the entire width of his over-sized head. His body is totally disproportionate, which irks me to my core.

"I do love hearing them scream…" He looks at me for the first time, sizing me up with eager eyes, before his shoulders hunch forward, totally deflated. "But I cannot take any more time away from this work." He shakes his head quickly as if trying to shoo the thought from his mind.

"But, Doctor—"

"You can throw her off yourself! The deadline is tomorrow, and we've lost all power except emergency remains!" He gestures toward the two lights, which flicker as if to prove his point. "And this idiot was utterly useless." He kicks the dentist chair, and the young man's body slouches forward, head drooping in an unnatural angle. Acid heaves up my throat. "Get back to work, and don't disturb me again." He returns to his computer screen.

"Doctor," Chantal says, standing upright and stiffening her posture. Though her voice softens, her grip on me doesn't. Dr. Souris whirls on her with an expression that would make anyone cower in fear, despite his small stature. But Chantal just speaks softly to him with the tender care of a loved one.

"You need to refill your inspiration tank," she says with a knowing smirk. I wonder how many times they've had this discussion or how long she's been in his "care." It creeps me out to think she was just an old lady tourist before, and now she's been brainwashed into being this creep's assistant. I wonder if she used to have a husband or children. Do they wonder what happened to her? Will my parents wonder what happened to me?

Dr. Souris relaxes his shoulders. "You're right," he huffs.

A beeping noise echoes through the air. Dr. Souris raises his tiny wrist and checks a large touch-screen watch. (Does everyone have watch alarms nowadays?)

"Mon deur!" he exclaims, then whirls back around and claps his gloved hands together triumphantly. "It is done!"

He eyes the computer screen. "The T.O.P.S.E.C.R.E.T. files have finished their decryption!"

I stifle an excited scream—his mention of T.O.P.S.E.C.R.E.T. proves the little thumb drive is The Backup. Now all I need is to steal it back.

"This is fabulous!" Chantal barks. I have to agree with her. It's just sitting right there on the counter. If I can find a way to snatch it...

"Prepare for last-minute funding!" Dr. Souris types furiously, and the computer screen changes from a list of passcodes and names with a white backdrop to a list of acronyms and titles with a black backdrop.

What does he mean "last-minute funding"?

Chantal shoves me forward so she can get a better look at the screen. The names of the columns on the digital sheet read, "Bidders," "Winners," "Assets," "Passwords,"—Oh my god! He's selling T.O.P.S.E.C.R.E.T. information on the black market!

This is so not good. Not only would it totally suck if the government's secrets were out in the open (let alone in the hands of the world's worst bad guys), but without that info, The Backup is useless. And with a useless Backup, I don't have a bargaining chip to get T.O.P.S.E.C.R.E.T. to remove The McGuffin from my brain.

An anchor drops in my stomach.

"Should we celebrate, Doctor?" Chantal asks. She leans closer to Dr. Souris with me between them, and I get a whiff of their nasty breath. Have they never heard of Listerine?

"Cell number twelve is unoccupied," Chantal continues. "We could go there for a few minutes…"

"Focus! I must tend to the bidding now." He waves her off once again. "You get rid of the prisoner."

Chantal cocks her bumpy hip to the side and gives me a glare. And that's when I notice what's wrapped around her waist. A shiny, reflective little bag.

My fanny pack.

I gasp, my eyes flick up to Chantal's, and she purses her lips in an amused sort of grin. She knows very well that that's my fanny pack. She probably enjoys holding my pockets hostage.

The thought makes me sick.

"Kids ruin everything," she mutters, then drags me toward a hallway opposite where we entered.

I struggle extra hard against her grip now, wondering how the heck I'm going to escape from this place with The Backup and my fanny pack intact.

As we reach another gate, slightly ajar from the power surge, Dr. Souris calls out, "Wait!" We both turn to him, though, to be fair, I do it entirely involuntarily as Chantal is currently my puppet master. The small man squints and holds his hand out, pointing right at me.

"You." He looks back at the computer screen as he continues, "Who are you?" Chantal is now squinting suspiciously, too.

I shrug my shoulders and say, in the most innocent tone I can muster, "Me? What do you mean?" Damn my shaky voice. "I'm just a tourist."

"You are speaking French, idiot," the small man says.

"Tourists can't practice the language of the place they're visiting?" I suggest.

"Why would a tourist be listed in the world's most coveted ledger of secrets?" He points to a black and white picture of me on his old computer screen. When did T.O.P.S.E.C.R.E.T. get a picture of me? And why did it have to be that picture? I stare in disgust at my college yearbook photo, the one where I'm mid-sneeze and the cap is way too big for my small head.

They wouldn't let me re-take it. Sigh.

"What are you hiding?" he continues, his voice rising in an accusatory manner. "Why are you here?"

"I'm not hiding anything! Your girlfriend kidnapped me and locked me in a cell!" I wriggle in her grasp, but Chantal yanks my arms back with her iron clasp. A loud POP sends a lightning bolt of pain down my arm— my shoulder! She must have popped it out of place, damn her!

I let out a gasp of pain. Holy snap that hurts. I glare up at the old lady (those platform heels really do add a considerable amount of height— mental note for future reference), and she shakes her head at me. She makes a dramatic frowny face like she's disappointed in me.

Dr. Souris turns back to the computer and begins typing away, occasionally clicking, then typing some more. He leans closer to the screen, a somewhat comical sight when you consider his glasses are already two inches thick. "Mon deur," he whispers.

"What is it, doctor?" Chantal asks.

He continues reading, then slowly turns to us, gears turning in his head. "Is this true?" he asks.

As if I know what he's talking about!

"What?" I say through clenched teeth. My shoulder really frickin' hurts, and the fact that my body is misaligned drives me mad.

"Do you hold the secrets of The Ledger in your mind!" he yells, his whiny voice echoing in the domed ceiling.

I consider my options. If I lie about who I am, Dr. Souris might torture me. Plus, he apparently has my file on his computer, so who knows what other stuff it might prompt him to search. But, if I tell him the truth, he might torture me. I sigh.

"Yes," I say.

Chantal looks between us, her wrinkly brow furrowed. "What's going on, doctor? Who is she?"

He scurries over to us much faster than I would have thought his tiny feet could take him. Then he stares up at me in awe.

"It has been done," he snickers to himself. The sound reminds me of a rat nibbling on cheese. "This changes everything," he says with eyes made even wider by his ridiculously magnified glasses. He takes a hand out of his glove and touches my face gingerly, his tiny fingers as soft as whiskers on my cheeks. It prompts another mental image of rats, and I'm officially creeped out. I jerk my head away.

"She is exactly what I've been looking for!" Dr. Souris claps his hands together once more in a triumphant manner. It's eerily similar to what Simon does when he's excited by a new way of "testing" me.

I shiver.

Chantal gives me a jealous glance, and I can feel her body go rigid as her grip on me tightens.

"What do you want with me?" I ask, but the tiny man ignores

my question and continues to appraise me from top to bottom. His beady eyes twinkle, and his hopeful face turns into a terrifying look of determination. The kind of look that an Evil Villain might get when he has a terribly inspired idea.

Then he says something that makes me wish I was back in that cramped bathroom stall.

"Put her in the chair."

22 / ANOTHER DAMN EXPERIMENT

The chair is even less comfortable than it looks. Especially since Dr. Souris kicked the poor young lad out of it, leaving a stain of eye juices and probably pee down its spine. Yuck. I try my hardest to avoid the puddle of liquids, but it seeps into my jeans all the same. I scream bloody murder.

"Stop squirming!" Chantal barks. She's holding me back with one arm to my gut, and her other is fastening my ankles in the leather straps attached to the torture device.

I can't even think of something to say to distract her or slow her down. My chest is heaving with each gulp of air I take. Suddenly sewage scented oxygen tastes excellent, and I can't get enough of it.

"If the information in T.O.P.S.E.C.R.E.T.'s file is correct, I am utterly baffled by the successful implementation of..." he squints at the screen and scrolls with the computer mouse, "... Project Mcguffin."

Chantal has managed to tie my left ankle down, and now I have one less limb to fight with. My efforts focused on stalling Chantal and compartmentalizing this experience as it's happening, I use what remaining brainpower I have left to try to figure a way out of here.

"So are we," I tell him. "None of us have any idea what's going on in my brain," I continue, hoping I can dissuade him from whatever it is he's planning, "or how it worked in the first place."

"Quiet! I'm plotting." He grabs a bunch of papers and scrolls through more notes on his computer. "This is exactly what I've needed from the start. I was so close, but I couldn't bridge the gap!" He points at a page with some kind of squiggly equations, a clear gap in the scrawl. "But if I can analyze your brain and implement a system for my own personal use, perhaps—"

"Oh, come on!" I whine. "Another test?" What is it with scientists and their squiggly readings? "I'm so over these damn brain tests!"

He whirls on me, his fingers gripping the air like he's holding a stress ball in each hand. Through gritted teeth, he says, "Do not interrupt me when I'm plotting!"

Chantal gets my second foot in the holster.

This isn't looking good.

I decide to appeal to this Evil Villain's ego. Maybe he'll reveal everything to me the way the bad guys do in all those movies. (Though, the last time I tried to take survival cues from the movies, I ended up turning myself into The McGuffin... However, I don't really see any other options at this point.)

"I'm sorry, Doctor," I say, bowing my head for effect. "I'm just so, er, grateful to be part of one of your legendary experiments."

His ears perk up at this statement. "Legendary?"

Ha! It's working.

"Oh, yes. You're all T.O.P.S.E.C.R.E.T. talks about. 'Dr. Souris' this 'Evil Villain' that..." I'm starting to babble. This happens when I'm nervous. Focus! "I couldn't wait to become part of all the action." I cringe on the inside. That's definitely overdoing it. For sure.

"Did you hear that Chantal?" He laces his fingers together in a thinking position as he paces. Chantal grunts, fastening my wrist into the leather belt.

"Doctor, please tell me what I get to be a part of," I say, batting my eyelashes by way of faux flirting. Chantal notices this and constricts the leather strap extra tight. My breath hitches.

In a few minutes, I won't be able to feel that hand at all, but I ignore the pain and the mental image of my circulation being cut off. "What are all these fascinating tests for?"

"Under normal circumstances, I would take this opportunity to explain everything," he checks his watch, "but since I'm running behind schedule, I must skip the monologuing and get right to the evil villain part."

"But what about—"

"Shut up, girl!" he shouts. Chantal smirks at this, clearly pleased Dr. Souris is no longer fascinated with my fake flirting.

So much for listening to the movies.

"It's time to give me your brain." Dr. Souris says this with eyes aglow and a creepy grin that reveals all his tiny teeth, even the ones in the way back.

"My brain? What?"

"You are the first person to ever have information digitally downloaded to your mind! I need this technology. I need to make it work for myself."

Alright, I always knew my brain was excellent (straight A's since Kindergarten, hello), but why the sudden interest from evil villains and Top Secret government programs?

"Even I don't understand how it works! It's not worth your incredibly precious time, doctor." Maybe if I pretend to care, he'll be more agreeable.

"Nonsense! If I cannot duplicate the system, I will simply take your brain."

My heart stops.

TAKE MY BRAIN?

"You don't understand," I start, "You-you can't just, even Simon doesn't," I search for something, anything, that might resonate with Dr. Souris. "But it's my brain!"

I admit it isn't exactly a compelling argument.

"And soon it will be mine."

Dr. Souris places the makeshift helmet over my head, and I realize it's the lacrosse helmet from my vision. Just like in my vision, it's covered in different colored wires and frayed copper mesh that attach to the computer selling all of T.O.P.S.E.C.R.E.T.'s goodies.

But unlike my vision, it doesn't seem like a toy. No, this helmet feels deadly as hell. There's no way I'm letting him put it on my head.

Then again, if it was in my vision, maybe that means I'm supposed to be here?

Gah, it's useless trying to come up with positives in this scenario. Not when the only thing I can do is watch an Evil Villain steal my own brain from my head!

My pulse quickens. My breathing turns shallow. I frantically search the place for some kind of solution, but I'm drawing a blank.

Chantal watches me with a cocked eyebrow. "It's pointless trying to get out of those, darling. If they can hold me, they can hold anyone," she says with a sultry voice. It occurs to me that this chair may have been used for worse things than experimentation. I fight the urge to vomit once more.

An incredibly loud metallic clanging shakes through the walls, followed by a raucous wailing and screeching. Wild animals must have been let loose in the sewers of Paris.

Chantal stops fastening my arms to stare down the hall where the noise came from.

"What was that?" she asks, now at full attention.

"Go find out," Dr. Souris tells her. He fiddles with The Backup on its little plastic platform.

Chantal gives me a pointed glare. "Do not try to escape again, girl. I will find you and throw you over the railing myself." She turns and darts down the hallway, her bumps and curves bouncing with each step.

The frightening speed at which she runs contrasts comically with the image of a frumpy old lady in pointy heels. Nevertheless, it sends a wave of creepiness down my spine.

Dr. Souris places some more wires in the helmet and grabs a remote control. He brings the germ-riddled device high above his head with eyes glimmering in the lamplight. The tiny man wiggles the oversized helmet to get it to lay on my head just right, then steps away from me cautiously, like someone distancing himself from a coming explosion.

"Do not fight it, girl," he says, raising his voice over the sudden electrical whirring that fills the room.

A salty tear makes its way to the corner of my mouth. It's my tear, I realize. Damn it! I don't want this to be the end.

The computer and the wires and the helmet all glow as electrical current fills them up. "In a moment you may be dead, or you may lose all original thoughts in your mind, or you may feel lighter, or—"

"You don't know what's going to happen?" I shriek.

"That's the nature of an experiment!" He laughs evilly (which is only one adjective off from Simon's unnerving giggle, though I'd much rather be in his electrocution chair right now) and presses the button on his little remote.

A surge of energy shoots through the wires, and I can feel heat build in the helmet on my head. I grit my teeth and scrunch my face up, expecting the worst. I make sure to keep my eyes clamped shut, in case they decide to start melting like the guy before me.

Dear God, I hope that doesn't happen.

"Yes!" he cries, the sound of the machine now so loud I can't even hear myself panting. "Surrender to the power, girl! Give me your mind!"

A jolt of energy explodes in my brain, sending commands to every muscle and joint to twitch like a person who just chugged twelve cups of espresso. I fight against it as hard as I can, but the twitching continues until something hot and heavy runs down my face. Is that... blood? It runs over my lips. I lick them but taste nothing. Is it all in my head? Is my brain leaking out?

BANG!

Something POPS off the helmet and a piece of metal flies across the room, lodging itself in the stone wall behind Dr. Souris. He furrows his unibrow and adjusts the dial on his little remote. The previously increasing electrical current noises reach a sudden halt, then begin to die down. The fans of the computer start purring as they cool the machinery. I can hear my panting again.

What's happening? I want to cry out, but my body is shaking from shock.

Dr. Souris presses every button on his remote with force. "What is wrong with you, you piece of shit?"

It merely beeps back at him. He smacks it against the wall with a huff, then rushes over to the computer. As he scans the readings on his screen, I wonder what Simon's readings are telling him now.

"Merde!" He slams his fist on the table, then he whirls around and tinkers with the helmet. "Agh! I need another piece of equipment." Dr. Souris trudges toward the hallway.

"What did you just do to me?" I yell after him.

"Nothing! That's the problem!" He shakes his head. "I will have to take your brain directly out," he continues, now muttering the details to himself as he shuffles down the hallway. "Subject fifty-nine could be of assistance…"

His voice fades, and I'm left alone to struggle against my leather bounds. Now is my chance to get out of here! I shake and twist and wriggle as hard as I can but to no avail. Chantal is damn good at tying people up.

I look to The Backup, taunting me from its perch on the little plastic platform. It's right there! And I can't even move.

Hot tears sting my eyes, and suddenly all the emotions hit me at once.

My bones ache from exhaustion. The one thing I ate in the last twenty-four hours drained me of all the energy I thought I had left, and now I'm trapped in an underground dungeon covered in the nasty stuff of my nightmares. I can't do anything about it. Except for cry. Like a baby. And wonder where the hell Eric is.

Maybe I can telepathically talk with The McGuffin. How do I get out of here, McGuffin? Tell me something useful! My eyes bulge from their sockets as I stare at The Backup, pretty sure I've gone crazy.

"Crrrk!" A faint static noise fills my ear. I gasp.

"Are you... talking to me?" I squint at The Backup, terrified and in awe at the same time. Maybe Dr. Souris' experiment gave me superpowers.

"Crrrk! Cccrrrrrkkk!" This time it seems farther away.

"Julie! Come in, over. Crrrk!"

Eric! He's talking to me through my earpiece. I let out a surprised little shriek.

"Eric!" I whisper loudly. "Eric, can you hear me?"

He doesn't answer.

"Over?" I add. Then I remember there's a way to adjust the volume. If I could only reach my earpiece, but my arms are no use. I push my head against the helmet, trying to use the frayed copper strands to adjust the dial in my ear. Almost there... gotcha!

"Eric? Do you come in?"

"Julie! Where the hell are you?" His voice screeches in my ear, the volume turned up to 100%. I quickly dial it down, banging my head against my helmet like an imbecile and blinking away the stars in my vision.

"Did you fall into the toilet or something? Jesus," he continues.

What a lovely partner.

"I was kidnapped, you ass!" I tell him all about how I was brought to an underground lair by a strong old lady, and now an Evil Villain is trying to sell The Backup to fund some type of experiment and steal my brain. Oh, and also that Greyson is here. I whisper that last part, realizing it would be terrible to add a conscious Greyson to the situation.

"You've experienced blunt force trauma."

"Just hurry up and find me before Dr. Souris turns me into another one of his deformed rejects!"

"Calm down. How did you get from the bathroom to where you are now?"

"Did you even listen to me?" This guy is unbelievable. "I was drugged and kidnapped!"

He laughs— actually laughs— and says, "I can't believe you were drugged again."

Why did I ever think this idiot would come to my rescue? Then I get an idea.

"I'm looking right at The Backup, but I can't get to it because I'm tied up," I tell him. Maybe that will get his attention.

"I'm coming, Julie," he says, suddenly serious. What a jerk.

"Hurry up! He's going to be back any second," I whisper loudly.

Silence.

"Eric?"

Nothing. A few moments pass. I wait with bated breath.

"Eric!" I whisper again.

"Crrrk! I'm currently approaching what looks to be a corridor of mutated slaves, probably the ones you were talking about. Just sit tight and I'll be right there."

How the hell did he find this place so quickly?

His voice crackles back in again. "Oh gosh, you poor little thing—"

A cacophony of chaos erupts in my ear, cutting Eric off. The call goes completely to static.

"Eric!" I say, but he's gone.

Oh boy. The little bird girl must have figured out he knows me.

Just then, multiple sets of footsteps echo down the hall.

23 / KRAV MAGA

When Dr. Souris returns, he brings with him a different assistant— a mutated overweight woman with multiple forearms protruding from a single elbow joint on each arm. The woman's smile extends wide enough to reveal slimy, sharp teeth. I grimace.

"What's your plan, Doctor?" I ask, an attempt to stall.

He places what looks like a metallic Yarmulke on the back of my head. It feels heavy and cool on my scalp. "My plan?"

"Does no one stick to their plans in this messed up world? Yes! Your plan! To rule the world, to avenge your dead mother or whatever it is that made you this way!"

"I do not wish to rule the world. I simply wish to be a Python."

A rat who wants to turn himself into a snake. Some evil villain he is. "Care to explain what that has to do with me?"

"Stop trying to stall, girl." He tells his multi-appendaged assistant to make sure I don't move. The woman, if she can still be called that, takes a step between us and places two of her slimy hands on my shoulders, pushing me back into the chair.

"Isn't this the part where you tell me all about your diabolical reasoning behind these disgusting experiments?"

"That would be an immense waste of time." Dr. Souris states. "Also, how dare you insult my creations? They're beautiful and ingenious." He gestures to the creature standing between us. "Look at Stella here. She is now able to perform with superior dexterity, and her reflexes are superb."

Stella wiggles her extra limbs to demonstrate.

"What about the family you stole her from? Do you even care that these people are people?"

"These people are my subjects. They're part of history, something anyone should be pleased to be a part of."

"Stella doesn't look too content about it."

The girl's eyes are downcast, though the rest of her features seem to blare at me, "I WANT TO KILL YOU." I wonder how he got Stella to listen to him. I doubt the bird girl obeys orders.

Dr. Souris powers on the headpiece, and the edges singe my skin.

"Yow!" I shake my head, trying to get it off. It doesn't budge.

"Don't be afraid, I'm a doctor." Dr. Souris flashes a self-satisfied grin at his little joke. "This little device has blades that will extend into your head, just around the edges of your brain, allowing me to remove the cerebrum while it remains intact."

My mouth drops. The mouse man giggles.

"It's finally my time!" Dr. Souris dramatically reaches out to press a button on his computer screen. When his finger is a centimeter away, something WHIZZES past with a whistle and lands right in the center of the giant computer, cracking the screen into a hundred pieces in an explosion of electric hissing.

Dr. Souris, Stella, and I whip our heads around to see Eric standing in the hallway, holding a T.O.P.S.E.C.R.E.T. pen as if it were a gun. His muscles glisten with sweat beneath the rips in his dirt-streaked cotton shirt. The bloody scratches on his face add ruggedness to his heroic entrance.

"Eric!" I say, incredibly relieved to see him.

"What have you done!" Dr. Souris shrieks. He pulls the dart from the screen, hands shaking. "My information!"

"That information belongs to T.O.P.S.E.C.R.E.T.," says Eric. He takes a step forward and drops the dart pen on the floor with a clatter. "Hand it over now."

A bubbling laugh emerges from the deepest recesses of Dr. Souris. "Absolutely not," he says, then he yanks the little USB from its plastic charging port (without properly ejecting it first!) and places the small piece of plastic in his lab coat pocket. He gives Eric a look that says, "Now what are you going to do?" Eric grits his teeth.

"Don't make me ask again," Eric says, stepping forward once more. The lights flicker, and only half remain on, bathing the area in an eerie fluorescent glow.

The harsh shadows accentuate Eric's downcast face as he glares at Dr. Souris, who glares right back through his thick-rimmed magnifying glasses.

"What the hell are you waiting for, Eric? Get us out of here!" I shout.

Dr. Souris slaps me with his rubber glove, sending a flurry of stars spinning across my vision. I gasp. Seriously, did he just fish-slap me?

"Quiet, girl!" He turns back to Eric. "I will give up neither," he says. Then he pulls a walkie talkie off the counter. "CCCR-RRK! Chantal, forget what I said earlier— send the subjects—"

But everything he's saying is being repeated back to us a second later. From Eric's belt, where Chantal's walkie hangs.

Eric picks up the walkie talkie and answers into it, "She's not available," with a smirk.

Dr. Souris lets out an angry groan and throws the walkie talkie into the cobblestone floor with surprising force, considering his tiny T-Rex arms. "What have you done to her?"

"Your saggy girlfriend was torn apart when she stepped

between me and the half-rat-half-girl abomination you call an experiment," he says.

"What was subject five-thirteen doing out of her cage?" Dr. Souris whispers worriedly to himself.

"There's a huge jailbreak down the hall, Doctor. You should get your locks fixed." Eric shakes his head disapprovingly. "It's a blood bath," he continues.

The tourists must have discovered the doors were unlocked.

"And I'm going to feed you to your own dogs unless you hand over The Backup. Now." Eric holds out his open palm expectantly.

Dr. Souris takes a deep breath, thinking for a moment. Then he says, "That doesn't sound very good to me."

"I don't care."

"How about I give you The Backup," Dr. Souris holds up a finger, prompting Eric to wait for the good part, "in exchange for the girl?"

Eric looks at me, tied up and covered in nastiness. Why hasn't he burst into a fit of kung fu awesomeness yet?

Eric nods once and says, "Deal."

"What!" I shriek.

Eric gives me a shrug, but it is burned in the waves of magma heat emanating from my fuming head.

"Toss it over," Eric says, and just as Dr. Souris reaches into his jacket pocket, the lights flicker out entirely, dissolving the whole room into shadows.

My eyes quickly adjust to the darkness as I scour the room. Eric lunges after Dr. Souris, but the freak with five arms jumps in the way, and now Eric and Stella are duking it out in the darkness.

To my right, something lets out a heavy grunt. I squint. Greyson's large lethargic body slowly stirs. Great. He's waking up. And I'm still sitting here like a helpless piece of crap! I yank against the leather straps, forgetting that my arm is totally out of place. Pain sears through my entire left side.

Eric's scuffling sounds grow louder with each passing second. C'mon, Julie!

I pull my left wrist free and quickly fumble through my jeans pocket for a pen. Aha! I grab the tiny handle and force my almost entirely non-responsive fingers to click the switch, sending a bright white beam of light across the room.

A flashlight pen! Thank goodness it wasn't another flash grenade.

I get a glimpse at the action unfolding in the dark before me. The grunting is coming from the multi-armed mutant— who is fighting herself! She's tangled up in her too-many limbs, slapping her own face. Dr. Souris fumbles for something in his desk drawer in the middle of the room and Eric is stretched out behind him, his hand inches from The Backup in Dr. Souris' pocket.

"Aahh!" Eric shields his eyes.

Dr. Souris grabs a giant rusty key from his drawer and shoots a conspiratorial glance over his shoulder in my direction before scurrying out of the room and down the other hallway. The mutant turns to Eric and me, its gaze locked on our positions.

Oops.

"What the hell, Julie!"

The mutant roars and jumps forward. Eric darts in front of me, blocking Stella's blow and knocking the flashlight out of my hand. It clicks itself off when it clatters to the ground, and our eyes are left to adjust to the darkness once more.

Full of fear and sweat and stress, I suddenly don't see a positive outcome for this situation. I scrunch my eyelids shut real tight and say one last prayer.

Dear God, please make my death quick and painless.

I realize perhaps that's asking for too much.

If pain is inevitable, please make it minimal.

Perhaps it's an answer to my prayer, or maybe it's just a coincidence, but just then, my back arches and my eyes fly open. I gulp down a deep breath. Karate fighting stances flash behind my eyes in a half-second before disappearing.

In an instant, I'm full of energy and confidence as I rip the leather straps off the rest of my limps and jump to my feet.

Though the room is still bathed in darkness, every movement around me is suddenly on my radar. It's like I just drank twenty jugs of carrot juice.

The mutant flings its arm toward Eric in a deadly blow, but I step between them and block it.

Who is taking over my body?

I watch, totally out of control, as my own body kicks ass and defeats the mutant in a few swift movements. Eric watches with his mouth slightly agape as the mutant falls to the floor with a sickening crunch. Each of her forearms breaks under her weight.

"Where did that come from?" he breathes.

"I have no idea. I'm so full of energy and power!" I punch the air in front of me. "I've never felt this way before. It's like I'm not in control of my body."

Eric's eyebrow shoots up. Somehow, he manages to make everything seem inappropriate. I roll my eyes at him.

"Focus. We need to get the backup," I say.

"He went this way." Eric points to the hallway and starts for the corridor. I follow suit.

"Wait, what happened to—" I start, but Greyson steps in between us and the exit. Eric's jaw drops.

"Greyson?"

Greyson smiles, fresh burn scars altering the way his lips bend.

"How the hell are you still alive?" Eric asks, more pissed off than incredulous.

Greyson ignores the question and takes a substantial step forward.

"Did all the 'almost dying' affect your voice box?" Eric goads. "Are you now the epitome of a sack of meat?"

Greyson answers with a mechanical whirring sound. His eyepatch lights up red, and a laser beam shoots from his eye, catching Stella on fire in the corner of the room. Flames erupt around her body.

"Now we're talking," Eric says. He jumps for Greyson. The movement looks like that of a flipbook in the flickering light of the flames. Greyson shoots another laser at Eric, but Eric anticipates this and ducks out of the way. He wraps his hand around Greyson's eyepatch, prepared to yank the dang thing off his face, but recoils in pain a moment later.

"Jesus, that's hot!"

Greyson smiles.

Eric does a perfect roundhouse kick to Greyson's side. It has no effect on the henchman, except maybe it's the reason he lets out a deep laugh.

Still full of unexplainable energy and power, I jump in between the two men, intending to stop this nonsense with my newfound fighting abilities.

But the surge of awesomeness wears off just as my puny, bony fist meets Greyson's rock-hard stomach. I hear the crunch before I feel it.

"Aah!" I gasp.

My hand is broken. I fight back an onslaught of tears and force myself to breathe as I crumple to the ground.

So much for being Super Woman.

Greyson steps right over me, an insignificant bump in the road, and shoots another laser beam at Eric. It catches on the soiled bed and erupts into a giant fireball.

"Julie, get up!" Eric tells me. His voice echoes in my head, which now feels utterly empty after all the hoopla. Was that the "big test" Simon mentioned in our phone call? If so, I'm going to have a word with him when we get back.

If we get back.

"Go after Dr. Souris, I'll handle this oaf," Eric continues. He raises his fists in a fighting stance as another laser beam singes the edge of his shirt. I scramble to my feet.

"Right. On it!" I dart down the hallway with absolutely no idea where I'm headed.

My head is throbbing, my pits are sweating profusely (either from the terror surging through my body or just a continued side effect of being the temporary McGuffin), my shoulder sears with pain, and my broken hand lies limp at my side, utterly useless.

As I continue my half-jog half-run through the somehow undiscovered secret evil lair in the sewers of Paris, I realize I've yet to see the Eiffel Tower.

24 / FOLLOW THAT RAT!

It's still pitch black, and the only thing I have to lead me to Dr. Souris is the sound of his tiny feet scuffling and echoing down the slimy sewer tunnels. I follow quickly but cautiously, careful not to trip on my own shoes at the very least.

As I near the rushing water, it becomes more challenging to distinguish Dr. Souris's soft shuffling feet from the rumble of the water. Where is this little dude headed?

"Dr. Souris!" I shout. "Wait! Let's just talk about this!" My own voice reverberates back to me. "I want you to win your competition." I try to be friendly. We're friends, right? I mean, besides the fact that he totally tried to steal my brain and kidnapped me and all.

I stop walking for a moment, anticipating a reaction, and the shuffling stops. Did Dr. Souris stop walking because I stopped walking? My eyes adjust, and I realize I'm standing at the edge of a tunnel opening. I peer around the corner, careful not to make too loud of a stepping noise on the wet stone ground.

The tunnel opens up into a grand hallway of sorts with multiple archways leading to other shafts on the opposite side of the opening. I stifle a groan. Dr. Souris could have gone through any one of them.

I step down into the open space, paralyzed by all the options before me. Which tunnel should I take? If I take the wrong one, Dr. Souris will have gotten away! Then again, if I actually do catch up to him, what exactly is my plan?

I shake the thought away. There's no room for doubt, as Penelope said before. She's right. I go with my instincts, something I remember Eric told me, and follow the hallway down to the left.

The tunnel opens into more tunnels, where the water funnels out through barred gates. I keep moving forward, half sprinting half scanning each tunnel for Dr. Souris. I wonder how long it took whoever built this to build it. I mean seriously, who has the time to not only plan but execute such a convoluted underground system?

"Not so fast, girlie," a raspy voice calls to me. I whip my head around.

Chantal slowly emerges from the darkest part of the tunnel. She's limping, and with each step she takes, her blubbery lumps of skin jiggle through the rips in her tight dress. Her stained old-people teeth stand out against the thick coat of blood and guts covering her from head to toe. One of her ankles is rolled under, hence the limping, and she's still wearing her red heels.

You gotta admire her for that, at least.

"There's no time for this, lady. Where is Dr. Souris?"

She wipes a bit of blood from her nose and rubs it on her fanny pack.

Gasp!

My fanny pack. And now it's stained with her mutant blood, damn her.

She just made this personal.

"Hand over the fanny pack, and I'll let you walk away."

She spits a wad of blood on the ground between us. "It looks better on me."

Oh no, she didn't.

Ready for this catfight, I step forward and curl my hands into fighting fists. YOW! My right wrist explodes with pain. I suck in a breath, blinking away black dots.

Yup, still broken.

Chantal takes advantage and runs at me, stumbling over her broken ankle. She's slowed down by the lagging limb, but still moving at a pace that would make any other seventy-year-old jealous.

What a couple of feisty ladies we are.

There's no way I'll last in a fight with this woman. Not with a broken hand and a useless arm. Think, Julie. Think!

Chantal is now ten feet away, seething at the teeth, arms outstretched, cursing at her broken ankle. She groans, stops walking long enough to force her ankle back in place with a sickening CRACK, then continues running five times her old-person pace.

She closes half the distance between us before I remember there's still one T.O.P.S.E.C.R.E.T. pen in my pocket. I yank it out and point the end right at her.

Click.

Nothing happens.

I inspect the tool and barely notice the tiny "PN" engraved on the side. Of course! A normal pen when I don't need one.

Chantal launches herself into the air and tackles me to the ground, knocking the wind out of me with her lumpy, blood-covered body. She slashes a wrinkly hand at me, her red acrylic nails slicing into my cheek.

I gasp for air and wriggle underneath her. My pen hand is pinned beneath her left boob. At least, I think that's a boob. She's so lumpy it could be anything. Uck.

She slashes for me again, and in the half-second she lifts her chest from my arm, I arc it upward to block her blow, pen still held tightly in my fist.

"Get off, old lady!" I yell, my voice echoing down the

deserted cobblestone halls.

"Grrgbldsk," she says.

Huh?

I open one of my eyes to find I've stabbed her in her goiter. She's bleeding through the small puncture wound, and the hot, sticky liquid spreads onto my hand.

"Ack!" I shove her off me and awkwardly crabwalk to the edge of the tunnel, grateful for the adrenaline surge masking the pain in my misaligned arm. She claws at her neck, her face, pulls at her hair. Her skin begins smoking and then melting.

Then I remember George telling me none of his pens are "normal." This is the pen he created with disintegrating ink to destroy T.O.P.S.E.C.R.E.T. messages.

Wait till he hears it destroys old ladies, too.

Chantal lets out her last strangled scream and then collapses to the floor in a melted heap of lumps and hormones and acrylic nails.

I wait for her remaining limbs to stop twitching before I let my shoulders down from my ears. It's another minute or two before I gather enough courage to poke her with my shoe.

No response.

What a pity.

I quickly yank the fanny pack from her pudgy waist before any of the acidic liquid touches it.

"Oh, I missed you!" I say, holding the fanny pack in front of me. It's dripping with blood and it smells absolutely disgusting, but damnit if I'm going to let these creeps steal the one thing that brings me joy in this insane spy world. I clasp the fanny pack around my hips like a boxing champion's trophy. I cinch it tighter and wipe off as much blood as I can with my shirt sleeve, feeling accomplished for the first time in the last few days. Checking inside, I see the pockets are still intact. Whew. But something crinkly and square-shaped has found a home in the middle pocket. I inspect it in my non-broken hand.

Condoms.

Yuck! I chuck them across the room and try not to puke. This fanny pack is getting a thorough wash when we get back to T.O.P.S.E.C.R.E.T. Head Quarters.

And we are getting back. I just decided. Right now.

My thoughts are cut short when there's a loud metallic CLACK and then a rusty sounding CREEEEAAKKKK coming from further down. I follow the sound around the corner to find Dr. Souris at the end of a short tunnel.

He's just opened an old metallic gate, and a rusty key protrudes from the lock. He taps a pattern into the stone wall. A few moments later, the wall opens to reveal a hidden safe, from which Dr. Souris pulls out a black briefcase.

"Hey!" I yell.

Dr. Souris whips his neck over his shoulder. He gives me a hunched over, beady-eyed hiss. The movement reminds me of the silhouette on The Director's computer at Head Quarters, and I remember he calls himself Dr. Mouse. Suddenly, he doesn't seem too scary.

Until he pulls a gun out.

BANG!

Thank God this man is practically blind. The bullet bounces off the cobblestone wall and ricochets on each corner of the four-way opening before disappearing into the water runoff. My heart races. I guess I spoke too soon. Even a half-blind mouse is still dangerous with a gun, Julie! I grit my teeth and run after him as he disappears down yet another corridor.

Luckily, this one seems to be heading somewhere a little less pitch black. I force my body to keep moving, ignoring my side stitch, my broken hand, and the growing numbness in my dislocated arm. Every breath feels like fire in my lungs, but all I'm focused on is the white blur down the tunnel as Dr. Souris somehow keeps the lead.

How can a person half my height and who knows how much

older than me be moving so quickly? Does he have rollerblades in his little black shoes or something?

I double my speed and lock eyes on my target. I'm catching up now, right on his heels, and just as we reach the light at the end of the tunnel (literally), a wave of sound and smell hits me like a brick wall, almost stopping me dead in my tracks.

We enter a cavernous space where three large tunnels come together to form a giant waterfall of sewage.

I gag at the smell, which has formed a sort of noxious gas. I hold my sleeve over my nose and peer through squinted watering eyes.

There!

Dr. Souris is so short I can barely see him under the gas, but there he is at the other side of the hallway. The tiny man is now racing toward the docked boat at the edge of the lapping sewer water. It's the boat I saw from the sewage bridge. Except now that I'm closer, I can see that there are two.

Oh great. Am I going to have to chase Dr. Souris on a boat? Because I really don't know if I can handle a boat chase. Especially considering I've never driven a boat before.

But Dr. Souris doesn't stop at the boats. In fact, he keeps going past the edges of the sewer waterfall and down a second tunnel. I continue after him, blinking the gas-induced fogginess from my brain. Where is he heading?

I round the tunnel entrance in time to witness Dr. Souris climbing up a rusty ladder toward a tiny shaft of light in the domed ceiling.

"Hey!" It comes out as a cough. "Not so fast, you… you turd!"

I could give Eric and his witty insults a run for their money.

But he climbs and climbs like a little rat until he disappears into the light, the black briefcase clanging against the metal with each step.

Shoot!

I race up to the ladder and grip a crusty rung just above my head. I take a deep breath and heave myself up with my one half-good arm, gripping the side of the ladder with the inner elbow of my broken-handed arm, forcing my brain to ignore the threat of tetanus.

Pretty soon, I reach the ceiling and climb over the ledge into blinding daylight.

We're on a rooftop overlooking the Seine. I run to the edge of the building and look over to find a series of pink awnings.

"Tout le Monde" café. How the hell did we get here? Weren't we just tens of floors underground?

A mechanical WHOOSHing calls my attention. Fifty yards behind me lies a helicopter pad with a small helicopter on top, and Dr. Souris is climbing inside.

"STOP!" I yell, but there's no way he can hear me over the blades of the vehicle. So, I keep running after him. I'm ten feet away when the helicopter lifts into the air.

No!

Without even thinking, I launch myself into the air.

It feels like an entire minute goes by in slow motion as I seriously wonder what the hell I'm doing jumping for a helicopter already taking flight. I witness my own foot land right at the edge of the open side door and push my body forward. I land on the metal floor with a SMACK and a loud POP and skid to the other edge.

Holy SHIT, I did it! "Yes," I cheer for myself absentmindedly. Oh, man, my high-school gym teacher would be proud.

I push myself up with my left arm, and when it doesn't hurt, I realize the POP sound was my shoulder popping back into place.

Just when it seems things are looking up, Dr. Souris whirls around, pointing a gun right between my eyes.

25 / UP, UP AND AWAY

"Just give me The Backup, and I won't hurt you," I say with as much authority as possible. Maybe if I act like I'm in charge, he'll believe I am. Though it's pretty unlikely, as Dr. Souris is the one holding a gun to my head, and my voice just fluctuated about three octaves.

The small man laughs at me, a piercing sound that sends chills down my spine.

"You idiot," he says with a thick French accent. I have to agree with him on that. "Now I have both The Backup and The McGuffin." He smirks. Crap. He's right again. I rack my brain for a solution.

"Look out!" I point out the front windshield and duck with overly dramatic wide eyes. Dr. Souris whips around. I take the opportunity to lunge forward and grab the briefcase resting on the passenger seat with my good hand. I recoil quickly, tumbling backward and fumbling with the latches.

Throwing the lid open reveals two large syringes. One of them holds a bright green liquid labeled "la guerison" and the other, a bright blue liquid labeled "la resistance."

I rack my brain for all the French verbs in my A.P. classes. Before I can figure out the translation, I'm overcome with a paralyzing sensation. Cold sweat forms on my forehead and in my armpits. My limbs begin convulsing.

Uh oh.

I grit my teeth and try to hold onto the briefcase before the oncoming flash of information takes over, but it's no use. My grip loosens involuntarily. My eyes scrunch tight, and the familiar onslaught of images comes at me like a tsunami.

Writhing snakes form into The N.E.S.T. logo from the brochure I found in Dr. Souris' lab, their scaly green skin shimmers in what appears to be moonlight. Then the scene fades as behind it a hundred names appear and disappear, like a ledger. They move too quickly for me to make any of them out, but one of them clearly stands out from the rest: "Dr. Souris."

The names turn to years: 1974, 1975, 1979, 1983… the numbers grow in size as the years go up, and soon, the figures morph into The N.E.S.T. logo once again, but this time it looks slightly different, less detailed as if it were drawn on an old sepia piece of paper. Dr. Souris's name appears written in ink on old parchment at the bottom of a list. A massive inky slash strikes through his name before the paper is ripped to shreds.

As the shreds fall, they morph into more snakes and form another version of THE N.E.S.T. logo, but this time it's a bit more detailed than before and made from the neat strokes of ballpoint pen ink rather than the messy smears of quill ink. And once more, Dr. Souris' name is crossed through and ripped to shreds. The cycle repeats again and again, faster and faster. The logo changes so quickly it's like a constant morphing transformation overlaying the constant slashing and deleting of Dr. Souris' name as the parchment turns to paper and then to computer screens.

The words "FAILED," "DELETED," "TERMINATED" appear and disappear throughout my vision until suddenly I'm transported into a cold, dark, wet corner with Dr. Souris. He huddles his knees to his chest and lets out a whimpering cry. I take a hesitant step toward him, but as soon as my foot hits the pavement, the scene changes around us.

Dr. Souris now stands gripping the two syringes in both hands. He looks down at them with adoring eyes, but then his expression changes. He's suddenly terrified. He looks up at me and pleads for help. Against my better judgment, I rush toward him. When I'm inches away from him, a gravitational pull sucks me into his black irises. I fall into darkness.

Gasp.

My eyes fly open, and I'm back in the helicopter above the Seine. My senses come back to me faster than they ever have before. I reach out and catch the open briefcase just before it slides over the edge of the open door.

"DO NOT TOUCH THOSE!" Dr. Souris yells. He grips one hand on the helicopter yoke and uses the other to aim the short barrel of his handgun at me. I wince, bracing for impact, but he doesn't shoot.

Oh, right, because I have his precious syringes dangling out the side of the helicopter. Duh! I pull it together, acting more appropriate for someone with the upper hand.

"Don't touch these?" I taunt, bouncing the briefcase in my hand outstretched over the Seine.

Dr. Souris lunges for the case, but as soon as he lets go of the yoke, the helicopter dips forward. He quickly returns his grip to the handle, waits for the aircraft to stabilize, and glares at me.

"I will drop these babies in a heartbeat unless you hand over The Backup," I say, this time confident that I'm the one in charge.

Dr. Souris bites his lip. "I cannot do that," he says.

I give a disappointed frown and shake the briefcase vigorously in a dramatic show of power.

A little too vigorously.

We both watch with dropped jaws as the green syringe falls out of view, right into the Seine.

Oops.

I pretend I meant to do that and raise my eyebrow at him.

"FINE," he says. "I'll tell you everything."

"I just want The Backup—"

He presses a button on the dashboard of a hundred dials and meters, sending the helicopter into "autopilot" mode. He then turns to me with a sudden somber mood about him, still pointing his gun at me.

"It all started when I was a child," he says, eyes wandering off to a place I can't follow, and then I realize what's happening.

It's monologue time.

26 / LOOK BEFORE YOU FALL

To be honest, I don't even hear what Dr. Souris is saying.

It's not that I'm not entirely intrigued by the twisted backstory fueling his evil ways— by all means, that's not what I'm saying. It's just that as soon as Dr. Souris starts talking, there's an explosion below us at the edge of the Seine, and I can't help but wonder if Eric is still alive down there.

My eyes dart to the left, where the open side door grants me a clear view of the events two hundred feet below. A silver deck boat surges through the flames, making a sharp turn into the Seine as it follows our general direction. If I squint my left eye and twitch my right eye slightly, I can just make out a black-haired man at the wheel.

Eric.

Just then, a second boat flies through the wall of fire, completely engulfed in flames. At first, it looks like no one is driving that second boat, but then the small vessel makes the same sharp turn and high speeds it after the first boat.

I can just make out the silhouette of a ridiculously large torso behind the wheel, standing tall in the flames.

Greyson?

A red laser beam erupts from the flaming boat and hits Eric's steering wheel, sending his boat swerving.

Yup. Definitely Greyson.

Dr. Souris shakes his pistol at me.

"Look at me when I'm monologuing!" he spits. I revert my eyes to him, trying hard to use my peripherals at the same time. The boats are following us.

Dr. Souris clears his throat. "As I was saying, by the time I turned fifteen, it was clear I would never grow a full head of hair." The static in my earpiece steals my attention.

"CCCCRRKKK!" I pretend to itch my ear and turn up the volume.

"Julie! God damn it, answer me, woman!" Eric's voice pierces my eardrum.

I bite my tongue, not too eager to be shot in the face today. Dr. Souris looks out the side of the helicopter as he continues his backstory. He has a particularly forlorn expression, and I think it's safe to say he's deep in his own self-pity. I whisper back at Eric.

"Can't talk— monologue time," I say. Dr. Souris throws me a warning look, but I play it off like a cough.

"Jesus, I've been calling for you ever since—"

A grunt cuts him off. I sneak a glance below in time to see Greyson's hulking body lunge for Eric's boat, just as his own water vehicle explodes behind them.

"And that was when I failed my first N.E.S.T. competition," Dr. Souris sniffs.

"What is The N.E.S.T.?" I ask, more to buy more monologue time than anything else.

Dr. Souris' nostrils flare, but not at me. He recalls something I can't see. I try to focus on his explanations and not on Eric's continuous, intense grunting in the background.

"The N.E.S.T. stands for The Nefarious Enterprise of Seasoned Transgressors." He huffs at my bewildered expression and adds, "It's an organization for the best Villains in the world." He says it like they're an all-knowing source of power, but I've never heard of them. Then again, I never heard of T.O.P.S.E.C.R.E.T., and they're anything but.

"They're always running low on henchmen," he continues, "but sometimes they require upper-level baddies, and that's where I come in." He smiles proudly, but it turns into a sour expression within seconds. "At least, that's always been my dream."

"So, wait a minute," I shake my head, trying to stay focused amidst a sudden plethora of questions about bad guy organizations. "What is the competition? How did you even find out about The N.E.S.T. in the first place?"

"Let me speak!" He slams his gun-toting fist on the chair next to him. The movement causes his small body to shake. While he recomposes himself, I sneak another peek down at Eric and Greyson.

They're still duking it out, but I don't see any more laser beams. It looks like one of them is performing karate moves on the other, but it's hard to tell who's winning. Judging by the continued grunting noises in my earpiece, Eric is still alive. Should I be helping him somehow? Maybe there's a turret or some sort of firing power in this helicopter. I turn back to Dr. Souris, secretly planning to take control of this vehicle once I somehow overpower him.

"The competition is the application," he continues.

"What do you have to do?" I ask, surprisingly intrigued by the whole logic behind this mysterious villain competition.

"Each year, the competition changes. However, the concept is always the same—pit all entrants against each other in a deathmatch."

"So, like The Hunger Games?"

"Some years' competitions were themed around the power

of starvation, yes," he says, my pop culture reference passing right over his head, "but that's only half of it."

"That sounds horrible."

"Oh, but it's my dream! The N.E.S.T. is a place for the brightest and most evil Evil Villains in the world. The N.E.S.T. has access to the most advanced technology— it's a playground for villains. And to be the best version of my villain self, I need to gain access to their plethora of information and knowledge. Working alongside the best will only train you to be the best."

I can't believe this actually makes sense. Maybe I was right earlier. Maybe I would make a good Evil Villain. I mean, the logic's there. Another grunt from Eric. No, focus, Julie. Not the time.

"But they still haven't accepted me into their ranks. Not even as a S.N.A.K.E. It's like they want me to have experience, but I can't get experience unless I already have experience."

"A catch 22." I nod.

"Exactly."

"You still haven't explained why you've been kidnapping and experimenting on tourists." I secretly hope he hasn't already gotten to that part, because I totally wasn't paying attention.

"Without knowing the details of the terrain or the competition requirements beforehand, even an Evil Villain like myself would have a hard time adapting to the stressful environment of gladiator-style bloodshed. Plus, I'm physically weak. That's why I began experimenting with methods for enhancing my mind and body, to prepare me for whatever fight I might find on the battlefield."

I furrow my brow. Dr. Souris rolls his beady black eyes at me.

"I use the tourists as test subjects, so I won't have to test myself."

"But then how could you know if the experiments would work on you?"

He stops to ponder this. "I suppose I wouldn't unless I tried." He shrugs. "But I wouldn't consider it unless my experiment worked successfully on someone else first."

"You mean this whole time you've been torturing and killing innocent people because you're too much of a wimp to test yourself?"

He glares at me.

"They should be proud to be part of such historical experiments!" he practically shouts.

"Give me a break," I say. "Your 'evil lair' is a sewer."

"Unfortunately, I had to perform under the streets of Paris to keep costs down. My attempts to avoid—" he shoots me a nervous glance, "I mean, my experiments were so elaborate that I simply had to stay hidden. Should anyone try to, uh, steal my work." He nods, pleased with his excuse.

"You ran out of money because you don't know what you're doing," I clarify.

"The McGuffin was about to provide me the last-minute boost I needed!"

"Because you were selling it on the black market," I add, putting the pieces together.

"Ha!" He cackles. "It's not worth pennies," he says, trying to catch his breath.

"What are you talking about? T.O.P.S.E.C.R.E.T. information must be worth a fortune."

He hisses through a fit of giggles. "Information that anyone can steal at any time they want isn't worth a dime!"

Note to self— tell Penelope to change the passcodes, or whatever it is she uses to keep the U.S. secrets secret.

"Then why did you steal it?"

"To see if anyone working for the United States government had successfully implemented something remotely related to what I'm trying to accomplish."

"Which is what, exactly?"

"To upgrade my physical abilities without the use of such—" his gaze flickers to the syringe— "primitive inventions."

I shiver along with him at the sight of the pointy needle glinting in the sunlight. "And what if your plan didn't work?"

He gives me a blank stare.

"You didn't have a backup plan?"

"I believe everything worked out tenfold better than I could have anticipated." He gives me an evil smirk. "I have the T.O.P.S.E.C.R.E.T. research files and a living subject to prove that they work."

Damn, he's right.

But not if I can steal the information back from him.

"What's your plan now?" I ask.

A red dot appears on his forehead, shaking slightly from left to right.

"Now I fly us to N.E.S.T. headquarters," he continues, unaware of the dot, "where I will no doubt be welcomed with open arms due to my discovery, and finish removing your brain in time to prepare myself for The N.E.S.T. competition."

The red dot finds its way onto Dr. Souris' eye. He blinks and swats it away. For the brief moment he's distracted, I kick the gun out of his hand. The tiny man gasps and lunges over the seat divider right at me, like a feral cat (or, I guess, a rat in this case).

I grab the syringe from its mesh cutout in the briefcase and let the metal encasing fall into the Seine below us. I've got the bright blue liquid held securely in my hand, far away from Dr. Souris's limited reach. The tiny man smacks and scratches at my arm.

"Give it back, girl!"

"Julie!" Eric's voice pierces my ear. I almost enter another fit of convulsions from the shocking volume ringing through my head.

"What?" I spit back.

"Give me the syringe, you idiot!" Dr. Souris replies. I'm not talking to you, I say in my head.

"Did you get The Backup yet?" Eric asks.

"Working on it!"

"Hurry up! Just grab it and jump before the missile hits you!" Eric's panting tells me he's still mid-fight with Greyson. I wonder who's winning. Then I realize he said missile.

"Missile? What missile? And stop yelling!" (The tables have turned, I see.)

"The one I just targeted to the helicopter with my pen!" He ignores my last comment.

Dr. Souris starts to climb on top of me. I hold the syringe as far above my head as possible and try to kick him away, but my long legs hit the yoke, and now we're spinning through the sky. Loud beeps fill the air once more. Damn it, does everything have to beep?

Dr. Souris gets his rubber gloved hands on my neck and squeezes with all his might. I can tell because the veins in his mostly bald head are popping out now, and it's causing my muscles to go weak.

Shit.

What do I have as a weapon? Nothing! I assess my options—helicopter falling to the Seine, gun kicked out the side door, no knowledge of flying a helicopter. The only thing I have is the syringe in my hand.

So, I use it.

Going against every vasovagal fiber in my body, I grab Dr. Souris' wrist to keep his arm in place, rearing back the syringe like a spear. His eyes widen with realization.

"Nooooo!" he shrieks.

I stab the pointy silver needle into his fleshy inner elbow. Somehow, I don't stop there. I press down on the edge of the syringe, forcing the blue liquid into his wriggling vein. Except I missed the mark by a good inch. The blue liquid spurts out all over the place, mixing with the spurting blood from Dr. Souris's new puncture wound.

Turns out, I don't think I'd make a good nurse.

I continue forcing the liquid out and onto Dr. Souris's arm until my muscles give out, and the familiar black stars of vasovagal syncope blur my vision. My grip loosens, and the syringe falls from my hand. It slides across the slippery metal floor and over the edge of the helicopter.

Dr. Souris and I look at each other for a moment, both covered in a mixture of blood and blue goo. Then we each simultaneously double over and retch.

At least I'm not the only one.

Ashamedly, I wipe my mouth on my shoulder sleeve.

Dr. Souris looks up at me like he wants to say something. His face is now even paler than it was before, almost translucent. He angrily stammers the start of a word, then loses consciousness and passes out. Right into his own puddle of vomit.

I'm tempted to follow his lead. My head grows heavier with the promise of sweet unconsciousness by the second, but unfortunately for me, I have Eric's loud voice in my inner ear to keep me conscious.

"What the hell is taking you so long?" Eric yells.

"I was a little busy!" I shove Dr. Souris's limp legs off mine and reach into his chest pocket. Though covered in slimy vomit (eew), The Backup otherwise appears to be intact.

"Got it!" I say. Relief floods every square inch of my body. I tuck The Backup into the back pocket of my jeans and grab hold of the handle at the edge of the open side door, trying to get my bearings as the helicopter continues to swerve midair. Wind whips through the cabin, blinding me in a dark brown tornado of hair.

"Do I just… jump?" I shout into the wind.

"Yes!" Eric yells.

"But what if I land on the water incorrectly?" I calculate all the possible different landing positions and their reciprocal levels of damage to my bone structure.

"I'll catch you in the boat— hurry!"

The entire sky sounds like it's being torn in half. I peer through my thick hair to see a shiny silver object flying straight toward me!

"JUMP!" Eric yells.

My stomach seizes tight, and I stop breathing momentarily. It all happens so fast that it feels like slow motion.

The missile approaches, glinting in the Parisian sunlight. I let go of the railing and take a deep breath. The beating of my heart is the only thing I can hear as I take a step forward, slip on Dr. Souris's vomit, and fall over the edge of the helicopter.

27 / PUKE BREATH

A million thoughts fly through my head in the brief time it takes me to fall from the helicopter.

Firstly, this is the second time I've jumped from a flying vehicle, and yet I still have no idea how to do this. I decide the flying squirrel method probably isn't a good idea in this situation, as I'd like to not break every limb. I curl into a cannonball (less surface area).

Secondly, is that the Eiffel tower? It's difficult to see through my flapping tendrils of hair. The glare of the sun on the water below me isn't helping either. It sure looks like a pointed building. There's really no way to know for sure, I suppose. Nevertheless, I take a small amount of joy from the thought that maybe I did get to see it after all.

And thirdly, I put The Backup in my pocket, right? 'Cuz, if I survive this fall and it isn't in my pocket, I might just kill myself before Eric can kill me. I should have double-checked.

A surge of energy erupts behind me as the missile hits the helicopter, sending it into a giant ball of flames on impact. The wave of heat and sound pushes me further toward the glistening water below. The explosion paints everything orange for a brief moment. It's oddly quiet and almost serene.

Until Eric flies right past me on his boat, allowing me to smack into the cold water at a hundred miles an hour.

I surge ten feet below the surface, thankfully still intact (the cannonball method apparently works!). The temperature shocks me back to life. I scramble to reach the surface before my lungs burst. I gulp down air and a bit of the Seine water as soon as I ascend.

A screeching sound reverberates through the air. I turn to witness the helicopter burst apart, sending multiple chunks of metal in all directions with an immense amount of force.

The propeller blade spins toward me and lands not even three inches to my right. I silently Thank God for not decapitating me today.

In front of me, Eric and Greyson continue to battle it out on Eric's boat. I wonder if this is why movies have cut scenes? This fighting part sure does take a long time. Greyson is covered in flames once again, yet he moves like he isn't bothered by it in the slightest. Maybe his skin really is made of rubber. Their fighting is cut short when a giant hunk of twisted, flaming metal shoots right at them. It narrowly misses Eric and catches on the top half of Greyson's body, taking the large man down into the water with it.

Whew.

All the normal sounds come back to me one at a time. The water lapping at the edges of the Seine. My own shallow breathing (pre-hypothermia perhaps?). An engine revving as Eric turns his boat around for me.

Could he move any slower? I signal for him to hurry up. He grunts.

Eric bends over the edge with an outstretched hand and grabs my upper arm, yanking me up out of the water.

But I'm a bit heavier than he expected.

We tumble onto the deck, and I land right on top of him, smacking his bottom lip with my forehead once more.

Except for this time, I don't have a helmet, so it hurts me, too.

"Uuuhhh..." I groan.

We lie there a moment, breathless and panting before having my body sprawled across his becomes awkward.

I jump back to my feet and wipe the water from my eyes.

"Where is it?" he asks with his annoyingly demanding voice.

"Where's what?" I feign confusion.

It works.

Eric practically bursts into flames. "The Backup."

I make a scrunched-up face. "Ooh, yeah. I almost had it. But then you shot a missile at me and told me to jump. So that's what I did."

He goes almost apoplectic. "You had the opportunity to get the one thing that could turn your life back to normal, and you let it slip through your fingers?"

"Who said I want to go back to my normal life?"

This really catches him off guard. He can't even hide his confusion.

"What if I want to be a spy?" I continue.

He snorts.

"Now I know you're joking," he says. "I'll admit, it's a miracle you survived this long, but there's no way you'd choose a life outside your little bubble."

I cock my hip to the side. "What's that supposed to mean?"

He takes a step closer. "It means you're an uptight goody two shoes, and as soon as you give me that Backup, we won't have to pretend you're necessary anymore." He holds his hand out.

Damn. He knows I have it.

"But Eric," I say with a smirk. "I am The McGuffin. You said so yourself. I am the almighty, the goddess divine ruler of your strange T.O.P.S.E.C.R.E.T. world."

"Just give me The Backup," he says, unmoving.

"Why? Once you have it, you'll just leave me behind again."

"Is that what this is about?" He scoffs. "I'd leave you right here in the Seine if it meant securing the fate of The McGuffin."

I swat my hand at his face, aiming for the perfect slap. And it really would be the ideal slap, except he grabs my arm mid-swing.

Damn it.

Instead of tossing me aside, Eric pulls me closer. He looks deep into my eyes. My breath hitches, and it's not from the cold.

Sirens fill the air around us. Is he going to kiss me? I've never been kissed. But I suppose Paris would be the best place of any to have a first kiss.

He reaches his other hand around my waist, slowly feeling my lower back. I hope he can't also feel my heart beating like a friggin' jackhammer. He leans almost imperceptibly closer to me. I close my eyes, preparing for kissage. He seductively traces the outline of my butt pocket...

And pulls out The Backup.

"Gotcha," he says with a wink. I can't even hide the shock on my face.

"You are such a jerk." I'd stomp my foot, but it'd just make me look more like a child. So, I sigh dramatically instead. Eric makes a sour face.

"Your breath smells like puke."

28 / TRIGGERED BY THE TRASH MAN

Mom hands me another Pina Colada. I take it with my non-broken hand and start sucking it down, thankful she used coconut milk instead of real milk, but somewhat disappointed it isn't her homemade chicken soup.

Right after they got home from their cruise last night, my parents went straight to CostCo and purchased their very own margarita maker. Which my mom has been using to try to re-create the Pina Coladas from the ship. Which she apparently hasn't perfected.

She keeps handing me her defects, but I'm happily drinking them down in an attempt to numb the pain in my healing hand. I idly admire the handiwork of the nurse who did my casting. It's a bright pink color, and it's waterproof.

Dad is sitting on the love seat across from me in the living room. He's got the Apple T.V. setup to stream his iPhone photos from their trip. He's telling me all about the differences in texture of the Pina Coladas on the ship versus the Pina Coladas in Inagua, but I haven't registered a word he's said.

I'm staring blankly, absentmindedly wondering for the hundredth time whether I should tell my parents what really happened to my broken hand, the only proof that my time at

T.O.P.S.E.C.R.E.T. was real. They think I broke it by "accidentally hitting a wall," which isn't too far from the truth.

Mom flashes dad a flirty grin from the kitchen, and he does a little growl and a snap with his teeth. She giggles and gets back to pouring another Pina Colada. I think I just threw up in my mouth.

It's a whole new world at the Richardson's residence.

Two nights ago, I was on the phone with Nicole, about to reveal everything, but she only had a few free minutes left on her break, so I let her tell me about her most recent date with Dr. Reeves. I guess it's a good thing, though, because The Director would have had to send someone to kill me if I'd leaked anything anyway.

So now I'm sitting on the couch, numb, mentally replaying my last moments as The McGuffin.

After we retrieved The Backup, Eric called for the P.I.L.O.T., and we headed back to Headquarters. I was debriefed in a cold, stark room before given another granola bar and a fresh set of clothes (a pair of jeans that actually fit and some good ol' granny panties).

Once I was cleaned up, and my shrunken stomach was filled with a granola bar, I entered another round of testing with Simon. He was instructed to remove The McGuffin from my brain, something he swore to The Director he had been prepared to do upon our arrival.

I expected Simon's testing to take forever, or at least involve a scalpel or a needle or something terrible. Probably it did require some of those things, but I wouldn't know because the moment my head hit the chair, I passed out. This time from exhaustion. I woke up feeling unnerved in my stomach and worried that Simon may have given me some sort of experimental mutant serum. Guess I'd spent too much time with Dr. Souris.

Speaking of the little mouse man, unfortunately,

T.O.P.S.E.C.R.E.T. couldn't question him about anything because Eric exploded him in his helicopter over the Seine. Most of his deformed inmates destroyed each other in the great sewer jailbreak of the century. The rest were discovered running through the streets of Paris, terrorizing other tourists. I don't know what happened to them after that. The T.O.P.S.E.C.R.E.T. team must have done a damn good job of covering it up, because not even my mom has found anything about it on Facebook.

The N.E.S.T. pamphlet was recovered from my back pocket, dried with a hairdryer, and examined by Simon and a few supplemental evidence analysts. They told me nothing of the clue. Then they thanked me for my cooperation and sent me home.

That was it.

I didn't even get a "Goodbye Julie, thanks for ruining everything," from Eric. My eyes do an involuntary roll at the thought of him. What a turd.

With an unsatisfied sigh, I finish my third Pina Colada and decide to take the trash out. My brain needs some fresh, humid Floridian air, I decide.

I'm tying the bag up in the kitchen when mom says, "Are you alright, sweetie?"

"Yeah, I'm just tired." And bored. I should absolutely be doing schoolwork to catch up on all the projects that were deleted on my laptop just days ago. But something about doing homework doesn't excite me anymore.

"I'm going to pack after I take the trash out," I say. Spring Break is over tomorrow, and I'll be headed back to college. Soon I'll graduate and get a generic business degree and... damn it, I still don't have a plan. I slam my forehead with the palm of my head.

It's fine. I'm fine. Everything's fine, I tell myself.

"Thanks for the drinks," I add.

"Alright," Mom says with a furrowed brow. She plants a kiss on my forehead where I slapped it, then rubs it affectionately. "You ready, Dan?" she asks my dad. He hops off the couch and nods his head.

"Yes, ma'am. After you, my dear." He motions toward the front door and grabs Mom's butt as she sashays past him with a giggle. I grimace.

"See you tonight, Julie," mom says, dipping into their silver Nissan sedan like it's a fancy limousine and not our old family car. I wonder how she could forget that time I hurled all over the back of her seat when I was seven and ate too many gummy bears. "Love you!"

"Bye, kid!" Dad waves through the front window.

I wave back until they're out of sight, then I go collect the trash and drop the heavy bag into our trashcan with a loud thud. It's pretty much empty, but I pull it to the curb anyway.

The deep mechanic whirring of a car engine snaps me to attention. A sizeable green garbage truck pulls to the curb next to the trash can, and a man in a reflective yellow vest steps out. He's a tall, burly guy with curly black hair and dark skin. He smiles and waves at me. I nod back politely.

Since when does the trash man come on Fridays? I probably have my days mixed up, I think, shrugging my shoulders.

The man walks around the back of the truck and steps toward me.

"Hola, Julie." His voice is gruff. There's something eerie about the way he says my name. Then I realize it's because he said my name.

"Uh, have we met before?" A sick feeling gnaws at my stomach. This doesn't seem right. Probably, I had too many Pina Coladas.

"Excuse me," I say, turning on my heel to head back inside.

The man grabs my forearm with a very tan, hairy arm. His grip is tight but not as strong as Chantal's. When I look down, I notice a tattoo peeking out from his sleeve. As he yanks me back toward him, his sleeve moves, revealing the rest of his tattoo.

A pile of snakes writhing on top of each other, forming the same image that was on the pamphlet at Dr. Souris' lab—The N.E.S.T. symbol.

I suck in a breath, realization sinking in. The tingling feeling on my spine returns, immediately followed by violent whole-body convulsions that I have no control over. The trash man grips my arms tighter. I vaguely hear him tell me to stop wriggling as my hearing becomes tunneled.

I close my eyes and let the wave of images crash down on my eyelids.

Everything is black as all get out (whatever that means), but I feel like I'm suffocating beneath something massive and squirming on top of me. I crack open my eyes to find I'm lying in an enormous pit of snakes. Thousands of the slimy creatures writhe in big piles above and beneath me, tightly winding themselves around my joints. The incessant hissing sends goosebumps and shivers to every inch of my body.

I scream for help, but my voice is too weak. A thick, scaly red viper stares me down with an angry hiss, rears its ugly fangs, and launches at my face. I jump. The bite sends a brief flicker of images through my head—tropical beaches, a jungle, the smirk of a woman wearing red lipstick—and then they disappear.

Before I can catch my breath, another snake stabs me with its fangs, and this time images of a snowcapped mountain fly through my mind. Pine trees, a crackling fireplace, a bubbling glass of champagne. These images blow away in a cold, snowy breeze, replaced by a crooked set of teeth featuring a giant silver fang protruding from the middle. A deep laugh reverberates through the air, and I'm snapped back to the snake pit.

I scream as another set of fangs penetrates my ankle,

followed by another bite on my thigh, then my wrist, my chest, my neck. I burst into a fit of convulsions as a rapid dance of sights, smells, and sounds transports me to places all over the world. Time's Square, Tokyo, the sea, the mountains, the smokey smell of a campfire, a citrusy orange breeze, fresh-cut grass—it's all so overwhelmingly fast that everything turns into one giant blur of colors.

The hissing in the snake pit mutates into a chorus of laughter. Deep, throaty chuckles, powerful booming laughter, high-pitched cackling—the mischievous song of villainy. The searing hot venom burns its way through my veins, growing closer to my heart with each erratic pump of blood until I finally blackout.

My eyes fly open, and I'm back in my front yard, in the trash man's tight grasp. I squirm to no avail. My pulse thumps rapidly, and I'm panting irregularly. Holy shit, a vision!

Why the hell did I have another vision? I'm going to give Simon a piece of my mind when I see him.

A smile spreads on my face, and I realize excitement is building in my stomach. I'm going to see that crazy kid scientist again because I'm still The McGuffin!

Before I can celebrate (or wonder why I feel like celebrating, let alone what must have gone wrong at T.O.P.S.E.C.R.E.T. for The McGuffin to still be sending me messages), the trash man hoists me over his shoulder and steps to his truck in two quick strides.

"Help!" I scream, but I know no one in this cul-de-sac can hear me. Tonight is bingo night at the neighborhood clubhouse, and all our old people neighbors are duking it out for the next week of bragging rights. Even if one of their hearing aids were strong enough to register my cries, I doubt an army of walkers and pace-makers would be much help.

The fake garbage man heaves me over the edge of the truck and slams me into the trash compactor. I wince from the impact and the putrid smell, quickly scan the trunk for anything helpful. A half-broken shovel and a dead potted sunflower spill out of a broken trash bag. Someone must have given up on their gardening hobby.

The man reaches for the trash compactor button. I grab the shovel with my good hand and swing it with all my force in the man's direction, eyes closed as to focus my efforts.

I make contact with his face to the sound of a sickening crunch.

Score 1 for Julie!

"Ouch!" says a voice that doesn't match the brawniness of the tough-looking man. What the heck?

I scramble out of the trash compactor to find Eric standing in front of me, nursing a broken, bloody nose.

"Eric!" I don't even try to hide my relief when I say it. He yanks the shovel from my hand with a glare.

"Thanks a lot!"

The trash man lunges at Eric from behind. Eric smoothly swivels out of the way, and I watch from the side as the man runs right into the trash compactor. Eric presses the button, and the heavy machinery slowly descends on the squirming burly man. Piercing screams fill the air.

I wince and turn away. "Is that really necessary?"

"What, no 'thank you?'" He snaps his nose back into place. Shrieks of terror and the crunching of bones twist my stomach into a knot as the trash man is compacted behind us. I grimace, willing the black dots to stay out of my vision.

It doesn't work.

I fumble back a step. Not now! I think. Not before I get my answers!

"What are you doing here?" I grumble.

"Aaaaagh!" The trash man's screams gurgle behind us.

"You're still The McGuffin," Eric says matter of fact.

"No, shit! I had a vision right before that creep tried to

kidnap me." I point to the trash compactor, now spurting blood into the air with each new crunch of force. The floor wobbles beneath my feet, and the dancing black dots crowd closer together.

Uh oh.

Eric straightens up at the mention of my vision. "What was it?"

"I'll tell you later," I spurt, trying to keep things short. The gurgling screams continue, now mixed with the compactor's mechanical whirring as it struggles to crunch down on the rest of the trash man.

"Tell me on the way," Eric says, sliding a pair of T.O.P.S.E.C.R.E.T. branded sunglasses on his face. "We gotta get back before The Director flips her shit."

I lose vision in one of my eyes. "Wait, wait—" I stammer, more so talking to my failing body than to Eric.

"No more waiting, Julie. We're heading back to T.O.P.S.E.C.R.E.T." He puts his sunglasses on. "What is that annoying sound?" He turns toward the trash compactor, still struggling to consume the trash man's body.

Eric presses the button on the remote. The heavy machinery slams down with a loud CRUNCH and a massive spurt of blood comes out in one final blow.

EPILOGUE
AKA CLAM CHOWDER

"That pretty much sums everything up," I tell the camera. I let out a satisfied sigh, feeling much better now that I got everything off my chest. Hashing through all the details helped me see things more clearly and, looking back, I realize nothing that happened to me was as bad as I'd thought. I mean, besides all the "almost dying," being kidnapped multiple times, and the continuing torturous experimentation.

It's been somewhat agonizing not being able to tell Nicole or my parents what happened. They'll never know what my real job is, and they'd never believe me if I told them. At least I can rest easy knowing they think I moved to New York for a fancy "business" job, whatever that means. It's safer for them to stay uninvolved, I keep telling myself. But that fact still doesn't make it any easier to keep this enormous secret from them.

"It's about time," Eric says from just behind me. I jump in my seat and whirl around. He's holding the box of pizza, now a platter of aromatic crumbs, and smacking on the last piece in his hand.

"How long have you been there?"

"Long enough." He crunches the crust down in three bites.

I roll my eyes. "Why are you in my space again?" If you can even call it that. There's barely enough breathing room for one person in this ridiculously small cabin in the woods, let alone two.

He shrugs. "I was bored. And you entertain me, Julie Richardson."

Honestly, I can't blame him. We've been locked in this safe house for the last week and a half, and I'm getting seriously stir crazy. With barely any breathing room and a pantry that was only stocked with canned clam chowder, I've been starving and in need of some fresh air since the first day we got here.

Eric drops his crummy pizza box on my temporary desk, spilling greasy flakes of cheese all over the laptop keyboard.

Seriously?

I glare at him, grab the box, and angrily stomp into the kitchen. Which is literally four strides away. Pinching my nose, I attempt to shove the large cardboard box into the overflowing trash can at the edge of the kitchen counter, but it causes the bag to rip, and a mix of sticky juices spurts out everywhere.

"Nice," I mutter, staring at the mess. We're out of trash bags and Lysol, and there's absolutely nothing I can do about it.

We're stuck in a pigsty.

"Goddamnit, this place is filthy and we can't even take the trash out!" I shout.

"Don't get mad at the pizza just because you couldn't eat it." Eric leans against the tiny center island, watching me with an amused half-grin.

"Eric, how can you deem it necessary to order a pizza and reveal our secret location, yet you won't take the damn trash out?" (How did he even get someone to deliver pizza to the middle of the woods anyway? God, he irks me!)

Eric shrugs again. "Priorities."

Priorities? Oh, how I want to slap that stupid grin from his face. "How about fresh air? Is fresh air not a priority? Why can't we at least open the damn windows?!" I pull at the metallic shades that have been blocking the sunlight from entering this musty safe house, but they don't budge an inch. The anger bubbling inside me finally boils over. I bang on the steel window blockers, yelling obscenities.

"Hey!" Eric grabs my wrists and yanks them behind my back, locking them in his tight grip.

"You know we can't go outside, Julie." Eric's voice is low, and the way he says my name draws my entire body to perky attention. You'd think I'd be used to him by now, but each time Eric comes close to me, my breath catches, and I find myself both wanting to scratch his eyes out and hoping he'll plant a kiss on my lips.

He adds in a warning tone, "Nestor is out looking for you, and it's a threat we don't take lightly here at T.O.P.S.E.C.R.E.T."

"What kind of an evil villain name is Nestor anyway? Nestor from The N.E.S.T.," I mock. "Sounds made up if you ask me."

"Stay focused, Julie," Eric says, his hot breath tickling my neck. How is his breath still minty? He just ate a whole pizza! "As our new McGuffin, you're T.O.P.S.E.C.R.E.T's biggest target in the world right now, and it's my job to keep you, er, The McGuffin safe."

Argh, he's making sense. I let my shoulders down slightly.

"Safe is different than locked up like a prisoner," I mutter. "Why couldn't we have gone to a safe house on the beach? Or to another one of those fancy hotels in someplace like, I don't know, the Bahamas," I whine, suddenly missing my breezy hometown.

Eric presses his lips together. Probably, he's wishing we were on the beach right now, too. "You should be thanking me, Julie. This safe house isn't even in the T.O.P.S.E.C.R.E.T. list of accessible locations anymore." He lowers his voice to a whisper. "It's strictly off-grid."

Gulp. No one will find me when I die of cabin fever.

"Let's try to have some fun," Eric says, straightening up behind me, my wrists still locked in his iron grip. That could have two very different meanings, but I'm sure he's not trying to be perverted. It's off-putting to think of Eric and fun in the same capacity. I doubt we have the same definition of the word. "Try to break free," he says.

Ugh. "I don't want to play your stupid game, Eric." He doesn't move at all. "Just let me go!" I wriggle with all my might and let out some embarrassing grunting sounds. If anything, I'd say Eric's grip tightened.

"That's what I thought." I can hear the smirk in his voice. "You're useless in the field without me."

"And you're useless as an agent without me," I counter.

His body stiffens against mine. He knows I'm right. I wriggle my wrists, but his grip doesn't loosen.

"You gonna let me go now?" I say to the wall in front of me.

Eric spins me around and pins me back.

"You've got a lot to learn, Agent Julie Richardson," he mocks.

We share a moment of electric silence, staring into each other's lively eyes. Eric leans forward, ever so slightly, and my heart rate hikes. Then I hear it. A slight buzzing sound.

"Did you hear that?" My ears stand perked like a terrier as I stand there, motionlessly straining my ears.

"What are you talking about?" Eric asks, looking around as if I'm insane. BZZZZZZZ.

"There it is again!" I follow the source of the buzzing and realize it's coming from Eric's ear. "Are you wearing an earpiece?"

"No." He hastily taps his ear, and the buzzing noise goes away.

"Who are you talking to?" I ask, realization that he's been up to something slowly sinking in. "Was that Simon?"

"No," he says, backing away from me.

"Have you been contacting him without telling me?" A rising tide of shock and anger swells in my veins.

"I mean, only for check-in purposes."

"You said we couldn't contact anyone." I take a step toward him, getting up close and personal. "You said The Director would contact us once the situation became stabilized."

He just stares back at me.

"What's going on here, Eric?"

"It's nothing you need to worry about."

"Tell me!" I grab a can of soup sitting on the counter and throw it at him. Eric ducks, letting the soup can burst against the cabinetry on the opposite wall, spewing clam chowder everywhere.

"Woah, no need to get crazy." Eric says with a shaky voice as he slowly backs away.

I may have overreacted. But then the thought crosses my mind that Eric has probably been lying about this entire situation—I mean, after all, would he really be able to order pizza to a secret, unaddressed cabin in the woods? "Are we even on lockdown?" I ask, just to be sure.

Eric sucks in a breath through his teeth, grimacing like he doesn't want to answer the question. It fills me with a panicky dread that sends my barometer way past crazy.

I grab another two cans and throw them at Eric with all my might. He uses the small kitchen island between us as a barrier and ducks. Soup explodes against the wall in the living room and the boarded window of the front door.

"Alright! Stop throwing things, and I'll tell you." The hanging pots and pans clank against each other as Eric backs up into the corner against the stove.

I'm holding the last can of soup in my hand, aimed and ready. "Well?"

Eric takes a moment before saying, in a low, serious voice, "This has been a test."

A test? I'm rendered entirely speechless. Another goddamn TEST?!

An audible SNAP fills the tiny space as what little remaining restraint I have breaks in two.

I haul the last can of soup at Eric, screeching like a madwoman. It actually catches him in the shoulder this time with an audible THUNK.

"Jesus, Julie!"

Religion won't save him now. I dart across the room for the knife brick in the corner, but Eric sees it coming and grabs the giant steak knife first.

"Stand back," he warns, terror in his eyes.

"What the hell kind of a test has this been? Haven't I been tested enough?!" I unsheathe a two-pronged carving fork from the wooden block of utensils and hold it in front of me like a sword, jutting it out to stab Eric in the gut. He expertly blocks the blow. His steak knife meets the middle of my fork with a metallic SHING.

"We—I mean, Simon just wanted to test your limits, you know? See how far you could go before breaking." He twists the fork out of my grip. It falls to the floor with a clatter.

"This was your idea?" I say, seething.

He stands up taller, puffing his chest out defensively. "Now that we're going to be working together, I think it's highly important to know your breaking points."

I stare him down, unable to speak without it coming out as unintelligible shrieking.

"It's not like we used any needles," he continues. "We made sure to skip out on the needles."

"I am going to kill you!" I growl. Eric drops the knife and turns away when he sees me lunge for him. I land on his back with a THUD, wrap my legs around his waist, and claw at his face, yelling into his earpiece, "You, too, Simon!"

"Damn it, Julie. Stop yelling!" Eric tries to throw me off of him, but my grip won't budge, and the weight of the motion sends us crashing into every doodad on the countertop. The pots and pans fall to the floor with an ear-shattering clatter.

"You asshole!" I shriek, yanking at his hair with all the pent-up energy that's been accumulating in me in this damn safe house. He yelps and reaches back to pull me away, his arm crashing into the empty wine glasses hanging from the cabinetry. The glasses break into jagged pieces, spreading out across the marble countertop.

"You better be getting this data, Simon," Eric gasps from beneath my arm wrapped around his neck. Drawers are caught on my jean belt loops, snapping into place with a loud clatter of silverware.

"Screw your data!" I shout. Eric trips over the corner of the counter and falls onto the couch in the living room. My grip breaks in the fall, and he lands on top of me in an awkward position, my elbow giving him a nice stab to the gut.

"You better take me back to headquarters right now," I say, struggling under his weight, "or I'll—"

"You'll what?" Eric asks from above me, pinning my arms down by my sides. He smirks down at me, and I suddenly become acutely aware of his body pressed against mine, our chests heaving from the adrenaline of the struggle. "You'll never have the upper hand, Julie."

"Oh yeah?" In a sheer act of will, I somehow manage to twist our bodies around with every remaining ounce of energy I have so that I'm on top of him, shoving the couch covers to the ground in the process. Eric's head hits the armrest, and I quickly grab his wrists, pinning him to the couch frame. "Don't test me, Eric. I'm The McGuffin." I say it with pride, feeling powerful for the first time since this shit show started.

Eric laughs, actually laughs at me, the bastard. "Did you get that, Simon? Julie thinks she's done being tested." He grins knowingly. "Not as long as you're The McGuffin."

I scoff. And then all my energy fizzes out of me like a balloon being popped by a pin. There's no point fighting it anymore. I'm The McGuffin, which means I'll always be Simon's lab rat.

At least the incessant testing comes with job security. Plus, my two imbecile partners remembered not to use needles this time.

Go figure.

Suddenly, the front door jostles. Eric and I share a shocked expression.

"Simon?" I mouth.

Eric furrows his brow.

Another jostling of the door handle. Eric throws me off of him, and I land on top of the glass table. Thankfully it doesn't break, but I hit my funny bone on the corner. And I'm not laughing.

I duck behind the couch as Eric gets into a fighting stance, carefully approaching the door. He taps his earpiece. "Simon, is that you? Come in. Over."

A moment later, the front door swings open. The silhouetted figure of a woman steps through the threshold. It takes a moment for my eyes to adjust to the glorious bright daylight behind her, but soon it's clear who she is.

Penelope Barnes. AKA The Director of T.O.P.S.E.C.R.E.T.

She's wearing a sundress, a sun hat, and sunglasses, pulling behind her a rolling brown suitcase and carrying a tote bag over her shoulder. The bag says, "You had me at Merlot," and it's overflowing with bottles of wine.

She steps inside the living room, bringing with her some much-needed fresh air. I jump up from the floor.

"Director!" I say, relieved to have some contact with the outside world.

"Er, what are you doing here?" Eric asks, standing awkwardly between us.

She looks like she's heading out on a beach vacation. But... to the middle of the woods?

The Director removes her sunglasses, slowly taking in the mess around us. The slight smile that was tugging at the corner of her lips when she walked in slowly slides off her face as she registers the scene. Clam chowder spattered on every wall, putrid trash overflowing and leaking in the corner, pots and pans spilled onto the counter, wine glasses broken all over the floor. Then her eyes land on Eric and me, skin flushed and hair crazy from our tussle.

It's not a pretty sight.

"What have you done to my house?" Her voice comes out like a squeaky toy.

"Your house?" Eric says.

She whirls to face him. "Yes! My safe house."

Eric and I share a confused expression. Eric speaks first.

"But Simon said it's off-grid—"

The Director flashes Eric the Evil Eye. Her voice becomes low and severe when she says, "Simon is behind this?"

Eric nods. "Yes, it was all Simon's idea."

Such an ass.

"And what idea was that, exactly?" she asks.

Eric fills her in on all the details, explaining that they created a fake Evil Villain (I knew that name was nonsense!) as the reason for keeping me locked up and that they wanted to expose me to all my personal trigger points until I reached my breaking point.

One look around this place, and it's pretty clear I reached it.

BEEP BEEP, BEEP BEEP—The Director's watch goes off once again. She calmly removes it from her wrist and sets it on the counter among the broken wine glass shards. She steps toward the nearest cabinet, her sandals crunching down on the broken shards on the floor. She pulls out a coffee mug from the cupboard and pours herself something red from the twist top wine bottle in her bag.

"Uh, Director?" I ask, suddenly worried for her mental health more than mine. She was probably coming here expecting a mini-vacation but found the two of us duking it out instead.

"Just… clean this mess up," The Director says with her eyes closed. Eric and I share a worried glance.

"There aren't any cleaning supplies—" I start, but Eric interrupts me with a pointed stare. He trudges over to the stovetop and types something into the tiles on the backsplash. A hidden cabinet is revealed with all sorts of cleaning supplies, towels, paper goods, snacks, feminine supplies, and even a sunchair shoved inside.

So that's where he hid everything. Sunovabitch.

He tosses me a container of Lysol wipes. I get to scrubbing the chowder off the nearest wall. Eric carefully sweeps the glass shards into a dustpan.

The Director takes a sip of her wine, grasping the mug close to her as if it were a cup of hot cocoa. Then she closes her eyes, probably imagining she was in the Bahamas right about now.

I give a sideways glance at Eric. He's pouting and shoving the broken trash bag into a new one, probably thinking the same thing as The Director.

I can't help but grin at the sight of him all grumpy. Eric notices and makes his way over to me, pretending to sweep something off the carpet nearby, the whole time keeping one eye on The Director who's still silently sipping her wine cocoa.

"I hope you're happy," he says in a low voice.

I chuckle again, unsure exactly why I feel like laughing. Being so close to Eric always turns me into a child.

"Did you just laugh?" he asks, incredulous, probably thinking that he and Simon did manage to break me.

"No. Get back to work." I turn back to scrubbing the wall, hiding the smirk on my face.

"You're crazy," he mutters so only I can hear.

No, I think with a smile. I'm The McGuffin.

DEAR READER

I hope you enjoyed reading this book as much as I loved writing it! My family calls me "The Giggler" because while I was writing *Over the Top Secret*, I could frequently be found hunched over my keyboard laughing my a** off.

If you're dying for more T.O.P.S.E.C.R.E.T. spy stuff, join the ranks of my newsletter subscribers (AKA Gigglers) for *exclusive* access to all sorts of highly classified goodies, such as REDACTED, REDACTED, and even REDACTED!

Visit alexatuttle.com/newsletter to join the fun! Can't wait to meet you.

Sincerely,
    Alexa

YOUR WORDS MATTER

Reviews are the most powerful tools in my arsenal when it comes to getting attention for my books. Though I don't have the financial muscle of a menacing organization like The N.E.S.T., I DO have something much more powerful and effective than that. It's something plenty of Evil Villains would love to get their hands on…

A committed and loyal bunch of readers. (That's YOU!)

Honest reviews of my books help bring them to the attention of other ~~goofballs~~ readers. If you've enjoyed *Over the Top Secret*, I would be very grateful if you could spend five minutes (or less) leaving a review on my book's online retail page where you purchased it. Even something as short as "Book good. Me like." works just fine!

Thank you very much in advance, lovely reader! Your words matter to me as much as mine do to you.

ABOUT THE AUTHOR

Alexa Tuttle is an award-winning director, writer, and voice actress, but above all, she's a big ol' goofball. Whether intended for the screen or the page, for kids or adults, Alexa's tales are best known for their humorous escapades, zany characters, and fun twists!

Alexa loves game nights, treasure hunts, secret doors, theme parks, and shenanigans of all kinds. Her frequent travels around the globe with her larger-than-life family members continue to provide hilarious inspiration behind her written adventures.

Curious to know more? Join Alexa's newsletter, check out her movies and other books, or send her a message at her website: www.alexatuttle.com!

ALSO BY ALEXA TUTTLE

Children's Picture Books

Rosie and Mr. Spooks

The Vegas Golden Knights: Defenders of the Ice

Visit alexatuttle.com for new release updates!

T.O.P.S.E.C.R.E.T.

www.ingramcontent.com/pod-product-compliance
Lightning Source LLC
Chambersburg PA
CBHW030432010526
44118CB00011B/603